Liberating Rites

Liberating Rites

Understanding the
Transformative Power
of Ritual

■ ■ ■

Tom F. Driver

WestviewPress
A Division of HarperCollins*Publishers*

Originally published in 1991 as *The Magic of Ritual: Our Need for Liberating Rites that Transform Our Lives & Our Communities* by HarperSanFrancisco.

Copyright © 1998 by Tom F. Driver

Published in 1998 in the United States of America by Westview Press, 5500 Central Avenue, Boulder, Colorado 80301-2877, and in the United Kingdom by Westview Press, 12 Hid's Copse Road, Cumnor Hill, Oxford OX2 9JJ

A CIP catalog record for this book is available from the Library of Congress.
ISBN 0-8133-3455-1

The paper used in this publication meets the requirements of the American National Standard for Permanence of Paper for Printed Library Materials Z39.48-1984.

10   9   8   7   6   5   4   3   2   1

For Daniel,
whose life so recently began.
May he find and follow pathways of freedom.

Contents

Acknowledgments

It was John David Maguire, a friend and colleague through the whole of my professional life, who best expressed the reason for the difficulty I face now in giving credit for work on this book where credit is due. While the project was still on the drawing board he asked me one day what it was about. Hearing my answer, and pausing only a moment to recall the several theological and cultural interests I have pursued over the years, he said, "Well! It's all coming together at last, isn't it?"

While a complete acknowledgment of all those who have personally helped me bring things together is impossible, I wish publicly to thank those who have gone out of their way to help me make the book better than it would otherwise have been. If I forget any who have done so, an event most likely, I thank them anyway and beg their indulgence.

Ronald Grimes, once a student of mine before either of us was working on rituals, and today a major figure in ritual studies who has taught me much, read through an entire draft of the book and sent voluminous, invaluable comments. Other scholars knowledgeable about rituals who personally gave me information, encouragement, and criticism include Catherine Bell, John Grim, Richard Schechner, Ivan Strenski, Mary Evelyn Tucker, Janet Walton, and Timothy Weiskel.

I am grateful to the Ritual Studies Group in the American Academy of Religion, especially its sometime chairperson, Tom Peterson, for its many helpful sessions, particularly one at which my evaluations of Victor Turner were heard and critiqued. For similar service I thank the members of the New Haven Theological Discussion Group.

The teaching staff of Auburn Theological Seminary read several manuscript chapters and spent a full day discussing them with me. On that occasion I received good suggestions from James Forbes, Maria Harris, Dwayne Huebner, Larry Rasmussen, Bob Reber, Barbara

Wheeler, and Walter Wink. The latter's words, both oral and written, about principalities, powers, and political resistance, have been particularly helpful during the course of a long friendship.

In 1982 I was assisted by a Summer Grant from the National Endowment for the Humanities to do research on *vodou* rituals in Haiti. I am very grateful for an experience that not only added to my information but also changed my understanding of rituals. While in Haiti I had constant, generous assistance from Jean-François Chalut, Newton Dougherty, Jean-Claude Flanquin, and Chantal Regnault. Before and after that summer I have greatly benefited from the friendship of Karen McCarthy Brown, whose knowledge of *vodou* is thorough and who encouraged me to go and experience it for myself.

In Papua New Guinea I was helped by Gary Trompf at the University in Port Moresby and by the Lutheran mission in Wabag in the Western Highlands. My stay in Japan was made possible by an invitation to teach at Doshisha University in Kyoto, where I was graciously welcomed by the Department of English Literature. In Korea my host was David Suh, who made it possible for me to attend some Korean shamanistic rituals accompanied by skilled translators.

For some years I have taught a course listed as "Systematic Theology 283: Rituals and Sacraments." The students in this course have contributed more to my thinking than they are likely to know. Without them I would not have realized how complex the subject of rituals is, how difficult its communication, how necessary the *practice* of ritual is to its understanding. For their courage, curiosity, and unflagging interest I am grateful indeed.

At HarperCollins encouragement and many helpful suggestions have come from my editor, John Loudon. At home Susannah Driver lent her professional expertise to assist me in final editing.

If not to read one's manuscripts and candidly respond, what are old friends for—especially if they are scholars and writers of distinction? James B. Carse, Carolyn G. Heilbrun, and Anne L. Barstow, who is both friend and spouse, did me that favor. I took all their counsels to heart, as any but a fool would do. Let the reader not hold them responsible for my errors but give them credit that there are not more. These friends are lights given by heaven to guide me.

Tom F. Driver
New York City
November 1990

Preface

This book was first published in 1991 as *The Magic of Ritual: Our Need for Liberating Rites that Transform Our Lives & Our Communities.* I am pleased that it is being reissued by Westview Press and am hopeful that its revised title will commend itself to readers both old and new.

What's in a name? The book has three major theses: (1) in spite of many contrary examples, rituals are often and ideally powerful; (2) this power is properly used not to instill conformity to what is old and entrenched but to facilitate various kinds of transformation; and (3) the truly ethical kind of transformation is that which results in the increase of freedom.

For people educated mainly along the lines of Western rationalism, the first two of these themes are counter-intuitive. So also was the use of the word "magic" in this book's original title, where it referred to ritual's surprising and not wholly rational power. In these pages one finds a defense of the word "magic" against its acquired pejorative connotations of mere superstition and wishful thinking.

This said, the more important theme of the book has to do with the role of ritual in processes both social and personal that move individuals, groups, and societies toward greater freedom. Most people in the world live in thrall to poverty, hunger, and disease. They are captive to the social, political, and economic systems that perpetuate these afflictions. Ideologies also enslave, among them sexism, racism, and the current idolatrous belief in free markets as the guarantors of human welfare. (The opposite idolatry of the "dictatorship of the proletariat" seems recently to have collapsed of its own weight.) Rich and poor alike are held captive by what the New Testament calls the "powers" of this world, which must, as Walter Wink says, be "engaged"—that is, opposed.[1] In such engagement, ritual has a far more important role to play than is often supposed. Therefore, the editors and I have chosen to re-christen this book as *Liberating Rites: Understanding the Transformative Power of Ritual.*

Here the word "liberating" carries a double meaning. It points toward the work that rituals can and should perform in the liberation of humankind from enslavement to powers that diminish freedom and bring more death than life. Rites can be liberating, provided their character is rightly understood and their practice creatively linked to the actual needs of living persons and groups. This requires, however, that rituals themselves need liberating. They need to be freed from misunderstanding and lack of creativity, from their presumed function as guardians and keepers of all that is ancient, stilted, incomprehensible, and conformist.

Modern Western history has had the effect of alienating liberal and progressive minds from positive appreciation of ritual. If something is dull or meaningless it is often said to have been turned into ritual. This has had the lamentable effect of leaving most ritual practice in the hands of the most conservative elements of society. If rites are to help liberate us, we must begin by liberating them from their Babylonian captivity—their subservience not only to our misunderstanding but also to powers both religious and secular that would hold the human spirit captive. Although this may sound like a daunting task, I hope to show that it includes much that is playful and brims with pleasure. The very real work that ritual can do, as I explain in the text, is work done playfully.

■

One benefit an author derives from the re-issue of a book is the chance to share second thoughts, which I have already had opportunity to do face-to-face with students and other audiences and may now do in print. Attention is directed to Part II, "Modalities of Performance." What follows should be helpful to readers both before and after their encounter with that material, especially the first part of Chapter 5.

The approach to the understanding of ritual that is taken in this book owes more to the study of performance than to the study of ritual texts. It is an approach I share with a number of recent analysts of ritual, notably Richard Schechner,[2] Ronald Grimes,[3] and Catherine Bell.[4] It is reflected also in the work of the Ritual Studies Group in the American Academy of Religion, which owes much to the twin influences of anthropology and performance studies.

The second of this book's four major parts is devoted to an analysis of "performance," which is an extremely rich phenomenon. Realizing that the word means many things to many people and that the reason for this lies in the very complexity of the phenomenon itself, I distinguished within it three "modes," discussing the first in Chapter 5 and the second and third in Chapter 6. I named them the ritual, the confessional, and the ethical modes.

Since the book's publication, I have come to see that this three-part scheme is somewhat confusing. Although I have yet found no reason to change the substance of what I was attempting to say, its exposition, I now think, could be improved by employing a four-part rather than a three-part scheme.

Unclarity resulted from my subsuming *theatrical* performance under the heading of performance's *ritual* mode. It is true that ritual and theater have much in common, as Chapter 5 insists. It is also true that they are significantly different, as the same chapter maintains. Bundling them both into the one modality, called "ritual," led to a "yes, but" form of exposition, needlessly tangling the thread of the argument.

Matters would have been simplified had I treated the theatrical and the ritual as two different modes, which would have been more in line with ordinary usage of the terms and would have resulted in a symmetrical scheme (see the accompanying figure).

Let it be clear that the diagram refers to *modes* and not *kinds* of performance. Any given ritual occasion will involve, or at least imply, all four modes. In other words, limiting ourselves for the moment to just two of the four, there is something theatrical about all ritual, just as every theatrical performance has something of ritual about it. What distinguishes one performative occasion from another is that a different quality, or dimension, is paramount in each, the complementary mode (shown on the opposite side of the circle in the diagram) becoming in some measure recessive.

To the dimensions that characterize both ritual and theater, I give names suggested by Richard Schechner. He proposed that we think of all performances as existing within a continuum that runs from a pole of *efficacy* on the one hand to that of *entertainment* on the other (see p. 94). If the dimension of entertainment in a ritual grows larger than that of its efficacy (unfortunately too often the case in contemporary America), we sense that the categories are shifting, that the ritual is becoming "nothing more" than theater. Conversely, although all theatrical performance aims to have an effect upon us and, therefore, has some dimension of efficacy, if the effect seems larger than or different from what can be described as entertainment, we again find the categories shifting. We may then think, as Sören Kierkegaard once said,

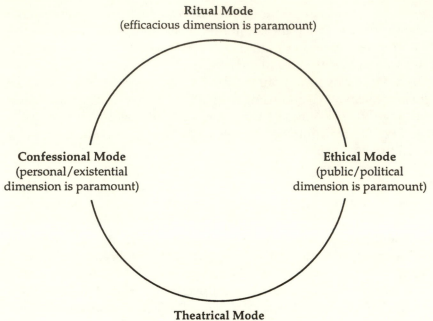

Ritual Mode
(efficacious dimension is paramount)

Confessional Mode
(personal/existential
dimension is paramount)

Ethical Mode
(public/political
dimension is paramount)

Theatrical Mode
(entertainment dimension is paramount)

MODES OF PERFORMANCE
Revision of scheme in Part II, "Modalities of Performance," pp. 79–127

that we are finding in the theater what we ought to, or once did, find in the church. He wisely observed that the reverse could happen, too: finding in the church what we ought to find in theater. These warnings heeded, we must nonetheless remember that ritual cannot and should not be purged of all that is theatrical, nor theater reduced to its entertainment dimension alone. Indeed, either would vanish without the complementary, albeit recessive, dimension.

Going beyond Schechner, I have distinguished also in performance two other modes, which I call the *confessional* and the *ethical.* Their explication is perhaps clear enough in Chapter 6. The confessional mode is distinguished by a dimension we may call personal or existential, since it has to do with conviction and commitment.

The diagram locates the confessional mode on the opposite side of the circle from the public and political dimension of the ethical mode. In some ritual, as also in some theater, the participant is pulled toward matters of deep personal moment. One feels that some kind of conversion or revelation, or at least commitment, is being summoned. Many persons experience this during certain performances of dance, drama, or music, as well as (some would say rather than) during participation in religious performances. When this occurs, the confessional mode has become paramount.

A rather different experience occurs when the public and political dimension of the event looms large. "Political" is used here in its broad sense as having to do with the contesting of power and policy within the body politic. The street or the public square becomes the locus of action, overshadowing the chambers of the heart. The transformation aimed at belongs to society more than to the individual. Even so, each dimension carries the other as its complement. We sense something wrong when a personal confession is heedless of, or irrelevant to, the social good. Something is amiss when a public demonstration is forgetful of the good of individuals. The twentieth century has seen too much of the latter in the massive marches and rallies of totalitarian regimes both fascist and communist. We have also seen too much of confessional religious performance of a type that seduces people to forget, or even deny, their public responsibility.

The co-inherence of all the dimensions of performance, all its modes, is suggested by the diagram's circle. On any given occasion, we should not be looking for just one or the other of these modes, but for the presence of them all in just the proportion that is appropriate to the particular performative event and the type of transformation it is intended to achieve.

Differences between modes of performance often have to do with style, or with the combined effect of all the specific elements that make up a performance. We are discussing, in the last analysis, matters of spirit and intentionality.

■

In May of 1992, about six months after this book had first been published, Ronald Grimes participated in a panel discussion of my professional work on the occasion of my retirement from the faculty of Union Theological Seminary. Choosing that moment to prod me into second thoughts about the book, he took issue with my strong emphasis upon ritual as a kind of work, even the kind that is done playfully. He asked me to consider that some ritual, perhaps the most important kind, has nothing to do with work but rather with "waiting."

The point was anticipated in Grimes' discussion of "liturgy" as one of the six "modes of ritual sensibility" that he had discussed in

Beginnings in Ritual Studies. There he had defined liturgy as "any ritual action with an ultimate frame of reference and the doing of which is felt to be of cosmic necessity."[5] I am in agreement with "ultimate frame of reference" as a distinguishing mark of liturgy but queasy with saying the same about "cosmic necessity," which seems to imply a bracketing or constraining of human will. Although there are, beyond doubt, religious traditions that regard the performance of their liturgies as a matter of "cosmic necessity," this is surely too strong a phrase to be applied to all.

In the same passage Grimes foreshadowed what he would say to me publicly in 1992:

> In liturgy we wait upon power. . . . In [liturgy] we actively await what gives itself and what is beyond our command. This is what separates liturgy from magic and what lends it an implicitly meditative and mystical character (43).

The reader of *Liberating Rites* will see that I do not separate liturgy from magic. On the contrary, I am at pains to show their coincidence. One will look here in vain for the "meditative and mystical character" of ritual. Would it be there if I were now to re-write the book, five years after Grimes' challenge?

No, I don't think so, although I am very aware that my view is a biased one. I have not wanted to say the last word about ritual but to supply a word that is too often ignored, leading to the "ritual misapprehension" that I discuss in the first chapter. One of the hats I wear is that of a Christian theologian concerned about the vitality of church liturgies. I recall a witticism uttered long ago by Ralph W. Sockman, a nationally known preacher: "The church has less to fear from the wolfishness of the wolves than from the sheepishness of the sheep." Ronald Grimes is no sheep, nor does he wish to placate them, but I have always seen it as my task to show that the moral life cannot be fulfilled by standing in wait.

There may be between me and Grimes, and is sure to be between me and some readers of this book, a philosophical and theological difference. My philosophical orientation owes much to pragmatism, especially as exemplified in William James and John Dewey. In the background is Aristotle, whom I quote on pages 79–80: "It is by their actions that we know what [people] are." This orientation is in line with the deep interest in all the forms of "act," "acting," and "action" that I have had since childhood and which led me eventually into professional training in both religion and theater.

My theological orientation has been taken in reaction to the neo-orthodox theology that prevailed during my seminary days. I first fled from its expression in Karl Barth to the more culturally astute theology of Paul Tillich. In time I realized that Tillich's ontology, the preeminence he gave to Being rather than to Doing, did not well help me to understand the character of the performing arts, of ritual, and of human agency.[6]

Whereas the "crisis theology" that arose in response to Nazism and World War II, especially Barth's version of it, dwelt upon the incommensurability of the human and the divine, I, along with much Feminist and Liberation theology, have stressed their mutual interaction. My theology of creation is one of co-creation. If we have fallen away from our original nature, it is from partnership that we have fallen, and partnership constitutes our greatest moral challenge.

The purpose of liturgy, according to this way of thinking, is only partly, but not primarily, to make us receptive. It is not to make us obedient but to make us free—free in the way that leads to freedom more abundant, not in ways that flourish only to die like grass in a dry season—free for what James Carse has called an "infinite game,"[7] which is an ever-flowering partnership with other human beings, with the living world that is our home, and with God.

■

Although this book is written by a Christian (and Protestant) theologian with certain churchly concerns that become most evident in the last chapter, it is not intended for Christians or other religiously minded readers alone. Although the values expressed are derived from my own religious orientation, the analyses of the place of ritual in human life, of its origins in pre-history (Part I), of the modalities of performance (Part II), and of the major gifts that ritual brings to society (Part III) are intended to be as nearly universal as possible. This in spite of the fact that I do not really believe in universals. I do not believe it is possible for human beings (nor even for God, come to think of it) to know what is everywhere and always the case. That is because life is made up of dynamic, ever-changing relationships. Some of the changes take place very slowly, however, enabling us to generalize for a time.

It has been said that the human mind is a world-making instrument. Although we cannot know what is universal, we can, do, and surely should, aspire to such knowing, for that is the way in which we make the worlds in which our minds and our values can dwell.

So I have wanted here to make some universal claims about ritual, knowing that I must fail, yet thinking that not to try would be failure of another kind. I invite the reader to see how much of what is here set forth is in harmony with his or her prior knowledge and experience, how much rings true, including things secretly longed for.

Tom F. Driver

Sheffield, Mass.

August 1997

NOTES

1. Walter Wink, *Engaging the Powers: Discernment and Resistance in a World of Domination* (Minneapolis: Fortress Press, 1992).

2. Since my book was written, Schechner has published another significant study: *The Future of Ritual: Writings on Culture and Performance* (London: New York: Routledge, 1993).

3. In addition to the two Grimes works in this book's list of References, see the following more recent ones: *Ritual Criticism: Case Studies in Its Practice, Essays on Its Theory* (Columbia, SC: University of South Carolina Press, 1990); *Reading, Writing, and Ritualizing: Ritual in Fictive, Liturgical, and Public Places* (Washington, DC: The Pastoral Press, 1993); *Marrying & Burying: Rites of Passage in a Man's Life* (Boulder, CO: Westview Press, 1995); and Ronald L. Grimes, ed., *Readings in Ritual Studies* (Upper Saddle River, NJ: Prentice Hall, 1996).

4. Catherine Bell's significant study, *Ritual Theory, Ritual Practice* (New York: Oxford University Press, 1992), includes a number of emphases similar to some of my own, although her methodology is quite different. We share certain thoughts: that ritual is better viewed as performative action than as symbolic structure, that it is always related to social power, and that it writes many of its meanings into the body language of its participants. I am not sure that she subscribes to the emphasis I lay upon transformation and freedom. Her book is recommended to scholarly readers for its explication of ritual in the context of recent social theory and political practice.

5. Grimes, *Beginnings* (1982), 43.

6. I have described this in some detail in *Patterns of Grace: The Word of God as Human Experience* (San Francisco: Harper & Row, 1977; reprinted New York: Union Theological Seminary, 1990).

7. James P. Carse, *Finite and Infinite Games: A Vision of Life as Possibility* (New York: The Free Press, 1986).

PART I

Ritual Pathways

1

Introduction

> . . . his servants came near and said to him, "My father, if the prophet had commanded you to do some great thing, would you not have done it? How much rather, then, when he says to you, 'Wash, and be clean?'" So he went down and dipped himself seven times in the Jordan, according to the word of the prophet of God; and his flesh was restored like the flesh of a little child, and he was clean.
>
> —2 Kings 5:13–14

Human longing for ritual is deep, and in our culture often frustrated.

The head of a large bank in New York City, much emotion in his voice, told his dinner companions that he had stopped going to Mass because "they have taken the drama out of it." I did not agree with his objection to the liturgical reforms of Vatican II, but I sympathized with his complaint that the ritual life in the churches—his Catholic, mine Protestant—is impoverished.

A number of women I know have quit going to church because they are not welcome as ritual leaders. The Catholic ones cannot get ordained, and the Protestants have trouble finding posts as ministers. These women feel "ritually abused."[1] Although the rites are very meaningful to them, they are controlled in such a way as to make women victims. I know many gays and lesbians who feel the same way. Their anguish is great because in addition to all kinds of social ostracism, they experience a barrier thrown up against their right to do ritual, which awakens knowledge of how deep their longing for it goes.

A woman has died. Her sister attends the funeral out of duty, not expecting it will do much for her. Sure enough, the service is pro forma, something everybody does at times like this, so hold your breath and go through with it. The ceremony is not in the least transforming, and the sister knows she will have to deal with her grief some other way.

A young mother in the hospital has given birth to her first child. All went well, she is very happy, and feels the need to express her joy in some sort of observance. A hospital chaplain (male, as usual) comes in, smiles at her good news, and immediately loses interest. The woman asks for a brief prayer service but he dashes off, saying that he has to attend to those who are sick. Neither she nor her friends know any rituals of thanksgiving for the birth of a child, and now she weeps to realize it.

A couple's marriage ends in divorce. At its start there had been a big wedding, into which a lot of time, talent, money, and care had gone. Scores of friends and relatives came, dancing far into the night. Now there is nothing but lawyers, courts, and papers. The same church that helped them to ritualize their marriage with gusto now looks the other way. There is no ritual anybody can perform to do something about the couple's sense of failure and guilt, nor to initiate the children into their new, frightening situation. Frustration and anguish hang over everyone like a dismal cloud, and no shaman comes with a billow of witnesses to beat drums, sing loud songs, draw magic circles, and blow that cloud away.

Young men and young women reach the age of sexual "maturity" (as it is rather optimistically called) but do not live in a culture that provides them any ritual pathways for becoming sexually mature. So they become simply active. When their situation is complicated by poverty, racism, broken homes, or drugs, it can seem a trackless waste.

To lose ritual is to lose the way. It is a condition not only painful and pathetic but also dangerous. Some people it destroys. As for the whole society, sooner or later it will find rituals again, but they may be of an oppressive rather than a liberating kind. Rituals have much to do with our fate.

■

The purposes of this book are several: to reflect upon the deep human longing for ritual; to interpret it in the light of our physical, social, political, sexual, moral, aesthetic, and religious existence; and to urge a reform of our ritual life, especially in religion, so that our longing for ritual and our longing for freedom may come together. It is a tragedy they were ever split. With enough knowledge and discipline, we can do something about it.

The book's research and writing have been an attempt to understand why, after all, we human beings are forever doing rituals. A great number of people, perhaps the majority in Western society, either take rituals for granted, raising few questions about them, or else try to avoid them. If, however, one begins to ask questions about ritual life, a door is opened to an immense terrain both familiar and mysterious. We are such stuff as ritual performances are made of, and these, like our dreams, would, if we knew their source, tell us much about what we are.

Upon reflection, is it not odd that human beings, in all societies, everywhere and in all ages, have engaged in the making and performing of rituals? Why have they done this, when life is full of dangers and challenges that would seem to require more practical kinds of activity? Contrary to common-sense expectation, rituals are not, in most cases, the product of affluence and leisure. Indeed, they seem to be born out of necessity, like an invention of that stern mother; and the people who best know that life is difficult are the ones most likely to cleave to ritual and make it work for them.

When John F. Kennedy was shot one Friday in Dallas, Texas, in 1963, the churches in the land were full the next Sunday. Preachers are tempted to give this a theological explanation, saying that the people, in their grief and fear, felt a need of God; but it may be closer the mark to suppose that the gut-level need was for ritual. Aside from the pictures of the President's motorcade under attack by gunfire, and later the shooting of Lee Harvey Oswald point blank, the most memorable images from that traumatic time are of the funeral cortege in procession through the streets of Washington, D.C. "The weight of this sad time we must obey," someone says at the end of *King Lear*, "Speak what we feel, not what we ought to say." At such times the impulse toward ritual is not so much to speak as to act: *act* what we feel, not what we ought to do.

Yet that is an odd thing for me to say. For in many peoples' minds—people somewhat out of touch with ritual life, I think—a ritual is indeed what one is obligated to do, not what one feels like doing. Perhaps it is both, depending on the circumstance and the angle of vision. Here is one of many ambiguities we shall come upon while pondering the use and abuse of ritual.

If the main purpose of this book is to inquire broadly into the place of ritual in human life, a second purpose is to consider rituals as part of religious life and to suggest a way of thinking about them that may foster their revitalization. To speak of ritual is not necessarily to speak of religion. Conversely, religion is not always thought of as ritual but perhaps as faith or theological opinion or the leading of an ethical life.

It has been truly argued, for example in a splendid book by David Kertzer on *Ritual, Politics, and Power*, that political life depends upon ritual every bit as much as does religion.[2] There are also rituals—such as birthday parties with their cakes, candles, cards, gifts, and songs—so much a part of social life that, as one author has noted, they do not require any formal instruction.[3]

Our study of rituals in religious life will place them in a context as wide as the whole of human existence. That is, we shall show that the making of rituals has not come from religion as such but from the evolution of the human species, an evolution that has both biological and cultural aspects. This being so, it is difficult, perhaps impossible, and certainly unwise for human beings to attempt to engage in social and political life, or establish intimate relations, or educate the young, or have a religious life, or to make and enjoy artistic things without also making and performing rituals. Rituals belong to us, and we to them, as surely as do our language and culture. The human choice is not *whether* to ritualize but when, how, where, and why.

The close association between religion and ritual is one of those often taken-for-granted subjects that needs to be asked about. I intend to ask in connection with my own religious tradition, which is Christian. I am hoping that the non-Christian reader, or the alienated Christian, will find my reflections upon ritual in general to be of interest in their own right. The person who, either from inside or outside, is concerned about the moral and spiritual health of Christianity is invited to follow my steps from the general to the particular, to entertain a vision of what Christian ritual could be if people were persuaded to play it, like very good music, in a new key. Even better: like variations upon a theme.

■

During the first part of my life, "ritual" seemed a dreary subject. That this has recently changed, that it has turned around at the very time when my social and religious ideas have become not more conservative but more radical, is for me a source of amazement; yet I sense that many others are making similar discoveries. Wishing I had made them when I was young, I realize today that I grew up in a milieu that did not encourage such thought, being too Protestant, too middle-class American, too much involved with having the right ideas, and too little interested in, even wary of, the things we learn through performance.

My religious heritage, which was that of Methodism in the American South, kept its distance from the word "ritual." We had "worship services," or "church services," or just plain "church," but not "rituals." Whatever they were called, as a child, I found them every bit as boring as they were obligatory for the members of my dedicated family. In our language "church service" referred to something God-given and true, while "ritual" was viewed with suspicion as some kind of esoteric activity practiced by people of "other faiths"—that is (in the order of their remoteness from our horizon) by Anglicans, Roman Catholics, Jews, Muslims, and all manner of pagans. I might now be ashamed to recall this Bible-belt attitude were it not for the fact that it carried within itself a hostility toward ritual that has been widespread in the culture, having roots not only in Protestant iconoclasm but also in the antireligious rationalism of the Enlightenment.

Except on rare occasions, church worship services proved no less tiresome to me as an adult than when I was a restless child. Nevertheless—or perhaps, as I sometimes think, because of this—I accepted a "call to the ministry." In that role I could stave off boredom by taking part in the leadership. After a time, however, even this ego boost stalled out in an atmosphere of increasingly pompous repetitiveness. I realized I would have to get out or look into the matter more deeply. But I resisted this looking for a long time.

At its most elemental level, this book is a response to what I shall call "ritual boredom." That is, a condition in which people have become fundamentally weary of the rituals available to them for giving their lives shape and meaning. I have mentioned its occurrence in church, but it is more widespread even than that. Political ritual in America is so vacuous that it has ceased to inspire most of the electorate to vote. Television is usually blamed for this, but it may be that TV is more the scapegoat than the culprit. Cameras may be used in all sorts of ways on all sorts of subjects. It seems likely that the kind of sound-bite political broadcasting we are used to is an ill-conceived attempt to fill a vacuum created by society's massive ritual boredom.

The causes of this boredom seem to me twofold: Either the rituals, in their form, content, and manner of performance, have lost touch with the actualities of people's lives and are thus simply arcane; or else the people have lost the ability to apprehend their very need of ritual, do not see what rituals are good for, and thus do not find them even potentially valuable. Often these two causes are present together. The second I call "ritual misapprehension." Its widespread occurrence in industrialized societies is one of the reasons that time-honored rituals often cease to change and fail to stay in touch with what people experience in the "real" world.

There are, then, two endemic ritual maladies that need address. First, many of the rituals that are available to people in our society are indeed dull and boring. We need either to find substitutes for them or learn how to revivify their form, content, and performance values. Second, many people do not understand what rituals do and why they are a necessary part of human life. This "ritual misapprehension" needs, as far as possible, to be corrected.

The tasks are more easily named than performed. Attempting to find a cure for the ritual impoverishment of our society, which extends into many churches, synagogues, and temples, we must avoid superficiality. Ritual impoverishment has many causes, and these reach into the cultural, political, moral, esthetic, and theological dimensions of our common life. To take a critical look at our relation to ritual is to call into question our existence in the world.

■

While the creation and performance of rituals belongs to what is best in human life, I have found it necessary also to keep in mind the power of rituals to do harm. At the present time, when many individuals and groups are finding rituals essential to renewed life, other people engage in ritualized acts of violence, including murder. Ritualized abuse can occur not only in Satanic cults but also, under certain circumstances, in church, synagogue, or temple.[4] Since people need ritual so much, it can, like sexual desire, be used as a weapon against them. Trusting a man she finds attractive, many a woman has found herself abused and perhaps raped by him; and those who long for ritual can find this longing used by people in power to keep them down (on their knees).

Rituals are like works of art in that no correlation exists between their power and their morality, and yet a society can scarcely exist, let alone be good, without fostering their growth. We might say a similar thing about religion, too, indeed any of the cultural activities of human beings: That they are necessary to our goodness does not mean that their every particular instance is good. As the devil can quote scripture or wear the mask of a saint, so there is nothing to stop wrongdoers from enacting quite marvelous rituals. Mahatma Gandhi was a consummate ritualist but so was Hitler's minister of propaganda, Joseph Goebbels.

Not forgetting, instead insisting upon, the power of rituals to do harm, my principal moral aim in this book is to show that rituals' power to do good is indispensable. And of the various kinds of good that may be ascribed to them, the one that interests me most is the one that seems the least sung. I am thinking of their liberating power.

Until recently, most educated thought in the Western world, whether liberal or radical, has been under sway of the Enlightenment's opinion that rituals belong to stages of human development destined for obsolescence by the triumph of reason. The liberal theological world has partaken of the same Enlightenment bias, while Protestantism inherited a Puritan suspicion of rituals as pagan, idolatrous, and popish. The chief result of such attitudes has been to leave interest in rituals in conservative hands. Mostly unchallenged is the assumption that rituals, by their very nature, either perpetuate the status quo or, worse, serve reactionary causes.

This particular form of ritual misapprehension seems now to be changing. One sign of the change is the rediscovery of ritual by the religious wing of the women's movement. Confronted with massive patriarchal resistance in the churches, women who struggle for the right to fulfill their call to religious leadership have found the performance of long-suppressed rituals (from the old Wicca traditions) and the making of newly improvised rituals to be invaluable for maintaining their solidarity, courage, and imaginative resource. As one group has written: "Ritual is the license we give one another and God to don bright colors and move in circles and claim this moment as a *kairos*. Only where there is death does ritual cease. Without it we literally die."[5]

Similarly, the Civil Rights Movement discovered in the 1950s and 1960s that much of its power came from the ritual traditions of the black church, which it could call upon and adapt when the time came to march in the streets. As Taylor Branch has shown in *Parting the Waters: America in the King Years 1954–63*, this is not merely a matter of whipping up the crowds but of tapping into deep moral roots and effecting, in a certain measure, a re-formation of the human spirit.

Rituals belonging to popular religion have had a prominent role during the last thirty or so years when the poor in Latin America, Asia, and Africa have risen up against economic, political, and military oppression. Where people are in movement, whether in a liberative or a reactionary direction, ritual is likely to be their strong ally. It is becoming clear that we should not let repulsion at the morally negative instances of this truth—found at one time in the great Nazi rallies and today in fanatic fundamentalisms in many countries—obscure the positive instances; for this would be to take away from oppressed people one of the principal means at their disposal for initiating and sustaining protest.

■

Another stimulus for renewed interest in rituals comes from anthropology. In my own life and work, the discovery of anthropological literature has been liberative. As long as my field of vision was confined to my own culture, I was blinded to the power of ritual. My training was in theology and the study of Western literature, particularly drama. The studies of ritual that I had come across were mostly conceived from a high-church point of view that virtually identified ritual with Christian liturgy and was totally uncritical of hierarchical sacramentalism. This had theological and socio-political implications with which I could not agree. In the early 1970s, owing to many changes that took place within society and within me during the 1960s, I decided to try to expand my cultural horizons by reading ethnography and anthropology, and this opened up for me an entirely new world. I decided also to travel in new directions. Before, whenever I left the United States, I journeyed across the Atlantic, seeking my own cultural roots in Britain, Europe, and the Near East. Now I went south—to Mexico, the Caribbean, Central America—and west across the Pacific—to New Zealand, New Guinea, Japan, China, Korea, India.

Soon I realized that my readings and travels were beginning to focus upon rituals. I had earlier given serious attention to Western theater. I had acted, directed, worked as a theater critic, written books and articles about theater. Now, with great excitement, I was discovering in the rites of Papua New Guineans, Haitians, Japanese Shintoists, Korean shamans, Nicaraguan members of the "people's church," and many others a "theater outside the theater." It was something the anthropologists already knew about and were leading me to find. When occasionally I came upon anthropologists, for example Clifford Geertz and Victor Turner, whose own sense of theater was particularly acute, I felt them to be kindred spirits.

Anthropology has discovered not only the prevalence of ritual in all societies but also its intimate linkage to social process. In a very real sense, to study humanity is to study ritual; and this has prompted me to think that to ponder the future of humanity is to consider the future of ritual.

In this book I will combine anthropological resources with moral and theological advocacy. Although I will draw upon cross-cultural materials, my aim is not to study all the varieties of ritual that exist in the world, nor to offer a theory of ritual that will be universally valid. That is certainly beyond my powers, and perhaps more than anyone could do. Margaret Mead used to say that the reason anthropologists study other cultures is to better understand their own. Although she has been criticized for that view, I take it to show a healthy sense of every person's particular cultural location, including the anthropologist's. Anthropology has broadened my cultural horizons immensely, has removed many of my cultural blind spots, and provided a liberation from parochialism; but it has not lifted me out of my skin nor made me a universal person. Like Mead, I speak from my culture and to my culture, nowadays trying to employ as much awareness of other cultures as I can absorb.

As Mead's concerns were often moral and religious, so, I do not hesitate to say, are mine. I wish to use whatever knowledge of rituals I can acquire to assist myself and my co-culturalists to do those things that promote peace, justice, and intercultural respect. The ideas about ritual, social justice, and religious practice that I shall advocate are by no means value free. They are meant to broaden and deepen the kind of life experience that people of my own Western culture may legitimately have as citizens of a world that grows more interconnected every day and is in urgent need of liberative justice as a condition of its survival.

■

I hope this book will be read by all people who are interested in the study and practice of rituals, people of various religious traditions or of none, laypeople as well as specialists. Rituals are part of the human condition, and their health or disease affects everyone.

I write also in hope of stimulating, or helping to stimulate, a transformation of the ritual life of the churches. Much Christian liturgical practice has become moribund. I believe the reason to be a certain unholy alliance between liturgical order and a social order that has set its face against the significant change that justice and peace require. I pray that my address to the subject of rituals and human transformation will be of use to the various theologies of liberation that are beginning to stir the churches out of their slumber.

2

Ritualizing: The Animals Do It and So Do We

When matters of origin are afoot we must consider ritual no less than myth.

—GENE KLAAREN[6]

I see no reason why we should not view ourselves as ritualizing animals.

—RONALD GRIMES[7]

Each morning when we are at the house in the country, my cat greets me as I open the bedroom door, and there we engage in certain nonverbal communications that are very much the same from day to day. Our little routine, which I will soon describe more fully, is now such a familiar, practiced part of the life the cat and I share that some might call it a ritual; but perhaps this would extend the word too far.

All over the world people perform rituals; and, from the archaeological evidence, it looks as if they always have. I find this an amazing fact. Most people in our society are not educated to think that the performance of rituals is as characteristic of human being as is speaking language and living in social groups; yet this is what the record seems to show. Three reasons for this miseducation occur to me.

First, our schooling is, by and large, so focused upon the modern ethos in Europe and North America and so little informed by world history and anthropology that the importance of rituals is overlooked. We do not realize that the modern (post-Enlightenment) attempt to get away from rituals and downplay their importance is very unusual in the history of the world.

Second, our thinking about rituals, as far as it goes, is directed toward the "big" ones: church services, funeral processions, state ceremonies, weddings, pilgrimages, festivals, and the like. These we tend to separate from the "little" ones: acts of greeting and leave-taking, table manners, making beds, issuing invitations, going to Grandma's house, making a date, and so on. Ignoring these because of their daily familiarity, we do not notice how greatly our lives are affected by ritualizing activities that have become, as they are supposed to do, our "second nature."

Third, we have thought too little about the animals. That is, we have learned not to take seriously our affinities with them, what in some societies would be called our kinship with other creatures. Hence we have not recognized that animals also ritualize their lives. Or if we have seen that, we have erroneously supposed that such ritualizing is "for the birds," not also for the humans. We have not understood that ritualizing is the bridge or pathway connecting animal ways to human. In short, we do not know where we have come from, nor where we are. If we did not ritualize, we would not speak. Ritualizing is our first language, not our "mother" but our "grandmother" tongue, and as such it is something we do not outgrow.

In this chapter, I want to draw a picture of ritualizing activity as something quite basic to the human condition. That is why I start with my cat. We are both ritualizing animals. This matters, for it is the basis of our relationship, and the same is true of my relation to human beings, and to all that is divine. If this is foolishness, I hope it is of the sort W. B. Yeats celebrated in one of his "Songs of a Fool":

> A speckled cat and a tame hare
> Eat at my hearthstone
> And sleep there;
> And both look up to me alone
> For learning and defence
> As I look up to Providence.
> I start out of my sleep to think
> Some day I may forget
> Their food and drink
> Or, the house door left unshut,
> The hare may run till it's found
> The horn's sweet note and the tooth of the hound.
> I bear a burden that might well try
> Men that do all by rule,
> And what can I
> That am a wandering-witted fool
> But pray to God that He ease
> My great responsibilities?"[8]

We shall not well understand what rituals are doing in human life unless we come to appreciate how deeply rooted they are in our animal natures. What goes on in churches, temples, state ceremonies, weddings, feasts, funerals, and arcane mysteries of high and low religion is built upon an urge to ritualize that we share with other animals and that has been part of our makeup since long before we evolved into our present form. That is part of the power that great ritual performances have: They link our most "advanced" ideas and aspirations with some of our most "primitive" tendencies. They are profoundly integrative. But let us go slowly and come to a sense of this by stages.

Human beings share with other animals a communicative world that depends upon gestural routines. Ethologists, who study animal behavior, have learned that animals of many different species engage in behaviors so highly patterned and so necessary for the animals' communication with each other that the scientists view them as akin to the rituals that humans perform. If my cat often seems ceremonious, that is because our evolutionary histories have something in common: Ritualized activities became, countless generations ago, necessary for our survival, and they have remained necessary to a far greater extent than is commonly recognized.

Between the cat's kind of ritualizing and the human's there are two main differences. One is that the cat does not employ words, but only mewings, purrings, hissings, and body language in her ceremonies. The humanoid line, within which our species evolved, had a potential for turning ritualized behavior into spoken word, which the other lines apparently did not have. In human rituals, then, words are usually (but not always) very important. Still, we must be aware that nonverbal behaviors precede and provide the basis for spoken language. This is a point to which I shall return.

The other principal difference is that the cat's ritualizings are based, to a high degree, on encodings in her genes, while the human's are mostly based on codes transmitted through culture. This also is a point we shall want to look at again.

Some people are most interested in the ways that humans and animals differ, but I find it more enlightening to focus upon similarities. I like to ask what it tells me about human beings to recognize that, in spite of our species differences, the cat and I are able to communicate so well that we have become mutually dependent.

The cat's behaviors are not exactly "rituals." But then neither are the acts that I perform with her—stroking her fur, reaching out with my hand for her to rub her head against it, talking to her in exaggerated tones of approval or admonishment, and so on. Her actions and mine are in some ways like rituals, they remind me of rituals, yet it would seem a bit pompous, in most contexts, to call them that.

It is better to speak of what the cat and I do together as "ritualizations." This word, though awkward, carries two useful connotations. Coined by students of animal life, it suggests, first, the similarity I mean to stress between the behaviors of human beings and other animals. One of the purposes of ritualizing is to communicate with individuals or groups with whom communication would otherwise be impossible. A ritualized behavior can be used by an animal not only to signal a member of its own species but also to deal with a predator: to make oneself big and threatening, like the cat with arched back and bristling fur, or to become invisible, like the rabbit that freezes. Humans also use ritualizations to communicate both with their own kind and with aliens. By ritualizing we make contact with animals, foreigners, and gods. I can better grasp a ritual performance from another culture than its spoken or written language. Of course, knowledge of the language would increase my understanding, but the ritualizations are basic because they display what the words interpret.

The second useful thought connoted by "ritualization" comes from its gerundive form, which emphasizes the making up of behavioral routines, their coming-to-be. Alongside the noun "ritual," we need the verb "ritualize" and the verbal-noun "ritualization." These invite us to think of ritual, using a developmental perspective, not as some kind of eternal form but as the result of *activity* in which both humans and animals engage. Contrary to some religious sensibilities, this perspective does not view rituals as having dropped from heaven but as having been created in the course of time on the basis of ritualizations evolved by many species, not least our own, to cope with danger, to communicate, and to celebrate. Whenever I use the words "ritualization," "ritualize," or "ritualizing," I hope the reader will think of *work*—often playful work, but nonetheless work—that animals as well as humans do. The animals ritualize, and so do we.

Let us glance first at the human side of ritualizing before looking to the other animals for a fuller picture.

■

To get a glimpse of our evolutionary past, it sometimes helps to look at infancy and childhood. Not that ontogeny necessarily recapitulates phylogeny but that the development of the individual offers some analogies to the evolution of the species.

Human beings are made, not born. A baby emerging from the womb
is a potential, not yet an actual, human being. Even if someone argues
that human endowments such as soul and rationality are innate, these
gifts are not sufficient to insure that an infant will become a truly
functional human being, capable of ethical and cultural responsibility. In
all senses but the purely genetic or purely theoretical, the humanity of
the infant has to be learned; and most of this learning takes place
through doing, through the activity of the learner as she or he imitates,
with some variation, the activity of others. In short, we enact, rehearse,
work, and play our way into the human condition.

The necessity to act or rehearse the way into a new state of being
seems to be as imperative for our entire species in its not-yet-finished
evolution as it is for specific cultures in their development, and for each
individual, never-quite-finished human person. The being of humanity
is a becoming. We become what we learn by doing—or what we do
while learning.

As participants in culture, we not only learn but also teach, mostly by
example. Collectively, we provide the means for our successors to take
their place in the human continuum, just as our own individual
learnings-by-doings were not left to pure invention and experiment but
mostly followed ways marked out by cultural predecessors. In this great
rhythm of learning and transmission, the principal technique is
ritualization.

To ritualize is to make (or utilize) a pathway through what would
otherwise be uncharted territory. What if no pathways for our behavior
had been blazed before we got here? It takes a strong act of imagination
to envision what our situation would be if our predecessors had not
marked out ways through which we can relate to one another and share
a common world of behavior. Consider a child as she finds out how to
exchange smiles, to crawl, to walk, and to dance. She learns a lot by
experiment but she is immensely aided by her society's pathways—that
is, examples for her to follow. A person from West Africa walks along a
road and dances at a gathering very differently from a North American.
The two have followed different pathways and ritualized themselves
into different ways of being human.

As a particular act of ritualizing becomes more and more familiar, as
it is repeated so often that it seems to circle round upon itself, it comes to
seem less like a pathway and more like a shelter. These two images—
pathway and shelter—reflect the tension in ritualization between the
verb and the noun. Some ritualizations have become in the course of
time such elaborate shelters that they are like architecture, and indeed
often have impressive buildings dedicated to their performance. What

once were newly blazed pathways are now old forms invested with rich symbolic content and carefully guarded by explicit traditions and rules. These are the great liturgies and ceremonies of stable institutions, like the coronation of a British monarch or the saying of Mass at St. Peter's in Rome. In Africa and in the South Pacific, there are ritual pathways so elaborate they are divided into cycles of performances that take many years to complete. They both guide and shelter the passing of generations.

Some ritual pathways are so much a part of everyday life that they pass largely unnoticed, thought of simply as normal behavior: shaking hands, saying "Hello" and "Goodbye," waiting for others at table before eating, and so on. While actions like this can scarcely be spoken of as rituals, they are the stuff of which rituals are made. To call them ritualizations is to emphasize that they are not reserved for special occasions, as full-blown rituals are, that they are clearly analogous to animal ways, and that they result from improvisation begun long ago and still continuing. In America the ritualized expression "Goodbye" is now often replaced by "Have a nice day," thanks, I believe, to an improvisation introduced, or at least popularized, by the telephone company. But let us lift the level of discussion by turning to species less motivated by business interests.

■

My cat, as I said, comes each morning to greet me at the bedroom door when I open it—provided, that is, she did not outwit me the night before and hide under my bed so as to pounce upon it hours later and disturb my sleep. If I have succeeded in confining her to that whole part of the house, excluding the bedroom, in which she is permitted to spend the night, and if she has not given too many nocturnal hours to wearing herself out chasing mice, she comes to the door as soon as she hears me up and waits there to be admitted.

When the door is opened, she stands for a moment for me to reach down and stroke her, and then she begins to make her little round, rubbing her cheek first against my hand, then my leg, then the door-frame, then the leg of the bedroom dresser, then back to my leg or hand. This may go on, round and round, for some time, until I move toward the kitchen, whither she half leads and half follows me in a deliberate pattern of underfootedness for which I have yet to find a motive. In the kitchen, she reenacts her cheek-rubbings at the door to the outside, letting me know she would like to make an exit.

Why this rubbing of the cheek against nearby objects? I learn from television that all cats do it, including the big ones in the wilds of Africa. A narrator tells me there are glands in the feline's cheeks that contain a scent. Rubbing up against something, the big cat leaves its odor there, presumably as some kind of message to other cats and, for all I know, to members of other species too. But my cat, it seems safe to say, did not learn from television what she is doing, let alone how to do it, nor to do it each morning. Hers is, some say, "instinctive behavior." It is, in any case, ritual-like behavior, a ritualization. How, and in what sense, does my cat know to do it?

In some animals many behaviors are learned by imitation and by trial and error. In this way, for example, a lion learns to stalk and kill the prey on which its own life depends. I do not know whether any of my cat's behaviors—rubbing her cheeks against things, stalking and pouncing on a mouse, going into the bushes for cover while defecating, then scratching dirt upon the leavings—were learned by observing other cats. I think very few, for she came to me so very young that it's hard to imagine she had already learned these things by imitation. I think most of her "learning" along these lines took place ages ago in cats' evolution.

How such learning passes from its first occurrences into some genetic code, so that my cat, aeons later, is repeating the gestures of her ancestors, I do not pretend to know. Scientists who study evolution have, for good reason, rejected theories of the inheritance of acquired characteristics, so the processes of evolution of these behaviors, depending on apparently random mutations of the genes, must be more complicated than I, a nonscientist, can fathom. What is clear is that the behaviors, as they have come to exist in my cat, are useful to her; and although she is free to adapt them to her own circumstances, she does not have to invent them from scratch.[9]

No doubt it took countless generations of cats' ritualizing (that is, improvising) with cheek movements before the ritualization now familiar to naturalists achieved its present more-or-less stable form. At the individual level, I can notice in my cat not only these inherited behaviors but also some ritualizing that seems particular to her. For example, when she is impatient with me to feed her, she makes an adaptation of her cheek rubbing, moving her head rapidly in that same gesture but touching nothing against her cheek except the air. Another example is her behavior in the car, where she seats herself in the lap of whoever is at the wheel, resting her forepaws on the driver's left arm and giving herself a view out the side window. She invented for herself this rather determined taking up of a position, adapting it from the lap-sitting she likes to do when I am in the armchair at home. Now she performs it during each journey at a time of her own choosing, going into a routine so familiar to her human companions that its every occurrence seems comic. Of course, our perspective is not hers. This only adds to the comedy.

■

Ritualizations do not start from nothing. They are elaborations upon simpler behaviors already known. If you watch the cat, you notice that her cheek-rubbing does not appear to be the most efficient way of merely leaving a mark upon the object she touches. The first sign of this is repetition: She goes round and round, making a circle, inscribing a path, adding one motion to another, and then going over the whole pattern once more with some minor variation. A second clue is her body language. Her tail is likely to point upward, quivering. She shakes her head and angles it as she goes. There is more energy concentrated in the event than the simple act of marking would require.

What cats' marking motions were like at an earlier stage of evolution, or even this cats' in the woods, I do not know, so I cannot well identify the "original" action upon which the ritualization has been built, but that does not matter. At whatever stage we notice ritualizing, we notice elaboration or refinement. As a good composer can sometimes make a melody more eloquent by simplifying it and at other times by adding flourishes, so I notice in the cat some movements that look like touches added and some that look like simplifications.

Julian Huxley's Introduction to "A Discussion on Ritualization of Behaviour in Animals and Man" [sic], published by the Royal Society of London in 1966, provides numerous examples of elaborate ritualizations, for instance the penguin dance, "the most elaborate of the great crested grebe's pair-bonding displays":

After a bout of intense head-shaking both birds dive, emerge with nest material (water-weed) in their bills, swim towards each other, and rear up breast to breast. They then indulge in a head-shaking display, which continues after they have dropped the weed and returned to a normal position.[10]

An astonishing example of ritualized elaboration has been observed by ornithologist Jared Diamond in the yellow-fronted gardener bowerbird in Papua New Guinea. The write-up in *The New York Times* is worth quoting at length:

Creeping forward, Dr. Diamond . . . came upon a brightly colored bird about the size of a blue jay standing in front of an edifice it had constructed, a four-foot-high bower of long sticks and fronds in the shape of a Maypole around a sapling. Three piles of brightly colored fruit—yellow figs and blue and green fruits—were meticulously laid out around the bower. A female was perched nearby, watching the male's performance. . . .

"The male bird held a bright blue fruit in its bill and pointed it toward the female so it always could be seen against the background of its brilliant orange crest," said Dr. Diamond in an interview. It was the kind of elaborate behavior typical of bowerbirds in courting, he said. As he watched, Dr. Diamond said, the male also raised his golden crest and caused it to quiver while displaying the fruit and uttering a variety of odd cries at the same time.

"I watched the performance for 20 minutes," the ornithologist said, "but the male didn't succeed in his wooing, and the female flew off." . . .

Male bowerbirds are known for their colorful plumage and their ability to use sticks, tree limbs, ferns, pebbles, key chains, flowers, fruit and other colorful objects to build exotically decorated "bowers" up to eight feet high. And, like only a few other animals, they use tools such as twigs or leaf stems to paint their bowers with vivid colors made from crushed fruit. Having finished the bowers, the males display their brilliantly colored crests, hold fruit in their bills and utter a variety of strange sounds, all for the sole purpose of luring and mating with an enthralled female. . . .

"And the males with the dullest plumage build the fanciest bowers," he said. "It's like the dull young man with a fancy sports car—even humans in their courtship go in for surrogate ornamentation."[11]

If the male is to get the female's consent to copulate, he must, at the very least, announce himself, something the bowerbird has done with extreme elaboration. That is to say, his "labor," which is here a performance, is drawn out extendedly. Ritualizing his actions, the bird piles up one colorful object after another. He underlines his meaning. We could say metaphorically that he piles word upon word. Literally, he heaps thing upon thing, taking care that the resulting heap has enough structure not to fall down, much as a rap artist piles one utterance upon another, taking care that his whole heap of words does not collapse into nonsense.

The bowerbird's behavior illustrates the link between ritualizing and the need to communicate. The earlier-stage form of a behavior is turned into a vehicle of expression. We find another instance in the gorilla's use of its penis erection to show strength in dominance contests with other males, or to threaten an aggressor. (This one causes me to wonder whether the roots of machismo may lie in male primates' search for something to do with their penises besides copulating.) I think also of the exaggerated thrust of my cat's head and the lift of her tail when she is impatient. Without going into the debatable matter of whether she *intends* to communicate (personally, I am satisfied that she does), the manifest fact is that her behavior announces her presence, makes me very aware of her, is attractive to me, results in my petting her, letting her outdoors, and, upon her return, putting food in her dish.

Jane Goodall witnessed a now-famous instance of communicative ritualization among the chimpanzees she has been observing in the wild in Tanzania since 1960. The example is particularly illuminating because it offers a glimpse of a ritual elaboration being improvised. An old chimp pathway was adapted for the occasion.

Male chimpanzees establish a hierarchy of dominance within their group. At the top of the group that Jane Goodall was studying, in the so-called alpha rank, was a male she called Goliath. It was to be expected that one day a younger male (who turned out to be one whom Goodall called Mike) would challenge the top male by putting on a display—that is, give a performance designed to intimidate Goliath and make him relinquish his king-of-the-mountain position. Such transference of power is regularly accomplished among chimpanzees, not by physical assaults but by ritualizations, which amount to contests in the *communication* of strength and ingenuity. Goodall describes a surprising occurrence on one particular day:

All at once Mike calmly walked over to our tent and took hold of an empty kerosene can by the handle. Then he picked up a second can and, walking upright, returned to the place where he had been sitting. Armed with his two cans Mike continued to stare toward the other males. After a few minutes he began to rock from side to side. At first the movement was almost imperceptible, but Hugo and I were watching him closely. Gradually he rocked more vigorously, his hair slowly began to stand erect, and then, softly at first, he started a series of pant-hoots. As he called, Mike got to his feet and suddenly he was off, charging toward the group of males, hitting the two cans ahead of him. The cans, together with Mike's crescendo of hooting, made the most appalling racket; no wonder the erstwhile peaceful males rushed out of the way. Mike and his cans vanished down a track, and after a few moments there was silence. . . . After a short interval that low-pitched hooting began again, followed almost immediately by the appearance of the two rackety cans with Mike closely behind them. Straight for the other males he charged, and once more they fled. This time, even before the group could reassemble, Mike set off again; but he made straight for Goliath—and even he hastened out of his way like all the others. Then Mike stopped and sat, all his hair on end, breathing hard. His eyes glared ahead and his lower lip was hanging slightly down so that the pink inside showed brightly and gave him a wild appearance.[12]

The result of this astonishing display was not long in coming:

Rudolf was the first of the males to approach Mike, uttering soft pant-grunts of submission, crouching low and pressing his lips to Mike's thigh. Next he began to groom Mike, and two other males approached, pant-grunting, and also began to groom him. Finally David Graybeard [an elderly chimp] went over to Mike, laid one hand on his groin, and joined in the grooming. Only Goliath kept away. . . .[13]

■

In the matter of ritualizing, humans are similar to other animals.[14] The group, whether it is a species or a culture, comes to "inherit" a behavior, the origins of which are often lost in time. "The domestic dog's turning round on a rug," said Huxley, "is a non-functional relic of a ritualization which was useful in the wild."[15]

Although the number of innate ritualizations in humans is no doubt fewer than in most other animals, we do have some of them, a notable example being the infant's smile.[16] Conversely, cultural and not merely genetic transmission of behaviors can occur in some other species, as was observed in some Japanese monkeys on Koshima Island in 1952.

A certain group of macaques, living near the water's edge, was fed sweet potatoes by researchers, who dumped the ration in the sand. Since macaques do not like gritty food, which injures their teeth, they cleaned the potatoes by tedious brushing and picking, until one day a young female (about a year and half old) took her food to the water and rinsed it. Pleased by the result, she repeated it. Soon her new behavior was imitated by others—first her mother, then her siblings, then members of her play group, and eventually all but a few adult males. Within ten years' time, rinsing of sandy food became habitual among this group of monkeys.[17]

I learned to wash my hands before meals years before I understood the dangers of infection. To wash before eating was "the way it is done," like putting the fork on the left and the knife and spoon on the right.

■

How much ought we to make of similarities between the ritualizations of animals and those of human beings? Some authorities, among them anthropologist Edmund Leach, think that the contrasts matter more than the likenesses because animal behavior is largely determined by genetic structure while human ritualization is generated by culture.

"It cannot be too strongly emphasized," Leach says, "that ritual, in the anthropologist's sense, is in no way whatsoever a genetic endowment of the species."[18] But this is to split animals' genes and humans' cultures too far apart. Mike's impressive use of kerosene cans is best understood as an elaboration upon an earlier ritualization customarily performed by male chimpanzees. Those ritualizations themselves were doubtless arrived at by elaboration upon still simpler ones. If we had the data to trace the line of development backward, we would doubtless come to a stage at which the behavior was very largely set by genetic endowment. Largely, but not totally.

Gregory Bateson has argued that it is an error, when analyzing a given structure or behavior of a living organism, to attribute its cause either to the environment or to the genes and not to their interaction.[19] He points out that the genetic code must contain instructions of a sort that will enable the individual to adapt and to learn. Otherwise, the adaptation of organisms to their environment would not be possible.[20]

Too simplistic an emphasis upon animal-human similarity can lead to superficial and prejudiced ascriptions to nature of human behaviors that are predominantly cultural and should be seen as expressing a specifically human creativity. At the same time, axiomatic insistence upon the categorical difference between culture and nature can deracinate human society, giving rise to the illusion that human projects are free from biological roots and constraints. This may lead to the rape of the earth and the exploitation of its people. As Ronald Grimes says in *Beginnings in Ritual Studies*, "If we forget our kinship with beasts and plants, we are likely to become in a perverse way what we deny."[21] Human beings are in all respects bio-cultural.[22]

■

My argument has been that human beings, like other animals, and for many of the same reasons, engage in ritualizations. We need them to give stability to our behaviors and to serve as vehicles of communication. In the primates, and probably in many other species, ritualizations seem to result from an interaction between genetic codes, group processes, the environment, and individual learning. This interaction is most clear in human beings. We can throw more light upon it by turning to what Clifford Geertz has said about the role of culture in human evolution. He reminds us that the evolution of our species has come about not simply through "natural selection" but through interaction between culture and biology.

Geertz's influential essay, "The Impact of the Concept of Culture on the Concept of Man [sic]," showed the fallacy of thinking that the physical evolution of humanity had ceased, or virtually ceased, before cultural development took over.[23] Geertz reasoned that some form of human culture must have appeared on the scene before physical evolution stopped (if it did stop), and that genetic evolution and culture must have interacted to produce the present physical form of our species. The major evidence for this is that we human beings depend on culture for our physical survival and, what is more, our mental functioning.

The brain of the newborn human is not suited for interaction with nature alone. It requires a *cultural* milieu. In order to function, it has to be nourished with words, symbols, and world-structuring patterns. These are as important to the young brain as warmth, bodily contact, and mother's milk are to the infant body. This dependence of the human brain upon a cultural environment indicates that culture became a significant part of human development *before* the physical evolution of the brain was complete. Otherwise, the brain would have evolved, like that of other mammals, with much less dependence on cultural factors. In short, culture and nature are deeply interdependent in our makeup.

Pointing out that culture is decisive for humanization, phylogenetically as well as ontogenetically, Geertz also reminded his readers that the cultural diversity in the world is not merely a set of variations upon a universal human nature. That is, in neither a logical nor a chronological sense does human nature precede culture, as if an original human nature were subsequently modified by culture. Rather, for the individual as well as the tribe and the species, humanization occurs along particular cultural pathways. No one can become human in a universal way; everyone does so in ways specific to this culture or that. Since ritualizations are such an important part of culture, Geertz's point adds strength to the argument that rituals spring from something essential to our humanity.

It is fun to speculate about the aspects of ritualization that are as useful to humans as to our sister species. Experimentation with certain gestures and repeating them over and over benefits the motoric system. In addition to strengthening and toning the muscles, it eventuates in a repertoire of rather distinct patterns of movement that are then available for later practical and communicative use. For example, movements of the head can be made to signify yes, no, and maybe.

On a visit to India, especially in the southern state of Tamil Nadu, I became fascinated with the way people seemed constantly to be shaking their heads from side to side. In my own culture, that is a movement meaning "no," and at first I mistook the Indians' signal. I soon realized their head-shaking signified assent rather than denial. It meant "yes,"

"OK," or "sure." I also noticed something else: The cattle that were everywhere to be seen drawing carts characteristically shook their heads from side to side in the same way! My fancy (how could I test it?) is that the people, being around the cattle so much and regarding them as sacred, have long ago picked up one of their gestures and used it for their own communicative purpose.

A people's repertoire of movement-patterns becomes more or less set through interaction between patterns encoded in the genes and patterns presented to the young by more mature members of the group. Eventually, these movements, a few innate, most of them learned, become useful in certain skills—for instance, in hunting or foraging for food. In such manner also appear the simple beginnings of technology.

For example, it is likely that playful routines in which chimpanzees fiddle with leaf-stems have led to their employment of these stems as tools for fishing edible ants from an anthill. Ritualization has provided the pathway to the use of a simple tool. Moreover, once such use is found, ritualization helps to spread it through the group and insure that it will be imitated by the young. Here, as so often in nature, we need to think of the principle of redundancy. Just as tens of thousands of a plant's seeds are scattered to insure that one will germinate, so in the animal world many, many gestures are formed, and some of these are repeated countless times, before one "catches on" in circumstances that prove its usefulness to the species.

The early motoric learnings have other potentials besides the directly pragmatic. They can also serve to mediate relations among members of the group: That is, they do double duty as signaling devices, helping to maintain order and give protection at moments of greeting, mating, food sharing, and social activities like mutual grooming in primates. Raymond Firth, highlighting the importance of ritualizations in determining relative status within groups, points out the similarity between animals and humans in greetings:

An important element in much greeting and parting behaviour is status demonstration. Relative posture and gesture, especially in degree of elevation, are used in very many cultures symbolically to indicate the relative status of the parties engaged. . . . social inferiority is expressed symbolically by a simulacrum of physical defencelessness. . . . Analogies with animal behaviour here are clear. . . . By visual, aural, tactile and olfactory means animals establish identity and social relationship. Human beings do not use the physical range of the senses so widely or so acutely—smell is rarely used in greeting behaviour, though sometimes it is discriminatory. But the bodily means of establishing relationship by touching—with hands, lips, noses—in such contexts is most marked, and would seem directly relatable to animal behaviour.[24]

The point here is not only that ritualized behaviors, since they are *patterned* and *repetitive,* can be employed as signaling devices, an important enough point in itself. Equally if not more significant is that ritualizations can be used to *store* and *transmit* information, across time and across generations. Leach reminds us that

> the Eskimos, Australian Aborigines, and Kalahari Bushmen all manage to live quite comfortably in conditions in which an ordinary white man [sic] would find himself incapable of sustaining life at all. This is possible because these people are somehow capable of transmitting from generation to generation an extremely elaborate body of information about the local topography, and its contents and how it may best be utilized. How is this achieved in the absence of any written documents or of any kind of formal schooling? In brief, my answer is that the performance of ritual serves to perpetuate knowledge which is essential for the survival of the performers.[25]

It seems likely that ritualizations were the first means evolved for doing this. Certainly they remain essential in the transmission of culture. Leach observes that for "ordinary non-literate people" in all societies "there are many kinds of information which are never verbalized but *only* expressed in action."[26] The same, I may add, is true of literate people, although they are less likely to notice it. If we had to do our business and educate our children with literate means only, we would not last long.

Ritualizations are the first symbols, carrying within themselves, just as chosen objects and words will later do, a whole complex of meanings. Such meanings do not have to be translated into words. They can generate intelligent responses in other members of the species before words are available. When the yellow-fronted gardener bowerbird puts a bright blue fruit in its bill and points this toward the female, the fruit alone is not carrying the message but rather the entire performance in which the fruit is used. The female's own action in return, whether she flees or remains to mate, is her sentient response. Such patterns of behavior survive generation to generation in the species. Whether by genetics or by protocultural transmission or (most likely) both together, complex information amounting to action-guides is transmitted along the intergenerational line. By the time the Eskimos and other human beings use ritualizing as the carrier of survival information, the mode of transmission is clearly cultural, though it remains to a large extent nonverbal. The code for learning how to be a human being is very largely a behavioral code, and this in a double sense: It is a code about behavior, and behavior is the code.

■

We are so used to putting human rituals in one category and animals' ritualizations in another that we may resist any assertion of continuity between them. Yet that connection seems to me essential for appreciating why we have rituals and are so dependent upon them. The link is signaled, no doubt, in the presence of animal masks and costumes in the rituals of many of the earth's peoples, as if it were widely sensed that to ritualize is to acknowledge a kinship with other species. A humane existence requires a mutual commerce with nature, a recognition of the ways we humans belong to other forms of life. This is best expressed and preserved through ritualizing.

A continuity between animal ritualization and human ritual is to be defended for reasons that are both developmental and logical. Concerning the developmental factors, I have to rely on Huxley, Lorenz, and other trained scientists; but on the logical side of the matter, I can offer a suggestion: In human culture the sense of ritual as ritual, that which makes it recognizable and intelligible as human behavior, presupposes a gestural context that goes beyond all formal ritual. No matter how symbolic human rituals may be, their sense requires the pre-understanding of a "world" in which the members of a group can communicate with each other through patterns of behavior. Language itself is made up of patterned behavior, some of it audible, some gestural, and some a combination.

The meaning-units of a language make sense within the "universe" of that language, but language itself—the very idea of speaking—is intelligible only within a horizon of action. As Wittgenstein said in *On Certainty*, "Language did not emerge from some kind of ratiocination. . . . Children do not learn that books exist, that armchairs exist, etc. etc.,—they learn to fetch books, sit in armchairs, etc. etc."[27] Language cannot give reasons for itself, nor can it supply final reasons for any of its propositions. "Giving grounds . . . comes to an end; —but the end is not certain propositions: . . . it is our *acting*, which lies at the bottom of the language-game."[28] Two of Wittgenstein's interpreter's say that language, "far from being a reflection of thought, is a form of behaviour."[29] Robert L. Moore writes:

Scholars and scientists have given increasing evidence that preverbal, instinctive acts or responses provide the verbal areas of the brain with the associations that constitute their basic meaning, emotion, and power for action; upon these associations the significance of the verbal elements of ritual depend.[30]

We may imagine three concentric circles. The innermost is speech, which has for its first horizon a field of nonverbal ritualizations, since speech is linked to body language, to gesture, tone of voice, and all manner of nonverbal behaviors on which it relies for emphasis, clarification, and grounding. The circle of ritualizations, in turn, has its own horizon—the environment of physical actions and objects that exist outside the coded realms of ritualization and speech.

This image of three concentric circles is intended to show that each inner circle assumes and relies upon those that surround it. But we need also an image that will suggest a certain ascendancy as we move from outer circle to inner, because what occurs in each circle is, after all, an elaboration upon and refinement of what is received from outside. That is why I speak of ritualization as a pathway: The elaborations produced by ritualizing activity have the intention of leading somewhere, of going from one condition to another, even though the end may not be clearly in view. Although the process employs randomness, it is not itself random.

Speech is elaboration upon nonverbal ritualizing. Huxley, and even Leach, both affirm this. Huxley says that symbolic language "can properly be regarded as ritualized (adaptively formalized) behavior."[31] This means that there is a potential in all ritualization to become symbolic. It also means that symbolic language, for all its abstraction, retains something of the character of formal behavior patterns. Leach says plainly that "speech itself is a form of ritual." (He says "ritual" where I would say "ritualizing.") Pointedly, he adds that "nonverbal ritual is simply a signal system of a different, less specialized, kind."[32]

Consider the ritualization of voice production. It is a necessary, not an accidental, precondition of language. If we did not first babble and cry like babies, we would not later talk. One piece of evidence is that the babbling and crying stage is not entirely left behind as speech matures, but remains in the background of all later articulation. To have a good feel for any human voice that addresses us, we must have some intuition of the cries and babbles out of which it has arisen and to which it has the possibility at any moment to return. The same holds for language's other behavioral roots, the gestures and the repertoire of "body language" with which the child, like the kitten, plays and becomes expressive. One function of play is to experiment—to produce and reproduce, invent and repeat, try things this way and that until a response, either from oneself or from outside, gives satisfaction. Such experiment serves to create channels in the form of behavior patterns that are then available for the discharge of energy, the expression of emotion, and other communications.

When my daughter was seven years old, I had the opportunity of watching her learn French. We were spending a year in a village in southern France, and she went to the one-room schoolhouse, where at first she understood not a word. Very soon she adopted a routine that I was able to watch. When she got home from school in the afternoon, she would set up a chalkboard and play teacher. Any members of the family who would sit in as students were welcome to do so, or else it would be just the cat we had then, or maybe just the flowers in their pots. No matter, she "taught" her audience in mock French. Out of her mouth came all the French phonemes I had ever heard, including those wonderful nasals, rolled Rs, and diphthongs that I, as an adult, found impossible to produce well. But at first she did not pronounce a single recognizable French word. It was a splendidly articulated gibberish, and yet at the end of three months' time she had turned it into perfectly good French and today earns her living by teaching that language.

Like a sculptor carving an image from raw stone, my daughter gradually discarded the combinations of phonemes that did not get satisfactory response in the French-speaking environment. From the welter of mock French a good French little by little appeared. It is the best example I have ever seen of language beginning as ritualized sound-making and later changing into the kind of verbal sense that the culture affirms. But, of course, a similar process goes on in every child's learning the mother tongue.

The child's babbling, of course, does not turn into English or Swahili all by itself. The infant, like some remote ancestor on the evolutionary tree, is not an actual but a potential human communicator. The transition from potential to actual, from genetic inheritance to cultural realization, requires interaction between self and others. This is done mostly through play, invention, and fooling around, in the course of which you notice that the behavior patterns you generate are getting signals in return—"answers" to messages you did not know you had sent. You may then consider, "What did I do to make that happen?"

It's what the drummer does on her drum, what the dancer does in his dance, the lover does in foreplay, what the adventurer does in the great, open world: the sending forth of something, and the discovery that it "works." Such probing, sending-out, and playing with the world to see what it will answer, is basic to ritual, to language, and to culture. An Ojibway shamanic chant declares:

> It will resound
> Clearly
> The sky
> When I come
> Making a sound.[33]

■

Like art, ritualization involves both improvisation and the establishment of repeatable form. These two elements provide a way of distinguishing the words "ritualization" and "ritual" in reference to human activity. The former (ritualization) emphasizes the making of new forms through which expressive behavior can flow, while the latter (ritual) connotes an already known, richly symbolic pattern of behavior, the emphasis falling less upon the making and more upon the valued pattern and its panoply of associations.

The difference between ritualization and ritual is not, however, categorical. A single event may be viewed under either aspect. We deal with a continuum, extending from the most inchoate and random behaviors imaginable to those with the greatest degree of formality and achieved cultural meaning. Throughout the gradient, differences are of degree more than kind. Without its ritualizing (new-making) component, ritual would be entirely repetitious and static. Without aiming at the condition of ritual, ritualizing would lack purpose and avoid form; it would fall back into that realm of informal, noncommunicative behavior from which it arose. As Ronald Grimes says, "Ritual begins with ritualization."[34]

Ritual, language, and culture are useful, then, not merely to store and repeat the known but also to extend the frontier. Ritualizing play, as J. Huizinga saw, provides a foundation for culture.[35] As Victor Turner well knew, and as we will argue later, ritual is a vital component in processes of social change.[36] In nine cases out of ten, no doubt, the soundings of ritual and language produce echoes of the already known, and these will confirm self-knowledge and world-knowledge; but the tenth case is the exception and the rule.

The frontier and its crossing validate all the probings that go on in more familiar territory day by day. The universe of logic and language, the web of meaning, as Wittgenstein calls it, cannot locate itself all by itself, cannot answer to itself. It calls for something other than itself, something not linguistic, something outside, something before, alongside, or yet-to-be, which can summon language to be language, can tell us that it makes sense to play and explore without yet knowing what we have in mind or whether we mean anything at all.

To be aware of the edge of the web, the otherness beyond the frontier, and the source still present in the later development, is necessary if we are to avoid an eventual intellectual cynicism.

Fortunately, such awareness, although sometimes lost by people in protected, privileged environments, is characteristic of the world's majority of downtrodden, suffering people, for whom praxis and meaning are not separate, who know, like Wittgenstein, that the ground of all meaning is an ungrounded way of acting.

Everything points to the supposition that our remote ancestors were ritualizing before they became human. This activity became the pathway to the human condition. Ritualization is a way, an experimental way, of going from the inchoate to the expressive, from the sheerly pragmatic to the communicative. Hence, in humans it is a close relative of art, especially the performing arts. In fact, we had best think of it as their progenitor, and as the source also of speech, of religion, of culture, and of ethics. It is not as true to say that we human beings invented rituals as that rituals have invented us.

3

Modern Warfare: The Loss of Ritual Pathways

Primitive warfare was usually highly formalized.

—*Encyclopedia Britannica*[37]

In the previous chapter, we have seen that the very human act of making rituals arises from ritualizing behavior that is prevalent throughout the animal world. We also saw that the making and performing of rituals is not just some curious thing that certain religious people like to do, but that it is as universal and essential to the human condition as is the speaking of language. It would be hard to overestimate the role that ritualizing has played in the evolution of our species and the development of all its cultures.

In the present chapter, we shall inquire further into the human dependence upon rituals. This time, instead of looking toward the animal kingdom, we shall consider our own human situation in the twentieth century; for this is an age in which the decline of ritual sensibility, particularly in the Western industrialized nations, has become a threat to the survival of life on earth.

It could be argued, I think, that the life-threatening pollution of the earth's oceans, streams, and atmosphere is partly due to the neglect and decline of rituals that once regulated people's relation to their habitat. At any rate, the attempt of modern civilization to live in a de-sacralized cosmos is coming more and more to look like the making of a catastrophe. This said, for present purposes, I am going to leave the ecological crisis aside and look instead at what may be its twin: the danger to all life that is presented by the twentieth century's practice of total warfare. The de-ritualization of war in our time means that modern warfare has become a horror that is conducted without moral constraint.

I do not go so far as to say that a loss of war-making ritual is the *cause* of the senseless way in which modern nations fight. Certainly, it is not the sole cause. It is, however, an important part of the process, along with technology and ideology, by which warfare has become in our century ever more dehumanized, irrational, and threatening to everything that lives.

One of the images for ritualization that I have employed is the making of a pathway. The image has several ramifications that are germane to our discussion. At the end of the chapter, we shall want to emphasize, as we did previously, the notion of cutting a path through new territory, or marking a new route to follow. At the start, however, I am most interested in the pathway as something already marked out, therefore something that has a boundary to define the range of acceptable behavior.

Many people in modern society dislike rituals because they see them as constraining. They do not want to engage in prescribed behavior but want to be free to do as they please. This is especially so in cultures like the North American, which put a high premium upon individuality and creativity. Often forgotten is the point that freedom cannot survive in conditions of moral chaos. One of the functions of ritual is to mark the pathways for morality to follow.

Traditionally, in most societies, warfare has been a highly ritualized activity. I will use as an example the people of the western highlands in Papua New Guinea, because I once had the opportunity to visit them. Although I did not witness any intertribal warfare, which has for the most part been suppressed under Australian and now independent central government, I attended a ceremony that was historically linked with combat and shared some of its qualities, the ritualized pig exchange.

Life in the New Guinea highlands, including warfare, pig exchange, agriculture, and domestic life has been beautifully depicted in a documentary film called *Dead Birds,* made by Robert Gardner in 1961 in Irian Barat (Irian Jaya), the Indonesian territory adjoining Papua New Guinea.[38] Writer Peter Matthiesen, who was a member of the expedition when the film was shot, produced a beautiful literary account called *Under the Mountain Wall* (1962). My own visit was to the Enga people of Papua New Guinea at a time when they were performing a pig exchange, which they call Te (pronounced "tay").

As is typical of traditional rituals, the Te serves many simultaneous purposes. The most ostensible one is to settle outstanding debts. Over the course of time, members of an Enga tribe will, for various reasons, incur debts to members of a neighboring tribe. These pile up until there is enough wealth to repay them, mostly in the form of pigs, which here as throughout Melanesia are a principal form of wealth. Other valuables used in payment are pearl shells, handsome bird feathers, axes, and nowadays paper money. I saw the latter folded and stuck into slits in long bamboo poles that were held high overhead by men wearing the traditional dress of a genital cover in front and pandana leaves behind.

The ceremony took place on the "Te ground," a clearing in the woods not proximate to any village, which we climbed up to by a steep and well-worn path for an hour and a half beyond the place our truck had to stop. As we neared the site, we came upon a row of stakes driven into the ground alongside the pathway. During the days preceding the Te, the pigs that were to change hands were staked out here by their several owners and given the once-over by their intended recipients. Then was the time for the latter to make sure that the pigs were big enough, healthy enough, and numerous enough to repay the obligations that were due. I was told that much haggling went on, because the Te should not take place until all parties were agreed upon the terms of repayment. These matters settled, the pigs had been taken forward to be staked out again at the Te ground itself, where, by the time I arrived, the ceremony was in full swing.

For the Te, a noncombative occasion that is nevertheless charged with latent hostilities, aggressiveness, and self-aggrandizement, the participants who are giving and receiving must be in full dress. This costume is the same as would be worn in intertribal combat. To speak of it as a military uniform, however, would be misleading, for it is not a standard garb prescribed by a military bureaucracy but a traditional one that is adapted by each individual to his own personality.

As I approached the Te ground, I discovered one participant surrounded by helpers grooming him for his entrance. He wore a broad headdress of matted black hair, shaped a bit (as I saw it) like the hat of Napoleon, into which was inserted magnificent multicolored plumage from the bird of paradise. Around his eyes was some kind of makeup that intensified his brows and lids, giving him what the people call "a dark look," signifying that he came bearing a grudge or at any rate was not to be trifled with. A thong around his neck supported a large pearl shell, which hung glistening upon the dark brown skin of his chest. Below his waist he wore a genital cover and pandana leaves. When I arrived, he was down on one knee while his assistants covered his body with pig fat to make it gleam in the sun.

Most of the time at the Te is given over to oratory, which is delivered as a kind of chant and accompanied by dancing, shouting, and parading up and down. What strikes an observer most of all is the energy given to display. It is not enough that I should give you these pigs, which are to repay you for the favors you have done to me in the past: It is important that you see me doing it, that all these other people here, surrounding us in a great circle and waiting to have a good time, should also see me doing it. And we should see and hear you accept the gift also. For on this occasion something important is happening: Instead of killing you, I am repaying my debt to you. But more. I am repaying you *more* than I owe you. Think of my generosity, that I give you more than I owe. And think of tomorrow, when I who was your debtor will be your creditor, and instead of me owing you, you will owe me. Think of this and hear this. For this change in our relationship is happening now, in front of all these people, and before your eyes and mine. When the sun goes down, all will not be the same.

These meanings and insinuations, these brandishes of power, make it clear that the pig exchange is not something to be called simply a transaction (though it is certainly that); it must also be called a ceremony or ritual. But what I want to call attention to now is the way the ritual works as a pathway for moral behavior, and its similarity to the ritualization of warfare.

The western highlands of New Guinea had no contact with the outside world until after World War II. Then the Australians moved in, establishing patrol posts and instituting civil government to protect the interests of gold miners, traders, and coffee planters.

The civil governors were offended by intertribal warfare and declared it illegal. As part of their campaign to eliminate it, they also outlawed the Te, having learned of the affinities that the Enga and other peoples saw between their ceremonies of exchange and their acts of war. In other words, the colonial authorities wished to establish a reign of total peace, which meant, of course, their own monopoly of war-making power. They declared there should be no more war and no more pig exchange.

Trade and combat, we must realize, are two closely related phenomena. Where there is contact and transaction, there is also the likelihood of combat. This is one reason why ritualization becomes morally significant and necessary for group survival; since without the channeling and moderation that ritualization provides, all contact between living things easily turns into combat without limit. If ritualization has provided the evolutionary pathways along which we have passed into the human condition, it also provides those that are necessary to keep us there.

In traditional Enga combat, any of three occurrences might bring an end to the fighting: (1) the going down of the sun (so the combatants could get home before dark, lest they be assailed by ghosts or ambushed by unprincipled opponents); (2) the falling of rain (which would spoil the feathers and cosmetics of the splendid fighting costume); (3) the killing or severe wounding of a single warrior on the opposing side (which constituted "payback" for previous injury). If any of these occurred, the battle was over, the warriors retired, and events awaited some new development.

I suggest that these limits imposed upon combat were not, to the participants' minds, so much a matter of abstract principles as they were features of the ritual combat itself. A man knew, as it were, how to fight and not to fight. When the conditions for not fighting were present, the ritual pathway pointed toward home. In like manner, women knew when and how to pursue their own activities.

Enga society, like most others, was very sexist, the roles for women and men rigidly prescribed; but its sexism, like its warfare, was more moderate than our own, being channeled by ritual. We moderns no doubt have the more insight into the problematic nature of sexism, but our behaviors are more given to extremes. To take Papua New Guinea's own example, the incidence of rape in its modernized cities like Port Moresby is greater than in its traditionalized hinterlands. Those who believe that modernism is the same as moral progress need to think again. Most of all, they need to think about the moderating influence of ritual.

My visit to Papua New Guinea prompted me to reconsider my received version of Christian theology, which had held that the Christian principle of forgiveness was superior to the *lex talionis:* "An eye for an eye and a tooth for a tooth." In the New Guinea context, I saw that the latter principle, which is there called "payback," had two sides: If it encouraged people to think that they had a right to take revenge for a killing, an injury, an insult, or some other damage, it also restrained their revengeful appetite by limiting the payback to the exact amount of the damage. This equilibrium or moderation was maintained not only by being abstractly stated but even more by ritualization, which indicated to members of the culture the appropriate forms for their fighting and their revenge to take.

■

The de-ritualization of war in modern societies does not, God knows, mean that we do not surround our wars with rituals. Tanks are paraded exultantly through the great public squares. Soldiers parade at goose step. Air shows featuring split-second maneuvers are held for excited audiences, thrilled the more because occasionally a plane will crash. Memorial Day parades and speeches are part of the American scene. Victory parades celebrate military triumphs. Military display seems to have lost none of its attraction.

When I speak of the de-ritualization of war, I am thinking of the way that the combat itself is conducted. Where warfare is ritualized, the combatants do everything possible to make themselves visible to one another. They display themselves vauntingly. They conduct the battle as much by self-advertisement as by their techniques of killing. The flamboyant costume of New Guinea fighters is ingredient to their military skill. The whole event is personalized, just as we find it in the epic traditions of Greece, India, and many other lands, where the idea is not simply to win but to win with honor.

We deal here with a cardinal principle of ritual: To ritualize is to make oneself present. It is to find a way of strongly presenting oneself, and by doing so to invoke the presence of that god, or person, or force whom it is necessary to confront. It is this, and not regimentation, which makes ritual often so scary.

Warfare in the twentieth century turns its back on all this. It knows nothing of honor but moves by stealth. It trusts naught to ritual process and everything to surprise and massive force. Submarines hide under the sea. Rockets hide under the ground. Soldiers wear "combat fatigues," designed to be invisible in the landscape. Modern warfare depends much on encryption, and the work that goes on in back rooms to break an enemy's codes. The CIA is authorized to engage in "covert operations," so called because they are never supposed to be seen in the light of day. Here we are far from ritual. We are in an ethos in which the ends are thought to justify the means, whereas in ritual the means and the ends are inseparable.

Having thought of these things in Papua New Guinea, I thought of them again some years later in Japan, where I made, somewhat reluctantly, a pilgrimage to Hiroshima. As it happened, I journeyed to the birthplace of atomic warfare by way of Izumo, one of Japan's most revered sites of ancient ritual.

■

On the northern side of the mountains, the sun was shining. That morning my companion and I concluded our visit to Izumo, ancient, much alive, prestigious, beautiful, mystery-enclosing shrine of Shinto, located in sacred hills near the Sea of Japan. It is difficult not to be romantic about Izumo, once you've seen it. On me the place exerted a kind of benign spell.

Arriving there on Children's Day, we had watched hours of Kagura (plays done for the gods, for children, and for the secret delight of grownups), had seen infants in large number undergo their first rite of purification, at the end of which the Miko had silkenly danced, to the sound of bell and drum, her serene celebration; and we had, after making a suitable contribution to the priest, ourselves undergone the purification rite, following into the inner court and bowing our heads as the robed priest waved over us his *gohei*, a wand with white paper streamers that rustled in the wind, followed by our ceremonious drinking of a cup of water from the shrine's fountain.

Before going to Japan, I had known nothing about Izumo. By the time I visited the sacred site, I was learning that Shinto has two sides. Long before it was the official religion of a modern nation-state, as it began to be under the Tokugawas in the seventeenth century, and as it became even more stridently after Japan's opening to the West in the nineteenth, Shinto had been the indigenous, nature-oriented religion of the countryside. Nowadays the two aspects of Shinto coexist without entirely melding. Popular shrines, mostly small and very local, and evidencing varying amounts of nationalistic pride, exist throughout Japan. Although Shinto is not a centralized, hierarchical religion, tradition is clear in recognizing that the two chief shrines are the one at Ise, near the old capitals, Nara and Kyoto, and the one at remote Izumo. Both have clear ties to the Imperial Household; but the one at Ise is saturated with the majesty of the state, while Izumo, though elegant, is imbued with the spirit of mountains, trees, water, and all manner of beneficent, occasionally mischievous, powers both human and divine, understood to live there.

Shinto, as is often said, is a religion not of theology but of ritual observance. In Japan I discovered that these observances are mostly happy. At Izumo I, a stranger with no deep knowledge of the religion or the customs and totally unable to understand the language, felt at home. There the world has been put together with simple ritual and with grace. The limits are very clear—so clear that even a stranger can be told without words what to do.

I would have been happy to stay in that benignly structured place a long time, but after two days we fulfilled our self-imposed vow to go to Hiroshima.

Clouds sat on the tops of the mountains. We drove into them, ascending into obscurity from the sunlit northern shores, and as we descended the mountains' southerly side a soft, steady rain began. It was not curiosity that was leading us to Hiroshima, and God knows there was no expectation of pleasure. I was on a pilgrimage I thought it my duty to make. My companion had suggested it first, and I wished she had not, for once the idea was spoken it was clear that conscience would compel me to that place. I could not live with myself if I, an American in uniform during World War II, came to spend five months in Japan as a guest of the Japanese, my first journey to that land, and did not look at the place where my government had introduced the Japanese firsthand to the hell of nuclear war, and the rest of humanity to the shock and fear of it.

I did not expect to gain much information there that I did not already know, and I could not quite imagine that my going would help anyone, but I felt at some deep level that I *ought* to go. If only my companion had kept silent; but she did not. Once she had said, "I want to go there," it was as if a voice inside me had spoken: "Thou shalt go! Thou shalt not stay away!"

We planned an itinerary that would take us by car from Kyoto, where we were living, to some sites and spas on the northern shore of Honshu, mainly to Izumo to observe its architecture and rituals. From there we would go by the cross-mountain highway to Hiroshima, destination of our quasi-ritual and pilgrimage. We stopped somewhere for lunch after the rain began and arrived at the city in early afternoon.

Hiroshima has recovered. We were already used to watching its baseball team win games on television. But I had to see the new, fast-moving metropolis with my own eyes, I had to hear its traffic, in order to comprehend that on the very place where atomic horror had happened new life had grown. I saw new buildings wherever I looked, not constructed along some futuristic plan but ordinary, mid-twentieth-century office buildings and apartment houses lining wide streets, through which moved cars and busses and trucks and streetcars and bicycles and the sounds of urgent vehicles and thousands of pedestrians as brisk in their stride as New Yorkers. The city's rejuvenation was palpable. My companion was encouraged by this, but I was terrified.

What, I asked myself, is to keep it from happening again? Where are the limits that we human beings need to protect us from ourselves? I live, I thought, in a century when the restraints have gone, one by one, away.

Rifles gave birth to machine guns. Explosives began to be dropped from the air. Armies let loose poison gasses. Scientists cooked up batches of deadly bacteria to be spilled out to cause public plague. Soldiers were no longer the main targets of war, but instead the civilian populations. Bombing of specific military targets gave way to "saturation" bombing and fire-bombing, which destroyed with no discrimination and were so massively destructive that they made it seem like a small and logical step to the atom bomb.

In our century we went beyond the thought of triumph in war and demanded the enemy's "total surrender." The idea of war became that of total war—war without limit.

The experts say that a nuclear war today would exceed the devastation at Hiroshima by a magnitude of thousands.

The year was 1983. Ronald Reagan was President, and many Americans seemed under the illusion that atomic wars are not really so bad, since it is possible to recover from them. Standing in rebuilt Hiroshima, I feared an amnesia, some immoral forgetfulness that would cast out all true memory of The Bomb. To me, at that moment, the thriving citizens of recovered Hiroshima were emblematic of the world's desire to believe that the nuclear volcano would never again erupt; or if it did, civilization would somehow get by. And I knew that there is a religious version of this callous optimism, according to which it is not civilization but rather those saved by Jesus who will "get by"—to heaven. In this accursed century, we become ever more inured to mass slaughter, often with religious blessing.

We do not like to face the truth that not only so and so many persons or cities or even nations might perish in nuclear war, but that the entire "fate of the earth," as Jonathan Schell has called it, is now in human hands. It is an awesome thought, one that in previous ages would have been sheer fantasy, like some wishful thinking of death-driven Samsons dreaming of colossal suicide by drawing down the pillars that supported the roof above them, taking all living beings to their deaths along with the hero-destroyer who pushed the button. Promethean technology has turned this nightmare possible.

The two of us drove through the busy thoroughfares, using a map to find our way to the Peace Park and the Museum, which lie at the center of the city, at the epicenter of the August 6, 1945, explosion.

The white museum stands in a green-grass park, a deep, rich green as we saw it in the rain, which covers the several acres on which the city decided not to rebuild. Left standing is one famous remnant, the shell of the nineteenth-century commercial exhibition center, with its now-skeletal dome conspicuous from all directions. From the museum, one looks at this hull across the green. Midway, set close to the ground, there burns an eternal flame.

Leave the car in the parking lot. Take umbrellas. Walk under a portico. Pay admission. Go upstairs. Begin to view the exhibit. Fall silent.

Wall-mounted text is informative about the bomber mission, the time and place of the explosion, the results, mostly in technical, quantitative language—how many degrees temperature, how many pounds explosive pressure, how many miles radius for this and that effect, how many victims, how many types of injury on and on—everything in dry, understated language, the effect not dramatic-sudden but cumulative, slow, sickening.

Interspersed among the words on the wall are photographs. Hundreds of those. And then what I had not, somehow, expected: encased specimens of actual objects and pieces of clothing, surviving in their burned-out, decomposed state. Words are one thing, especially the laconic, information-loaded words chosen here. Photos are another, especially these documentary images, also understated in their way, even when they show corpses or, worse, the walking dead. But these material objects, these pieces of wood, cloth, and steel, were—what? For a long time I stared at them awestruck, not having the word for them. Then I knew: relics. They had been there. They had survived their own destruction, mute witness to the life they had once been part of, to the violence committed upon them, to everything that was once here and had in an instant become nothing.

From these holy-unholy objects, I would repeatedly remove myself, seeking respite. The museum is designed in such a way that one can turn at times from the display walls to an expanse of glass overlooking the greensward, the eternal flame, and the bombed-out shell some half-mile away. To this scene I would repeatedly go to give some balm, some perspective of time and place, to my horror-bulged eyes. And then I would realize that I was standing in the actual space where the devastation described on the wall behind me had come down. This was The Very Place. It. Not far away in some other country but Here. And I felt: This is not my place. I do not belong here. No one belongs here.

In *The Idea of the Holy*, Rudolf Otto says that an experience of the holy is characterized by an emotional response that combines fascination and fear. That was my experience at the museum in Hiroshima. Holiness is not always goodness. When it came to light that Oedipus had murdered his father and married his own mother, evils that drove Oedipus to gouge out his eyes and send himself into permanent exile, he became a holy figure. Socrates dramatized that aspect of him in *Oedipus at Colonus*. I had the feeling at Hiroshima that the place was holy not in spite of but because something unspeakably bad had happened there. But this is the kind of awareness that needs to be ritualized. It is not so much a piece of knowledge to be analyzed as it is a moral awareness asking for an appropriate action. We will look later at the ways in which ritual is freeing, but first we must see the affinity between ritual and the sense of moral obligation.

My going to Hiroshima was in itself a ritualization, and I had recognized it as a pilgrimage. By pilgrimage I mean a journey undertaken not so much for empirical as for moral reasons, although some pilgrimages (to Lourdes, for example) may promise very practical benefits as well.

Ordinarily, we think of pilgrimages as religious events. Well and good; but since I believe that ritualizations exist before religions do, and since I think that theology comes *after* and not *before* religion's rituals, I beg the reader's leave to insist that a pilgrimage be viewed, first of all, as a journey undertaken out of felt necessity. We may ask whether this need arises from some moral imperative or from some other quarter, but the crucial point is the *obligation* one feels.

At first the museum had been quiet. My companion and I were, it seemed, the only foreigners in the building. The other visitors were Japanese, mostly of middle age and up, and there were a good many of them, considering the day was mid-week and the weather inclement. They were of my generation, and this was about the only thing I felt we had in common. I was acutely aware of myself as an American, one who belonged to the nation that had perpetrated the destruction pictured around us. "Don't you realize," my Japanese colleagues in Kyoto had said, "the Japanese do not blame America for The Bomb. They blame the war." But here in the museum I had no way to know what the Japanese around me thought of the two Americans present. Perhaps they gave us little thought, although they would glance in our direction from time to time. For myself, I felt stained, guilt-ridden, in need of purgation. My existence, our existence, the life of all who had survived, perhaps like the lives of those who survived Auschwitz, I don't know, seemed somehow illicit. I was in the grip of an odd logic: Since so many innocent have died, all those who have not died are guilty. And those who must count themselves among "the victors" are the most guilty of all. I felt then what I have often felt when watching films or photos from the death camps in Germany: that my eyes were guilty for having looked, especially as I could not think what to do about what my eyes had seen, and so I was of evil, nothing better than a voyeur.

To ease this grief I would go stand at the window, looking at green grass in rain, relieved now to see beyond the park the movement of city life apparently untroubled by the grotesqueries that hissed and moaned like devils in my mind.

Then came the children.

Bus loads debarked. They were in blue school uniforms with yellow caps. They swarm like bees over every shrine, temple, and monument in Japan. Had I been thinking dispassionately about the museum, I might have anticipated their coming, but I had got lost in a world desecrated long before these youth were born, and their arrival jolted me. They entered running and screaming. I don't know how many score of them invaded all at once. For the other visitors that afternoon, the place held the quiet of a sanctuary, but to the schoolchildren it was a playground. They ran from wall to wall, pointing, reading snatches of legend out loud, shrieking, not with fright but excitement, yelling at each other, rushing to the next wall, next room, their decibels scarcely diminishing as they went, since the whole building was full of their sound, and they arrived now in wave after wave with almost no pause.

What was for me a dolorous pilgrimage to a place of horror, many times worse than the bloodstained palace at Mycenae or the bed-chamber of Oedipus at Thebes, was to the schoolchildren a festivity. They got their history lesson on the run, and they tumbled forward like white water not caring from what source they came nor into what sea they would debouch.

I was standing on the forlorn side of the knowledge of good and evil, feeling I was about to plunge into a depth in which all morality would be drowned, or perhaps had already been destroyed at the dawn of the nuclear age. These children acted as if good and evil had never yet been born. They knew only themselves, their own energy and play.

After a time, quiet returned. The children were gone. I finished making my way slowly to the end of the exhibit, and then I came once more to the great glass windows, as did my companion, and we stood side by side for the first time since entering. In spite of the skill of the museum builders and the exhibit's designers, in spite of the cultivated emptiness of the park land in front of us now, in spite of every sign of thriving civilization around us, beginning with the souvenir stand doing brisk business a few yards away, I felt that I was in a totally unstructured space.

There were no limits here. Once the bomb had fallen, *anything* could happen. What atomic weapons meant, what the death camps in Europe had meant, was that nothing ever more was sacred. In our day, it had been revealed that human beings are capable of demolishing every imaginable boundary. Morality is not innate. There are times and places from which it disappears. These instances are awesome. They are the reversed image, the diabolical mirror image of the holiness of God.

And that is the most terrifying thought of all, for it means that the *lack* of moral limit speaks more clearly of divinity to many people now than its presence does. This moral void is therefore something we desire as much as we fear.

I had now the urge to flee from the bomb site. It was as strong as the urge that had got me to come there. The inner voice came to me again and said, "Go! Get you away from this place!"

Touching my arm, my companion whispered, "Let's go."

We descended the stairs, wordless. Retrieved umbrellas but did not open them, walking wet through rain to the car. Once in it, we found the way to the superhighway.

The rain was heavy now, and darkness came. The return to Kyoto took six hours, stopping only for gas and coffee. Outside the car, rain and darkness. Silence within. Neither of us spoke. Slowly, it began to feel good to be encircled by something as small as an automobile and to have the way charted by the course of the road. My imagination retreated to a known world.

Perhaps it was to find and possess the known once more that I had made the pilgrimage. But this thought is after the fact. I made the journey not knowing why, only that I must.

■

The desire for ritual seems to grow most urgent when people feel a prolonged or acute absence of moral guidance. That is the first lesson that I have drawn from my Hiroshima experience. The second is that too much of modern life, including its warfare, has turned away from ritual, pursuing instead the technologies of genes, machines, electrons, and particles. I shall comment on these two points in turn.

At Hiroshima, although the museum and the park gave me a defined space, offered me symbols and icons, and provided factual information to encourage meditation upon the event of The Bomb, it did not strongly suggest anything of a performative or ritual nature for me to *do* then and there. One could say that it is not the business of a public memorial to do that, especially at a place that will be visited by the followers of many different religions or of none at all. Yet this does not alter the fact that I felt strongly the need of a Hiroshima ritual that day, and had to provide one for myself, such as it was, by making my journey into a pilgrimage, and by offering several silent prayers.

It is also the case that I have not found an adequate Hiroshima ritual anywhere, although I am aware of several attempts at making one. On August 6 every year there is a ceremonial in Hiroshima that has been televised the world over. The people of the city go to the river's edge by the thousands and place upon the water floating candles. They create an image, very beautiful to see, of life inextinguishable and of peace. In recent years, rituals of protest have been conducted on Hiroshima Day in Nevada, at the place where nuclear-bomb tests are conducted by the U.S. government. Observances on that day are held in a number (not the majority) of churches, synagogues, and temples. Yet there appears to be no ritual, certainly none widely performed, to express what Hiroshima means for the fate of the earth.

My spouse and I go each year to a Hiroshima Day observance in Pittsfield, Massachusetts, where perhaps a score of people stand in the main square holding aloft antinuclear placards before the eyes of motorists and pedestrians going to work. Although our political clout is near zero, I feel the need to do something with my body in response to the nuclear danger, to bear witness, to keep company with others who care, and through this activity to search for a nuclear-age morality.

This kind of pragmatically inadequate, half-certain, ethically driven, expressive behavior is an instance of "ritualizing." It is like trying to beat a pathway through wilderness, through a terrain of human, moral bewilderment. It is analogous to what our forebears did as animals when they laid out, surely unconsciously, the ritualizations their offspring would follow. Analogous, but not identical; for as human beings the major threats we face to our species' survival are of our own making, and the terrain we most need to know is that of culture and morality.

At Hiroshima I was like a child, perhaps even a blind child, groping its way. It was this sense of blindness and dependency that impelled me to make the pilgrimage in the first place, and later to grope my way as best I could. The urge to ritualize is strongest where there is a prolonged or acute absence of pertinent moral guidance. To be sure, this urge is not always acted upon. In modern society, it comes most often to nothing because the climate is so full of ritual misapprehension.

■

Just as strongly as Hiroshima spoke to me of the need to ritualize, it spoke also of modernity's turning away from ritual to pursue, as I have said, the technologies of genes, machines, atoms, and particles. If my readers understand me, signaling as I do through the flames that have consumed so many victims in our day, they will recognize that modernity's loss of ritual's moderation pertains not only to warfare. The chief desires of human beings that are most in need of ritual constraint, because most lacking in it today, are sex, food, the power to dominate, and violence.

These four human desires link us closely to our animal heritage, but no less closely to the divine in us. For both reasons, they have traditionally been major subjects of ritual, through which societies have sought to link their members with animals, with gods, and with each other in patterns of ethical behavior.

I do not, of course, mean that I agree with all of the values and behaviors that have ever been celebrated in ritual. For example, most rituals in recorded history have linked sex and power in a way that upholds male domination and female subservience. Morally wrong as I, a twentieth-century opponent of patriarchalism, think these rituals have been, I must acknowledge that most of them expressed the best ethical insight of their epochs, and served to moderate the very male dominance that they justified. I share the conviction of many feminists that what we need today is not the abolition of rituals having to do with sex and power but their transformation or replacement so that newly conceived values in sexual ethics can create pathways along which more just and humane sexual behavior, as we envision it, may go.

In a later chapter, we shall look at the link between ritual and violence which has led to practices of human and animal sacrifice that have been, and remain, spread throughout the world. Today, as far as I know, human sacrifice is illegal everywhere, but it is also rumored to survive in some locales. Even the rumor is enough to show the historic and psychological link between ritual and violence. In any case, the link is very clear in various activities that are either criminal or in the twilight zone of legality. Structures of violent power, including who murders whom and how, are highly ritualized in the Mafia, as they were also in the Manson family. Certain types of pornography (not all) depict ritualized acts of assault and murder against both women and men.

As for warfare, even in modern society, many rituals surround it. An argument has been made that the nuclear arms race itself is conducted like a ritual.[39] Yet, as I have already mentioned, modern societies tend not to conceive of the actual business of war, the fighting and the violence, within a ritual context. Where there is still to be found some sense of this, as in Iran under the influence of Shiite Islamicism, for example, the Western world tends to regard it as barbaric, as if our own destructiveness, carried out in the name of science, democracy, and progress, were not even greater. It is the United States of America, and not any practitioners of ritualized warfare, that has dropped the atom bomb.

Ritual belongs to what the ancient Greeks would have called *techné*, the root of our words technical, technique, and technology. Ritual is a sort of technology because it is a method (a time-honored one) for accomplishing something in the real world. We shall have more to say about this in our chapter on ritual as transformation. The *techné* of ritual, however, is utterly different from modern technology. Its field of action is not an objectified physical world but a divine, human, animal, and vegetative cosmos of mores, moralities, and mutual relationships.

When the techniques of ritual are cast off in favor of the apparently more rational technologies of genes, machines, atoms, and particles, humane values are jeopardized, because something essential to the self-regulation of humanity, its ritual processes, are shunted. We enter then upon a time of ritual misapprehension and ritual boredom, which cannot but be a time of dehumanization. The world becomes an impersonal thing, defined by numbers and not by ceremonial actions. Of this development, the atom bomb may serve as our preeminent symbol.

■

A ritual is moral territory, sometimes secular, sometimes religious, that has been staked out. Ritual marks the boundary at which wilderness, moral desert, or profane life stop.

One of the more vivid examples of such demarcation that I have seen is the sacred rope (*shimenawa*) that marks the entrance to Shinto shrines. At some of these, the rope has reached gigantic proportions (the one suspended over the main gateway at Izumo, for example, is about three feet in diameter); but the ceremonial rope in Japan that made the greatest impression on me was not outsize. It was simply, to my eye, out of place.

At Kamigamo Shrine in Kyoto, while walking through a wooded area to pass the time before the start of a Noh performance at ceremonies held to mark rice-planting time, I was startled to come upon an otherwise ordinary looking rock, perhaps three feet in diameter,

girdled with a rope. A length of hemp had been wrapped once around
the girth of the stone and tied in a simple knot. My feet coming full halt,
I stared several moments in astonishment. The encircling cord made of
the rock a thing apart, like a circle of stones one might come upon in a
desert or on top of a mountain, or for that matter at Stonehenge on
Salisbury plain. Only after a time did I notice that in fact this stone was
surrounded by a circle of smaller, low-lying ones, and that the plain-
looking rope was embellished with two or three colorless tassels.

The "territory" that rituals mark is both literal and metaphoric. It is
well and good to speak of "sacred space," provided we remember that
in and of itself the space is not what is sacred. Neither is time itself
sacred when a calendrical mark is made to set off a sabbath day or a
holy week or any other ritual time in the calendar. These demarcations
of sacred regions in time or space are part of ritual's techniques to
spotlight and re-form human behaviors.

The more important thing is not the stone with the rope around it but
the behavioral result: Confronting it, I stop in my tracks. Here is the
similarity, despite all differences, between law, ritual, and art.

In one of his perceptive, felicitous essays, this one elegantly called
"The Bare Facts of Ritual," Jonathan Z. Smith speaks of a sacred place as
"a focusing lens."

When one enters a temple, one enters marked-off space in which, at least in
principle, nothing is accidental; everything, at least potentially, is of significance. The temple serves as a *focusing lens*, marking and revealing significance.
. . . The ordinary (which remains, to the observer's eye, wholly ordinary)
becomes significant, becomes sacred, simply by *being there.* It becomes sacred by
having our attention directed to it in a special way.[40]

Smith notes that a similar point had been made by Arnold Van
Gennep in *The Rites of Passage* when he spoke of the pivoting of the
scared. Van Gennep wrote:

A man at home, in his tribe, lives in the secular realm; he moves into the realm of
the sacred when he goes on a journey and finds himself a foreigner near a camp
of strangers. ... Every woman, though congenitally impure, is sacred to all adult
men; if she is pregnant, she also becomes sacred to all other women of the tribe
except her close relatives; and these other women constitute in relation to her a
profane world. . . . Thus the "magic circles" pivot, shifting as a person moves
from one place in society to another.[41]

We may add that the "magic circles" also pivot when an entire
society moves from one historical epoch to another.

Rituals mark locations in time and in space, but they do so in order to define ethical behavior. We do well to attend carefully to the defining and delimiting functions of ritual, not in order to keep forever inviolate any particular limits our traditions may have set for us, but in order to see the heroic work performed by our ritualizing ancestors. Among these predecessors, we should count not only the remembered pioneers of given traditions but also our so-called animal forebears who preceded all human societies and from whom, as we saw in the previous chapter, we have received the ritualizing possibilities that make civilization possible.

The horror represented by Hiroshima is the destruction of moral limit. Those who dropped The Bomb profaned everything, which results in a kind of moral devastation. The nuclear arms race that has ensued continues this atrocity by holding in hostage all life, animal and vegetable, on the planet. And with this transgression, a great deal of our moral life has collapsed, as it must do when people live with the sense that any and all behavior is allowed. The ways, paths, or channels that guide behavior are felt to disintegrate, leaving individuals and groups in a condition known to psychologists and sociologists as *anomie*, the absence of law or norm.

This lawless atmosphere, however, contains also its apparent opposite: totalitarianism. Nuclear weapons are themselves totalitarian. Their construction and strategic placement at the ready shares with political totalitarianism the idea that there is no limit to what one is permitted to do for the "good" of the state, or perhaps for some other "holy" cause. It is forgotten that one of the functions of ritual has been not only to place limits upon the behavior of persons but also at times to restrain the actions of divinities who might otherwise imagine themselves as all-powerful, under no obligation to place ethical discipline upon themselves.

Manufactured and deployed by America, the atomic bomb is part of the history of totalitarianism, which willfully regiments, incarcerates, tortures, and murders people, imposing narrow limits beyond which ordinary people dare not pass, while arrogating to armies and governments the right to stride heedless over all moral limits. Totalitarian ambition is shared alike by capitalist and Communist powers, and both are skilled at devising rituals that constrain the populace while elevating governmental power to godlike omnipotence. Think of the rituals of Nazi Germany or Maoist China.

At a deep level, then, our situation is a bewildering zone of moral devastation, even though, at a more superficial level, we are bound tight by rules, regulations, and idolatrous rites that glorify totalitarian power.

With The Bomb we come to the outer limit of moral existence, facing the edge of what can be mapped as human reality. From here, morally speaking, we must grope our way forward.

■

Groping in the face of danger has much to do with rituals. It is paradigmatic, not for rituals as such but for the *engendering* of ritual and the establishment, or reestablishment, of human society. It is precisely when we do not know in our conscious minds what we ought to do that the ritualizing impulse, laid down for us in structures older than consciousness, is brought into play.

Ours is an age that needs both the marking of known ways that are worthy of repetition and the groping for new ways in situations with scant precedent. Humanity's ritual traditions are rich but they were not devised to deal with the split atom, nor space flight, nor the hole in the ozone layer. Neither were most of them fashioned to uphold sexual, racial, cultural, and social-class equality.

When we do not know what to do, confronted with challenges that baffle and frighten us, we have to rehearse in the dark, so to speak, without a script. We have then to improvise on the basis of gut feelings, following primal motivations.

Whereas received rituals guide practitioners along known paths, *ritualizings* create pathways in response to new moral obligations. As the child babbles playfully before it can talk, as the infant gropes with wandering hand before it can see or even know the target, as the dancing begins before the dance has any name and before there is any idea what dancing is, so too in times of crisis when received wisdom is inadequate to the new situation, groping may come to our aid. Confronting radically new dangers and moral challenges, we need to shift our magic circles and redefine the sacred.

■

I have stressed in this chapter the principle of moderation and limit that ritual incorporates. But this is not ritual's whole point. Even traditional ritual has also an innovative and a liberating side, the exploration of which is the major task of this book. Limit and innovation, formation and transformation, are complementary in human life. They constitute a polarity within which ritual practice moves. Where limit is given too great a value, there ritual becomes the servant of oppression. Where innovation is sought without regard for restraint, there ritual will lose itself in chaos and confusion. Our next step will be to look at this polarity as it manifests itself in rituals that are specifically religious.

4

Priest and Shaman: Two Pathways of Religious Ritual

It does not matter whether you believe in the loa, as long as you serve them.

—HAITIAN PROVERB

In Haiti one hears it said that the country is 95 percent Catholic and 90 percent *vodou*. These two sides of Haitian religion exemplify the two poles between which religious ritual moves. At one pole, the paramount consideration is order, regularity, and limit. At the other, creativity and infusion of spirit. Of course, since both Roman Catholicism and *vodou* are living religions, and furthermore are closely related, both poles are represented in all of their rituals; but the emphasis is strikingly different in the two traditions, which may go a long way to explain why there is so much tension between them.

Let us give these traditions generic names, calling the one priestly and the other shamanic. These names suggest "ideal" types of religious ritual. In practice the priestly and the shamanic are mixed, and indeed it is customary to speak of the Haitian *houngan* as a priest, his female counterpart, the *mambo*, as a priestess. Even so, as I have said, Haiti provides us with a clear enough example of the difference between the two types, which may be found also in any American town as a contrast between church congregations devoted to "high" liturgical practices and those given to being filled with the Spirit.

Except to scholars, the very word "ritual" often suggests "high" liturgies only. What goes on in more popular religious gatherings, where there is apt to be a lot of hymn-singing, shouting, and other forms of enthusiasm, is not, in popular idiom, called ritual at all. For this reason, it is very important that the reader be able to visualize, when the word "ritual" occurs, the more popular as well as the more "classical" practices. Hence I invite the reader with me to Haiti, where I found the contrast to be particularly vivid.

Most of this chapter will be given over to description of two particular rituals that I was able to photograph and tape record in the summer of 1982. My aim is not only to project pictures onto the screen of the reader's imagination but also to convey something of the experiential feel that the two events provided. Afterward we will turn to some general comment.

As we shall see, my role as photographer did not prohibit me from "getting inside" the celebrations as a participant. My participation could not, of course, be as full as the Haitians', since my command of the language was poor and I was a cultural outsider; but my participation was welcomed on both occasions, and I cannot bear to be present at lively rituals and neither move nor be moved.

I start with the priestly example, since its features are probably more familiar to my readers. It is also the type of ritual that most Westerners from the middle and upper classes regard as normative, a judgment I would like to challenge.

■

Jean-Claude and I had spent ten exhausting days and nights going to almost as many *services vodou* in Port-au-Prince. He was my right and left hand during that summer of Haitian research, my interpreter and the opener of doors to *hounfors* (places of worship) I could not easily have found nor walked into unannounced. Tired from the very successes of our "ritual-hunting" in the capital, and deciding to go away for a bit of rest, we drove down to Les Cayes and took a room in a *pension*. When Sunday came, I surprised Jean-Claude by announcing I would like to go to church.

"I thought you came down here to find out about *vodou*."

"That's right."

"Church is not *vodou*."

"I know it, but I go to church when I am at home, and I need to see what it's like here." His look told me that was not a good reason for dragging him out today, so I went on. "If I don't know how they do church here, I won't well understand *vodou*." It was true, and the right thing to say. He was ready to go before I was.

We walked toward the center of town, aiming for the cathedral. We were not yet in sight of it when Jean-Claude said softly: "I think there is going to be a *grand manifestation*."

"How do you know?"

"Do you see those men walking? Look what they're carrying."

I woke up. Two or three men ahead of us in the street had what I now saw to be liturgical vestments draped over their arms as they, in casual clothing, moved neither swift nor slow but with clear intent toward the town square. Glancing around, I saw others approaching along side streets. We quickened our pace.

At the square, the cathedral was to our left, receiving a stream of pedestrians. The men with robes in hand were disappearing into a building on another side of the square, which Jean-Claude said was the bishop's house.

Going into the cathedral, we found it nearly full. Immaculately groomed, as Haitians usually are on Sunday, the men wore business suits, the women colorful dresses, mostly in reds or blues, or else the habits of the religious. They were all singing, led by a robed priest waving his arms, swaying his whole body, and eliciting from the people waves of lilting and joyful noise. I thought to myself: "If this be priestly ritual, it is better than most." Here the priestly had been blessed by infusion of Caribbean rhythms. The congregational voices were backed up by a small combo, which had no brilliance but did mix a sweetness of tone with a beat just well enough syncopated to help the singing swell as if forever. In my experience, the priestly type of ritual often lacks rhythm this good, so I was delighted.

We taped some of the singing and then went out once more into the town square, where we learned that the occasion for the festivity was the ordination of seven diocesan priests. I stood on the cathedral steps facing outward, edging as far as possible to the left because the bishop's house was to that side, and I expected the clerical procession from there.

It came arrayed all in white with a boy crucifer at its head, he flanked by two other youths. The white-robed, mostly black-skinned processionalists were dazzling in the morning sun. Their albs of white linen were allowed to hang loosely about them and had very wide sleeves, which gave the men a look of being at ease even in the midst of formality. Each had a stole of different design with soft-hued embroidery on a field of cream or pastel. The priests walked in two columns rather wide apart, making their procession appear to fill the street. They were not a vast number, perhaps forty in all, but their eye-catching appearance and graceful way of walking (a Haitian specialty) created a most imposing image, even before we caught sight of the bishop.

He came at the end of the formation, of course, and was far and away the largest person in it. All I could think of when he came into view was the New Guinea expression "Big Man," an epithet that refers to a self-appointed entrepreneurial leader. I knew that a Catholic bishop could not appoint himself to his office, but this one looked as if he were perhaps an exception. At any rate, he was very big, both vertically and horizontally, yet gave no impression of lethargy. If he walked slowly, that was because he *wanted* to walk that way. He did not go to the left or the right side of the street as the others did, but came right down the middle; so that although he was the last member of the procession (except for the two who managed the tail of his cope), no person but the crucifer far ahead was directly in front of him.

He wore crimson. His gown was of that color, over which he wore a white lace surplice. This was topped by his great red cope, which covered his shoulders completely and was fastened together over his chest and would have covered his back to the ground if the two train-bearers were not holding it up out of the dirt. The stiff breeze tried to whip it out of their hands, so they held on with tight fingers while the cape billowed so much that it made the bishop in profile look as if he might turn into a balloon and fly away; but from the front he seemed as massive and firmly in place as the church he represented. On his head was a four-cornered chapeau the same color as his robes, and on his face a large pair of gold-rimmed spectacles. His missal was carried by a white-skinned, white-robed priest walking one step ahead and to the left.

Jean-Claude and I decide not to wait for the procession to get all the way inside but push in through a side door so as to be able to watch the parade go down the center aisle. Now the congregation is singing a song with a refrain beginning, "*Attendez, attendez*" ("Await, await"). The procession advances straight down the middle and up about three steps into the "choir."

The bishop advances to an altar table that is covered by a linen cloth on which the number "7" has been embroidered at the left and right—for the seven new priests? He walks around this table on the right, climbs three more steps, and stands in front of his chair, which is placed before of a second altar. He is flanked by seven attendants. Behind his head is a ciborium, above that a bas-relief of a white dove descending, above that a painted carving of Jesus on the cross, at the foot of which stand the Blessed Virgin and a disciple, the latter looking up, she with head bowed. Above the cross is a framed painting of heavenly angels.

During the service, the bishop's outer vestments and head-covering are changed frequently. Part of the time, his great crimson robe is replaced by a shorter white cape with a blue trim at the neck. The four-cornered red hat is exchanged for a skull-cap of the same color, and at times the assistant places over this the bishop's miter, tall and golden with red lining and red trim.

Early along in the service there is a sermon. It is in French, not the Creole that is the only language most Haitians understand. The substance is fairly progressive. It looks to the future and alludes to a time when Haiti will be free of poverty and oppression. Its main emphasis, however, is on faithfulness and obedience within the church.

The motif of obedience is later enacted in a powerful way. The ordinands stand seven-abreast at the front of the choir, facing the altars and the bishop. He leaves his position and comes down the steps to the same level as they, where he comes in front of them, turning to face the altars himself. He is in white, like the ordinands, except for the blue trim of his cape and the red of his skull cap. He is flanked by two bare-headed attendants also wearing white with blue trim. He kneels, and the seven ordinands behind him go flat to the floor, lying prostrate upon their stomachs, their faces buried in their folded arms. The bishop prays. Then, having submitted himself to the higher authority of pope and Trinitarian God, he stands, turning to face the ordinands with his back to the altars. They rise and face him. Now comes the litany of promises.

One by one, each ordinand comes forward and kneels at the bishop's feet, arms folded. The bishop places his right had upon the kneeler's head and asks: *"Promessez moi . . . ?"* ("Do you promise me . . . ?"). A vow of obedience is taken. After this the ordinands receive new albs decorated with blue trim and yellow sunbursts on the back. The bishop's throne is brought forward and the miter placed upon his head. He sits, the picture of royalty surrounded by his court. The ordinands again come before him one by one, standing with bowed head to show respect and receive blessing. This done, the bishop returns to his place before the higher altar, his throne being returned there as well.

Now the diocesan clergy, who had formed most of the original procession and have been sitting in chairs along each side of the "choir," come to greet their newly ordained colleagues. It is a splendidly warm moment with embraces, kisses of peace, a relaxed circulation of men from one to the other, the mitered bishop looking on paternally from his high seat, and the congregation happily singing. The brotherhood of it was sweet to my eyes and ears until, looking down at the scene from on top, I noticed that it was a brotherhood defined by the exclusion of women.

To make some pictures, Jean-Claude and I had climbed some stairs into a balcony running the full length of the cathedral. From up there the hierarchical division was clear to the eye: The cathedral was divided into two major zones, the choir and the nave, which seemed related to each other as the shore to the ocean. On the one side, stretching far to the left of our position, was the vast company of laity. On the other side, to our right, was the much smaller group of clergy. On the left were street clothes; on the right, clerical vestments. On the left were a mixture of men and women, but mostly women, including a good number of nuns; on the right, men only. At the shoreline between the two areas was the bank of steps demarcating the choir from the nave. The building was split from one end to the other by an axis down its middle, the long center aisle, which ran from the street entrance at the back right through the middle of everything and up the steps into the choir and up more steps to the bishop's seat, in which he sat, at the highest end of this longitudinal line, and at the middle of anyone's view who looked from the lay into the clerical zone of the church. He was lifted up, and this elevation pointed to things higher still, for his miter was pointed, and behind and above him rose the vertical cross of Jesus; and the spectator's eye traveled, as it almost always does in cathedrals, to tall columns and arches and high windows and decorated ceilings where the mind's eye takes over and gazes still further up to the infinity of heaven.

Although I am not much in sympathy with displays of hierarchical authority, I found this Haitian version easier to take than many. The music had the common touch. The ceremony exuded warmth, howsoever stratified and male-centered it was. At one point, in fact, the male/female division of territory was breached. At the offertory, a group of six young girls, dressed in white frocks, white stockings, white shoes, and flowered straw hats, rose from the first pew and danced their way right up into the choir. There they continued to dance for several minutes before making their way back again to the first pew. It was without question the most sedate dance I saw in Haiti, but it was not without charm; and by introducing females into the choir area, albeit in tokenized form, it was not without point.

The *manifestation* ended with Holy Eucharist. The bishop was the celebrant, and the servers were the new priests. They stood at what I call the shoreline, at first taking up their positions at the top of the steps and then going down them to stand on the laity's own level, getting their feet wet, as I came to think of it, at the edge of the sea. The singing was again joyous, and when people had communed and returned to their places they added a thunderous percussion of hand-clapping to the song's beat.

Of its kind, the service that morning was among the best. Even Jean-Claude said he was glad he had been there. But his resistance, like mine, came from the tension we felt between the ritual impulse to unite all souls as one and the priestly advertisement of its own mediating role. Shamanic ritual is different.

■

Leaving Port-au-Prince for the west and south, the main road passes through a region of third-world urban sprawl known as Carrefour. Here are not the worst slums of the city, but perhaps for that very reason the poverty seems somehow more real, as if it is entirely normal and will last for ages. Here people with almost no money, mostly unemployed, manage somehow to survive in a city offering no welfare programs, very few medical clinics, no employment agencies, no counseling services. People live by whatever temporary jobs for the unskilled they can find, by the aid of friends and family, and by their wits. In this milieu, the *hounfor*, a place of worship presided over by a *houngan* (a male shamanic type leader) or *mambo* (female), offers both a spiritual and material resource. In the city, a *hounfor* can be a substitute family, a community to lean on.

The *hounfor* of Marc Jerome is located on an unpaved street crowded with houses and small shops. We arrive on Tuesday evening just before dark to find a vendor of cigarettes and rum established at her little table just outside the *hounfor* entrance, where a number of young people are hanging out. They look like people waiting for a dance to start, and this is correct, for a *vodou* service is essentially a party combining great conviviality with its seriousness of purpose. A ritual, I remind myself, is work done playfully.

A single doorway, standing wide and full open, gives entrance to a cinder-block building some forty by sixty feet. The walls, except where there are murals, are painted blue and pink. Although there are no windows, numerous openings at the top where the walls meet the tin roof allow ventilation and symbolize connection between the *service* and its material and spiritual environment. The floor is unpaved, so that the bare feet of the *serviteurs* of the *loa* (spirits) may be in direct contact with the earth. The *hounfor* is a crossroad, a place of connection. The *loa* may arrive from any direction.

Near but not exactly at the center of the room is a large *poteau mitan* or center-pole. This off-centered center gives to the room an architectural energy the plain rectangular space would otherwise lack. The concrete post is fairly massive, being about fifteen inches in diameter and standing on a circular base about three times its own width and almost hip high. Its top seeming to disappear through the roof, the column is painted in spiraled stripes like a barber's pole except that its colors are brown, white, light blue, yellow, dark blue, red, and green. From rafters all over the room hang paper pennants in the same set of colors.

Three drums are leaning against the wall to the right of the door as I face into the room. Near them several young men stand joking with each other, occasionally tapping out a rhythm. When the drums were new, they were christened, using a Christian rite of baptism, but the drums are not sacred objects. There is magic in their use during a *service*, but otherwise they are just drums with names.

Stretching the full length of the long wall at right angles to the row of drums is a permanent set of tiered benches for the choir, who now, resplendent in their white knee-length dresses and white head-wrappings, are waiting for something to start. By far the majority are women, but a few are bareheaded men in white shirts and white slacks. The choir leader is a man whose tailored white sport shirt, worn loose over the top of his slacks, gives him a look of breezy elegance. The choir members are *hounsi*, who have undergone one degree of initiation into the mysteries of *vodou* and who make up the core of the *hounfor's* constituency. I estimate there are more than fifty of them tonight.

The wall opposite the entrance has three small doors, all closed. These go to the *cayes mystères*, "houses of mysteries"—that is, rooms dedicated to particular *loa*, who are the spirits (deities) sacred to *vodou*. In each *hounfor* about three of these will be particularly honored. A *caye mystère* will contain objects associated with one of these by tradition or dedication. The doors themselves are plain, except that the one in the middle has pinned to it a photograph of François Duvalier, Haiti's dictatorial President-for-Life, who ruled from 1957 to 1971.

Near the door on the right, a mural depicts a long-haired, short-bearded St. André wearing a brown robe, standing tall, and carrying a cross. I read in black letters just to the left of this figure, "3 *fois* 3," a message that will appear again during the evening.

Some chairs for visitors have been set in front of this third wall, and there are more along the fourth side. In fact, chairs for visitors take up perhaps a quarter of the floor space. Moving a little further in, and turning around to look back at the doorway, I see above it in red block letters: "CASPARD, MELCHIOR, BALTHAZAR." Near this door, on what I have called the fourth wall, a lively bull leads a painted existence. His tail is raised high and curled, while his head is lowered for a charge, his legs appearing already to have sprung into action. He looks as if he

is on his way down from the wall to spring over the heads of those
seated near him and join the festivities.

Adjacent to the bull is a poster picture of Jean-Claude Duvalier and
his wife, he the son and successor of François Duvalier until he will be
forced to abdicate in 1986. There are several such posters in this *hounfor*,
as in most. The relation between *vodou* and the unscrupulous Duvaliers
was troublesome and ambiguous. The father attempted to form a
network of support among the *houngans* and *mambos*, and some say that
he was a *houngan* himself. Had the policy succeeded, it would have
pushed *vodou* ritual from the shamanic toward the priestly type. But this
seems not to have gone very far. Every *houngan* and *mambo* had reason
to cloak the matter in ambiguity, since open opposition to the regime
was not tolerated and too-open support of it, except in outward things
like posters on the wall, was in many places unpopular. Moreover, since
Marc Jerome was the *serviteur* of a deity (Simbi) who specialized in
ambiguity and in-between-ness as well as in magic and luck, I knew that
the politics of this *hounfor* could not possibly become clear to a short-
term visitor.

Jean-Claude introduces me to M. Jerome, a large-framed man
dressed in white sport shirt and slacks, like the choir director.
Permission for me to visit and to make photos and tape recordings had
been sought earlier in the day by Jean-Claude, who promised that in
return for such courtesy we would be glad to make a contribution of
several bottles of rum, which I now present to our host. He receives
them in a dignified manner and places them with other such bottles on a
table near one of the *cayes mystères*. He tells me I am most welcome and
should feel free to use my tape recorder, camera, and flash and to move
about the room as necessary. I feel truly welcome, but he does not linger,
for in fact there are quite a number of visitors tonight with whom he
needs to speak, all Haitians except me.

The ceremony to be performed is known as *Chiré d'Ayizan*, or
Shredding of Palm. The name Ayizan also belongs to one of the *loa*, and
as it happens she has particular concern for ritual life. Calling her "the
first priestess," Maya Deren says that in her "are the last echoes of the
androgynous divinity. In some regions she is referred to as 'he'; and in
songs she is related to the ancient androgynous founders of the race. . . ."[42]

Here is part of Deren's portrait of her:

. . . she is patron . . . of the ritual stages of initiation which culminate, finally, in
the canzo ceremony of spiritual birth. It is her palm leaf which purifies and
protects when shredded into a fringe; it is worn as a sort of mask by the initiate
on the occasion of his [sic] first emergence into the world. Thus she is the loa of

the psychic womb of the race and she is guardian of the place of spiritual birth, the hounfor.[43]

These thoughts direct attention to the priestly elements within *vodou*. Deren says, for example, that Ayizan is a "mediator," which is a priestly attribute.[44] We must be aware, however, that the ritual life over which Ayizan watches (that of *vodou* in general) is based upon ecstatic possession, which means a ritual life intended either to bring about or to recognize an *un*mediated presence of the divine in the human.

Chiré d'Ayizan is part of a lengthy initiation process. After the *Chiré*, initiates are taken into seclusion, where they remain for a week, solitary much of the time but also receiving instruction and undergoing experiences that are secret. At this *service* at Marc Jerome's, the initiates were a mother and her daughter; yet the two of them were not conspicuous until the very end.

Most *services* begin with a litany of invocations to a long list of Catholic saints. I did not see or hear this on the occasion being described: Perhaps it had been got out of the way before I arrived, since it is often done perfunctorily, or perhaps it was omitted. The *service* began when the drums began, which soon brought the choir into song, which soon after prompted some of its members to dance. This was around eight o'clock. The *service* lasted about five hours. I shall not attempt to describe it all but rather to highlight its performance qualities.

Except for brief periods when the drummers rested, there was no break in the music the whole time. Everything I describe now is done to the drums' rhythms, with dancing and singing. The songs change. The rhythms vary. Intensity builds or relaxes according to the beat. We come under the sway of the drums and stay there until we go home. It is quite intoxicating, even without any rum to go with it, but rum is here, too. Haitians drink a lot of it, yet drunken behavior is a disgrace, and one almost never sees it. In the *service*, the rum, drum, dancing, and singing produce an elevation of spirit, not a sloppiness.

After I got back to New York, I sat one day at my desk wearing headphones to make notes on the many hours of *vodou* drumming I had recorded. I remember once putting the headphones down and going to the kitchen for coffee and realizing as I walked through the hall that I was quite high. No chemicals had done it, only the drums.

While the drums beat now on Tuesday night *chez* Marc Jerome, a man and a woman begin a *salutation*, an action of such courtly, rhythmic, and fluid beauty that I was glad to find it repeated many times throughout the *service*. The woman is one of the *hounsi*, dressed in white.

In her left hand, a lighted candle; in her right, an opened bottle of Barbancourt rum. The man is a visiting *houngan*, one of several here tonight. Bareheaded, wearing brown slacks and a white knit pullover shirt, he carries in his left hand an ordinary white enameled kitchen pot with a looped handle. This holds water. In his right hand is an *asson*, emblem of the *houngan* and *mambo*. It is a hollow gourd rattle, painted red, blue, and gold, laced around with vertebrae from a snake. With such an instrument, Marc Jerome subtly leads the entire *service*, establishing now this rhythm and now that for the drums to pick up, summoning the *loa* or asking them to leave if they create too much havoc. The *asson* speaks its own language, which is often irresistible.

Moving like courtly dancers, the couple first approach the drums, in front of which, as I now notice, someone has sketched three different *vevés* on the floor. In *vodou* each *loa* has an individual *vevé*, an elaborate design that is his or her symbol. Drawn on the floor, it offers a point in the room through which that *loa* may choose to arrive.[45] Since the designs are executed with cornmeal, they soon disappear, rubbed out by the dancers' feet.

The couple curtsy, whether to the busy drummers or to the drums, who is to say? Their salutation is to *drumming*, the magic which the instruments, together with their players, can perform. Squatting down, laying his *asson* and water pot on the floor, the man lights four small candles and stands one upon each *vevé* and one in front of a tambourine near the drums. This done, the couple curtsy again and pour libations on the ground, she dispensing a bit of rum from her bottle, he a dash of water from the white pot. Except for the placement and lighting of the candles, all this is done very rhythmically, with gently swaying motions.

They move to the *poteau mitan*, circle it once, then step forward, step backward, curtsy, and make libation. They move to the far end of the room, near one of the *cayes mystères*. Here Melanie and her son are sitting among numerous guests. She is a *mambo* whom Jean-Claude and I know well, having been to her home several times. Now a *salutation* is made to her, the libation poured at her feet. This is partly to welcome her as a visiting colleague, and partly to recognize that, like the *vevés* and the *poteau mitan*, she is a *point* through which a *loa* may choose to arrive. I begin to realize that almost every artifact and behavior here tonight is preparation for the arrival of *loa*. This is done not by directing attention heavenward but by directing it *here*, and by increasing people's awareness of each other. The *service* is not only like a party; it is one.

The couple now go to the main doorway, on the earthen threshold of which they place another lighted candle, then curtsy and pour libations. The rum and the water splash onto the ground, coloring it dark, so that a mark has been left. It will soon disappear like the *vevés*, but for the moment it creates another *point* through which the hoped-for *loa* may come upon the scene. Teenagers still hang around the door, some inside, some out. It's nice to be on the edge of a party, especially at first.

Another *houngan* replaces the first, and *salutations* continue. There are quite a few visiting shamans (as I call them) to be saluted. The *poteau mitan* is visited several times. More and more of the *hounsi* are dancing now, leaving fewer and fewer in the bleachers. Marc Jerome is not conspicuous. Had I not met him earlier and kept my eye out for him, it would have taken me a long time to figure out who, if anybody, was in charge. Excellent host of the party, he moves about quietly, making sure that everything is all right, that everyone who needs greeting gets it. He also gives signals to the drummers from time to time. He does not speak much to me, but I soon realize he is aware of my every movement, and this reassures me. I know that if my camera and flash get in anybody's way he will instruct me. But this is not necessary, as it turns out.

People seemed to recognize and accept my presence, and they thought it best not only to let me do my thing but to make something of it. I moved around a lot, partly to take pictures from all angles, partly because everybody else was moving, and partly to respond to the drums in my own fashion. I do not know how to dance in a Haitian way, yet the drums would not let me stay motionless, so I swayed and danced little improvised steps, and I moved on impulse from one part of the room to another, prompted as often by the drumbeats as by anything visual. People not only noticed this but found ways of playing to it. Once a man who had paraded the room with palm leaves ended his routine with a flourish by turning full face to the camera, placing hands on hips, grinning broadly, and stopping his movement as if to say, "Shoot!" I did; and in perfect synchronization with my flash-gun came a thunderclap from the drums. They had played a joke on me with such good humor that it was a sign of welcome. The distraction my photography might have created was avoided not by denial but by recognition, and the party flowed on.

I see a parade of banners. Two of the *hounsi* come dancing while carrying flags, dazzling things made of rich colors and shiny sequins on heavy cloth. The one on the left is mostly white and blue, with yellow fringe. It suggests water and serpent, and on it I read "Damballah," the name of the creator spirit always visualized as a snake. The banner on the right is mostly dark red, with a bit of blue and the same yellow fringe. In the center of the red field there is a white horse being ridden by a man in medieval dress. I know this is St. Jacques, in Haiti a stand-in for Ogoun, a very popular *loa* characterized by independence of spirit, toughness, and skill in surviving. Between the two flag-bearers a man holds a sword, unsheathed, painted red, and carried point upward. It is the sword of Ogoun.

The banners and sword are dance-paraded about the room. At one place, they are met by the folk with rum and water, and the sword receives a *salutation*. The woman with the rum pours some of it out to make a long line on the floor, then kneels and kisses the fringe of Damballah's flag. The grace of movement with which this encounter takes place astonishes me. It somehow combines nonchalance with strong determination. The flag-bearers approach a visiting *houngan* sitting not far from Melanie. They hold the flags out to him, and he kisses them. I see that on the back Damballah's flag is a rich velvet in solid blue.

A number of the dancing *hounsi* encircle the flag-bearers, and all continue to move counterclockwise about the room. During one passage, the flags are carried to the *caye mystère* on the right. Its door is opened, and the flags are dipped as if in salute to what is inside (and invisible to most of us).

A man now suddenly appears from the *caye mystère* in the middle, wearing about his neck an astonishing number (dozens) of necklaces made of colored beads. He is approached by the libation bearers, and a *salutation* is made—not to him, I think, but to his treasure. Then he and the libation-bearers move in parade, with a jaunty, bouncy step, the *houngan* broadly grinning, throwing first one white-trousered leg and bare foot and then the other high in front of him as he goes. The flags, too, are in parade.

Each of the many necklaces belongs to a particular *hounsi*. They are worn during *services*, kept in the *caye mystère* between times. Their bearer knows which necklace belongs to whom. He begins to distribute them. Some of the *hounsi*, when he approaches with the necklaces, kneel and kiss the ground.

The rum-bearer pours out another libation, making a wet line on the ground. A broom appears in the hands of a *hounsi*, and a small area of the floor is swept clean. Beside her stands another *hounsi* in white, a man, holding a wooden bowl that contains cornmeal. On his left is the *hounsi* with the lighted candle. Taking a fist full of meal from the bowl and stooping down, he begins to create a large *vevé*. A few people stop and watch him, but most keep on dancing. The flag-bearers hover nearby, never stopping their own motion. A visiting *houngan, asson* in lap, sits causally upon the base of the *poteau mitan*. A pattern of white upon the gray floor, the *vevé* grows, line by line. Jean-Claude tells me what I had supposed, that it is the *vevé* of Ayizan. When it's done, the man who drew it stands back to inspect his work. Then he looks up at me, for I have been photographing his activity. When I signal my approval, he beams broadly and walks away.

A ladder-back wooden chair with cane bottom is brought and placed squarely upon the *vevé*. A visiting *houngan* gets up from his seat on the base of the *poteau mitan* as a large white linen sheet is brought to him. He drapes it over the chair, contouring it to the back and seat, letting it hang to the ground on all sides. For a moment, everyone moves away, so that the draped chair sits isolated, an empty throne. The *vevé* beneath it is mostly hidden.

From amid the dancing, and without stopping it, a parade emerges, to move with spring step and high spirit counterclockwise about the room. A couple with the paraphernalia of the *salutation* come first, flanked on their left by a man in white bearing a palm branch. It is perhaps six feet in length, its tightly furled leaves girt by a white cloth wrapped around the middle. He holds this object in front of him with outstretched arms, the left end pointed slightly upward. Next comes the red sword of Ogoun, pointed straight to the sky, and then the two flag-bearers. They all circle the *poteau mitan*, where a *salutation* is made, then move around the room to an accelerating rhythm. Finally, the palm leaf is deposited near the *poteau mitan*.

While the dancing continues, the palm branch is unrolled and some of the leaves cut from it, others left attached to the stem. Several people, male and female, using pocket knives or fingernails, shred the leaves into long strands. The free strands are laid across the seat of Ayizan's chair, the empty fullness of which is becoming more evident each moment. The strands still attached to the branch are draped down the back of the chair, so that it begins to look as if it is made entirely of palm. A woman wearing a linen skirt almost the same straw color as the palm strands (the only such skirt in the room) kneels on one knee before the chair, staying a moment or so in prayer, then moves away, to be followed by several others kneeling in turn. Still another visiting *houngan*, this one in blue slacks and blue-striped shirt, comes forward with the white pot and makes *salutation* to the chair.

The palm-bearer returns, lifts the strand-sheaf from the back of the chair to hold it high in front of him with both hands and dance with it round and round the room, joyously. Returning the strand to the chair, he turns suddenly to me, striking that pose in expectation of my flash-gun that I have already described.

The party continues. Marc Jerome supervises the distribution of drinks. Low, square tables are placed here and there among the chairs, to hold paper cups and bottles of rum and Coca Cola, which people

open and pour. Melanie and her son signal me to come have a drink.
The young people at the door move further into the room, dance with
each other. Festivity.

After a time, the dancing becomes more intense. The rhythms have
changed. They are less affable, more like fire and storm. I find it
exhilarating yet feel a touch of anxiety. Suddenly, I am jolted by a loud
noise, sharp as a pistol shot. Turning, I see that it was the crack of a large
whip.

Near the doorway and drums, a man is wielding the whip.
Unnoticed by me, he has taken it from where it hung on the *poteau mitan.*
Now he cracks it repeatedly while moving about near the drums. It
dawns on me that this is a slaver's whip. The agitation in the drums I
have been noticing is an echo of the violence of Haitian life, beginning
with slavery and continuing to the present day.

In Haiti the focus of religion shifted from the challenges of nature
(gardening, drought, storms, and the like) to the challenges of a brutal
society (slavery, politics, poverty, and passion).[46] The slave whip is here
not to frighten the likes of me, but as a sign of the oppression under
which Haitians have lived for hundreds of years, during slavery and
since.

As the whip continues to crack, punctuating the drums' own
percussions, I begin to feel a certain strength in the room. Having been
taken from the slavers' hands, the whip is now wielded ritually in the
hounfor. Like the Christian cross, the *vodou* whip is the relic of a people's
oppression. I thought to myself, "There is power in the whip."

Long after, I would remember that Augustine had said of hope that
she has two lovely daughters—anger and courage. All I knew at the
time was that my initial fear soon gave way to a feeling of strength.

The music shifts again, this time abruptly. It has suddenly gone from
fire and storm to water and gurgle. What does it signal? In the crowd of
dancers it takes my eyes a few moments to discover the presence of a
figure who seems to have materialized from nowhere. He looks a little
bit like a pirate.

His white trousers were rolled up to his calves. His head was
wrapped in a red and gold bandana, the ends hanging down his back.
His short-sleeved shirt was bright red. On the back of it, in white, was a
fairly large cross, under the arms of which were two smaller crosses, and
a small cross at its base also. Above this design was written: "3 *fois* 3." In
his left hand, he carried a pipe. He was wearing dark glasses. When I
first noticed him, he was holding the hands of a woman as he spoke
directly into her ear, she intently listening. I realized I was looking at
Marc Jerome possessed by Simbi.

There are a few *loa* in the Haitian pantheon who stand "in between," and Simbi is one of these. The *loa* are divided into two major groups, known as Rada and Petro. Those of the Rada group are gentler, have ancient African roots and seem to belong to one's extended family. The Petro group are fiercer. They are thought by scholars to have their origin in the New World during the harshness of slavery.

When the music had changed from the softer to the more agitated rhythms, and the whip began to crack, it was a sign that the *service* had shifted from the Rada to the Petro. Simbi stands between these two categories, partaking of them both, committed to neither. Similarly, he is between water and fire, between male and female, between the lawful and the unlawful, between the beneficent and the malevolent potentialities of magic, between all symbolism of the right hand and the left.[47]

Simbi is thus a master of ambiguity, and hence a comfort and a resource for people who find themselves in ambiguous situations or endowed with ambiguous personalities. He is the patron of gamblers and also of magicians. His motto is "Three times three," which in French is a triple rhyme: *"Trois fois trois."* Over the doorway I had read the names of the three "magi," Caspard, Melchior, and Balthazar.

Soon the flag bearers and the *salutation* team get in front of Simbi and lead him in a little parade. This soon dissolves, and Simbi begins to circulate again among the dancers, inviting some to dance with him, holding little conversations, or both at once. He often twirls his partner under his right arm, right hand holding right hand, a turn that appears frequently in the dancing of the *hounsis*. He seems exotic and awe-inspiring, while at the same time benign and avuncular. Not everyone pays attention to him. If they did, the party's rhythm would break, but it goes on and on. The music periodically returns to the driving force of the Petro style, then goes back to that watery sound that had announced Simbi's arrival. The whip cracks now and then, but Simbi pays it no attention. By this time, I have understood that the attention of the room is never given to any one thing all at once.

Another parade forms. Walking in front of the flags of Damballah and Ogoun is one of the two persons being initiated, the mother. In her right hand is an *asson* (lent to her now, not yet her own). Her white head-wrap comes so low over her eyes that she is partially blindfolded, and she is guided by the woman in the linen skirt holding her left arm. The parade grows larger, and the daughter being initiated joins it, accompanied by Melanie. Assisted by a *hounsi*, Simbi approaches the mother and places upon her head a large pot or bucket completely wrapped in red cloth. I have no idea what's in it, but it seems fairly heavy. The mother continues in the procession balancing the burden. Later Simbi shifts the pot to the head of the daughter.

Simbi returns to dancing. The procession has dissolved and I see him dance with the younger initiate, holding her hands close to his chest and looking straight into her eyes. Her attitude is demure, pliant. Simbi dances with several women, young and old, appearing to listen and give counsel to most of them in the process; then he dances with several men. One of them is a youth wearing blue jeans and a gold lamé shirt, with whom Simbi dances in a very flirtatious way, the youth becoming excited. Then there's another young man, also in blue jeans, his shirt a less flashy dark green. With him Simbi's dance is sexually charged. A kerchief tucked into his trousers gives the suggestion of a protruding phallus, but the partner's response is cool. I seem to be almost the only person paying these exchanges any attention. The party gets more high-spirited. Simbi's next partner is a middle-aged woman who has donned a man's straw hat, wearing it tilted forward at a rakish angle while shaking her shoulders and hips in a who's-to-stop-me attitude. Simbi steps back, throws up his hands rejoicing.

Another procession emerges as if from nowhere, led by a young woman *hounsi* with an *asson* in her right hand. (There are now quite a number of *assons* in the room.) As she dances forward, she arches her body first to one side then the other, arms extended gracefully over her head. She could be a swaying palm tree. One of the women following her goes into possession. I see her right foot suddenly plant itself to the floor, her body lurch forward, and then swerve to the left. Her eyes roll upward and seem to turn around in their sockets. Then she contracts at the waist and bends forward in a paroxysm. A woman near her takes her hand to keep her from falling, and soon she regains some balance and is able to walk stiffly.

Trance possession is so common in the *services* that it does not interrupt other activity. One or two persons near the affected person (the "horse" being "mounted" by the *loa*, as the Haitians express it) will take care that no bodily injury occurs, but otherwise the flow of things continues, unless the *loa* who has thus entered upon the scene should choose to do something to command attention. I learned later that several persons had been possessed that night, but this was the only one I noticed apart from Marc Jerome's possession by Simbi.

Now my attention is diverted from the possessed woman to the procession of which she had been a part. The two initiates are coming, completely blindfolded. Each is guided by the hands of a woman walking behind her, holding her at the waist. The mother and her guide are followed by the daughter and Melanie, and the latter pair are flanked by the flag- and sword-bearers. They all come down the length of the room, make a horseshoe turn leftward around the *poteau mitan,* and head for the *caye mystère* on the right, their pace quickening into a trot. Someone opens the door and the two initiates are pushed inside. It is as if they go blindfolded into a darkness.

The door is swung shut. The drums rise in crescendo to a great flourish. Cheers ring out from all over the room. Then silence. The *service* is suddenly over.

Everyone is leaving. Jean-Claude and I say good night to Melanie and her son. I wave to a few others whose names I don't know but have had some exchange with during the evening, including the drummers. Simbi is still here. I approach, thinking I should say thanks to Marc Jerome for letting me come; but ambiguity reigns. I realize I do not know whether I am about to greet the horse or the rider. If I say anything, the ground will shift under me, and I'm not ready for that. So I simply lower my head, raise it again and look into his eyes. He returns this gesture and stares at me. I nod once again and leave.

We walk into the open air after 1:00 A.M. As we head for the highway to find transportation, I realize that I am utterly refreshed. Not in the least tired, not disturbed, not solemn, not giddy. Refreshed. This was my feeling after every one of the many Haitian *services* that I attended. Nothing that I had ever read or heard prepared me for this up-beat, cathartic effect from *vodou.* It was a gift.

■

Although it is customary to refer to a Haitian *houngan* as a priest and a *mambo* as a priestess, it is clear that the *houngan* is a very different figure from a priest of the Roman Catholic church. In that church, moreover, it is decreed that there shall be no priestesses at all. *Houngan* and *mambo* are far closer to the shamanic than to the priestly prototype. They are descended from the religions of Africa, with some influence also, people say, from the Carib Indians who inhabited the land before the Europeans and slavery came.

Priesthood comes later than shamanism and is an adaptation of it to hierarchical patterns of social organization. We should associate the priestly type with the rise of kingship, the priest being a shaman who has become "courtly," finding a place within the ranks of the king's ministers, appointed to serve the religious interests of the monarchy, and providing the king a divine mandate in rituals of anointing and crowning. The priest retains some of the attributes of the shaman but loses others. For the most part, shamanism is then left to "outsiders," especially women.[48]

As the Haitian examples demonstrate, often there are marked differences in performance styles between shaman and priest, to which we shall return. Theologically, however, the main difference has to do with vocation and accountability.

In the southern Protestantism in which I grew up, much emphasis was placed upon a preacher's "call." If you were going to enter the ministry, you were supposed to have received a "call to preach." I myself received such a call when I was in high school. It came to me during a period of struggle within my soul, which lasted for many months and had its roots in early childhood, when I felt very attracted to what went on in the pulpit of the Methodist church I attended regularly with my parents. My months of agony during high school culminated in a clear awareness of divine calling, which came to a climax one afternoon after school. I was in the basement of my home, shoveling coal into the furnace fire and feeling very angry that a mark of some sort had been put upon me so that I would have to become a preacher in spite of myself and be the laughingstock of all my friends. On this particular afternoon, an inner voice whispered, "Would that be so bad?" and I knew that the struggle was over. I had the call, and there was nothing to be done about it.

The word "shaman" was not in my vocabulary then, and "priest" was something I understood dimly. Some priests were mentioned in the Bible, but I didn't know what they did. I knew of preaching, and pastoring, and getting the call. Looking back, I see that my particular kind of call was midway between the shamanic and the priestly poles. I have remained there my whole life, drawn in both directions.

Since priesthood is a function of a well-organized religious institution, the priest's call is to serve that institution. The priest may indeed have a call direct from God, but it is the church, temple, or other organized religious body that has the power to ordain. This gift is bestowed, during a rite of passage such as the laying on of hands, in exchange for the priest's becoming accountable to that religious body, and to none other. The priest is its servant. The priest serves God by serving the previously ordained elders, bishops, and such like who form the institution's ordered ranks, often with the national sovereign at the top. Taking his (usually his, up to the present time) place within the institutional ranks, below some authorities and above others, including all laity (ordinary people), "the priest mediates between the people and the transcendent deity."[49] He is a link between lower and higher.

Max Weber's concept, "the routinization of charisma,"[50] well describes the priestly role and indicates why it is found in so many religions and denominations, particularly in those that have developed strong "connectional" and hierarchical forms of organization, in Protestant denominations as well as Catholic. Like the shaman, the priest (or the preacher, pastor, rabbi, imam, or any other who is of the priestly type) has a divine calling; but this charisma has become subordinated to the regularities of the religious institution. Such routinization may occur even when the "priest" is under no bishop or other superior but is beholden to a congregation for appointment and salary.

Subordination of charisma to institutional regularity occurs under a wide variety of religious "polities," structures, and theologies. One result is that the "priest" becomes the steward of the religious rites, charged with keeping them in order. If possible, the priest is also expected to see that the rites are effective channels of divine power, but this becomes a secondary consideration. A theology often grows up to maintain that there is little a priest or any other human being can do to invoke divine power. Instead, the purpose of ritual is to encourage obedience.

Later in this book, we shall examine three major functions of ritual: making and preserving order, fostering community, and effecting transformation. Within the priestly type, the first of those functions is paramount. The others are not absent, but they take their places within an overarching concern for the preservation of a given order. We are speaking of social order, cosmic order, and the ordering of the religious life, especially its rituals. Within the priestly type, it is almost safe to say that ordering is what ritual *means*.

This sense of ritual as order, presided over by priestly functionaries whose main business is to preserve tradition and whose rites inevitably become routines, is what many people regard as the paradigm of ritual. However, there is an older and still widespread type, one more open to the principle of change, offering a contrasting paradigm.

■

In the ritual pathways of shamanism, transformation takes precedence. This does not mean, of course, that no order is to be found in shamanic rituals. It means instead that the order in them is of a kind that can become infused with Spirit. Hence it is order in the service of the unpredictable. Whereas priestly ritual is mostly concerned with regularity and a predictable future, shamanic ritual is mostly concerned with transformative powers and experiment. Like any adventuresome artist (not the courtly artist who aims to satisfy well-placed patrons), the shaman does not know what will come of his or her activity. The techniques may be familiar in the shaman's community, but their performance is somewhat different every time, as when a really good cook makes bread. Variations are prized if they turn out to have point. A shamanic ritual is the opening of a window, the casting of a net, the hurling of a cry into the night. It involves risk-taking.

Since for the most part shamanism is practiced by nonliterate peoples, it does not exist under the control of scripture or written rules. It is handed down by apprenticeship and oral tradition. For the shaman, the "call" is crucial. One reason is that the shaman is very much on his or her own, since there is no institution to ordain or certify the practitioner, although the call that he or she receives must be validated less formally by communal acceptance.

Typically, the call comes after an illness, which is accompanied or else followed by a period of severe emotional distress, a breakdown. During this episode, it is said in many cultures that the soul of the shaman takes leave of the body. It journeys to the spirit world, where it is taught many mysteries, of which perhaps the most important is the revelation that these sufferings in body and soul are the sign of a shamanic vocation: The shaman is a wounded healer. Upon the soul's return to the body, the person is "resurrected," that is, restored to health and given a new way of life. She or he now seeks out some already established shaman from whom to learn the craft.

The relation between established shaman and new learner is ad hoc. No regulating institution supervises it. In Haiti, Korea, and many other places, the relation is expressed in familial language: The Haitian *mambo* or *houngan* is the learner's mother or father, both during and after the time of training. The learning period, which is also a process of successive initiations, culminates in a *service* held deep in the woods when the initiate receives from the "parent" the *asson*, the instrument used not only to establish rhythms while conducting the *vodou* rites but also to intimidate and gain control over the *loa* themselves. At Marc

Jerome's *hounfor*, Melanie proudly introduced me to her "father, who gave me the *asson*."

Shamanic rituals do not occupy a mediating space between the people and the spirits. On the contrary, they provide an occasion for the gods to come forth boldly and possess whomever they choose. Whereas in the priestly type, the rite serves to insure that divine-human transactions are proper, in the shamanic type, the rite is a technique for summoning spirits whose behavior is not entirely predictable. And the rite is not strictly necessary, because the gods can take possession of anyone, whenever and wherever they please, just as they can call the shaman without going through ordination committees and seminaries and hierarchical channels.

If we shift to the language of theater, we may say that the shaman's performance is done for *effect*. Everyone notices the theatricality of shamanic performance, which is probably the source of popular entertainments.[51] The shaman performs for effect because the shaman understands himself or herself to be an agent of transformative power. I distinguish this role from that of a mediator. What is the difference?

In the religious world, a mediator is needed to make a bridge between two incommensurate realities, the human and the divine. Gods and humans (like kings and subjects) are so different that something is needed to connect them. Yet because they are so different, they must also be kept separate. That which connects them must also keep them apart.

I saw this graphically in the cathedral at Les Cayes, at that shoreline dividing the ocean of laity from the island of the ordained. When the Eucharist was celebrated, the new priests brought the elements from the altar where the bishop had consecrated them, to the shoreline, where the priests gave them to the laity, one by one. It was the meeting of two worlds, and the priests who gave out the sacrament also signified that the laity should not come to the altar. This connecting while dividing is what I call mediation.

If the priest is a mediator, the shaman is a matchmaker. The shaman's role is not so much to interpret as to manifest. The shaman does not sit or stand in the middle, like the priests and bishop at Les Cayes, making themselves the points of connection through whom all others relate. The shaman flits all over, like Marc Jerome at Carrefour, cuing others to their tasks, directing music, playing music, dancing, becoming possessed, disappearing and reappearing, greeting people, admonishing people, manipulating the scene, not representing the spirits but creating the conditions through which they come here and now and connect. Like a matchmaker, the shaman aims to be upstaged, not always, but for the sake of the present connection. This active standing in, standing for, and standing out of the way is what the shaman performs.

Shamanic ritual is relatively uncentered. As a westerner, this was the hardest thing for me to grasp at first. I kept wanting to look at some fixed point, and indeed there were no lack of candidates for my attention: in Haiti the *poteau mitan* or "center-post"; in Korea the altar laden with food-offerings. But these focal points turned out not to function as I expected. If you looked in their direction, you missed most of what went on. No matter how many times dancers and processioners went counterclockwise around the *poteau mitan*, it was not at the post that possessions took place. They could occur anywhere. Except for the time when a *salutation* was made to it, the *poteau mitan* was not the object of anyone's attention; and in receiving the *salutation* the *poteau mitan* took its turn as one among many recipients throughout the space. Likewise, the altar piled high with food and other offerings at the Korean *kut*, splendid to look at, was not the locus of any action.

■

Jesus said that the wind (spirit) blows where it will. So also the spirits summoned by shamanism arrive when, where, and how they will. This does not mean the shaman does not actively direct the ritual, nor that it has no predictability. On the contrary, the shaman is typically very much in charge, and shamanic ritual traditions are often very strong. It does mean, however, that the chief end of shamanic ritual is neither to symbolize the spirits nor to plot their movements, but instead to provide as many pathways as possible for spirits to become present and exercise their powers.

In the New Testament, especially in Matthew, Mark, and Luke, Jesus is portrayed more like a shaman than a priest. Probably the earliest Christian rituals were of the shamanic type, occasions when worshipers invoked the spirit of the crucified Jesus and became ecstatically possessed by him. This is something scarcely dreamt of in Christian ritual today, a situation indicative of a ritual impoverishment that might perhaps be overcome.

The move away from the shamanic pole of religious ritual toward the priestly may be described as a move away from performative power toward static symbolism. The shaman invokes; the priest represents. These differences are not absolute but are strong tendencies within the two types. Revitalization of religious ritual in Westernized societies today would require overcoming the dominance of the priestly type by moving again toward the shamanic. This in turn means to set free the performative power of ritual which is corseted by liturgical rigidities, many of them cherished by conservative communities precisely *because* they keep the performative and transformative power of ritual under wraps.

Wishing to free ritual from these constraints, our next task is to look closely and sympathetically at the fact that rituals are quasi-theatrical performances. As such they are full of potential for both good and evil. In other words, they are closely intertwined with morality, and with the ambiguity that belongs to all power, whether human or divine.

PART II

Modalities of Performance

5

Ritual, Theater,
and Sacrifice

Human beings are by nature actors, who cannot become something
until first they have pretended to be it. They are therefore to be
divided, not into the hypocritical and the sincere, but into the sane,
who know they are acting, and the mad who do not.
—ATTRIBUTED TO W. H. AUDEN

Ritual, religion, and social action do not necessarily go together. Not
all rituals are religious; some religious communities are hostile toward
ritual; and some kinds of ritual and religion turn away from social
action. At a deep level, however, they are all connected. We shall
explore this connection by looking at three different yet related modes of
performance, which I call the ritual, the confessional, and the ethical.
The ritual mode will be considered in the present chapter, the
confessional and the ethical in the next.

Our discussion of performance in its ritual mode will begin quietly
but end with fearful matters. Ritual is a many-sided thing. It seems often
to be mere make-believe, yet it can lead to death and destruction. There
is, as we shall see, something within ritual performance that can lead to
blood sacrifice; yet there is also something about it that aims toward
creativity and freedom. It is often hard to say which of these, blood
sacrifice or freedom, is the more fearful. But let us hold that thought in
abeyance until we come to it.

Wishing now to look at ritual as a kind of performance, let us start by
recalling that human lives are shaped not only, not even principally, by
the ideas we have in our minds, but even more by the actions we
perform with our bodies, which Roland Delattre has eloquently called
"the carefully rehearsed motions through which we regularly go."[52] In
the *Poetics*, Aristotle said, "It is by their actions that we know what

[people] are." Actions, so the saying goes, speak louder than words. Human selves, John Macmurray has argued, are to be understood as agents.[53] A similar point of view is to be found in William James and other pragmatic philosophers and in the Gestalt psychologists. In performance we come upon something quite basic about human beings—that we constitute ourselves through our actions. The activities of human beings, however, are most peculiar, for they are pervaded by an ambiguity that is inherent in the very thought of "acting" and "performing."

One of the ways in which ritual, religion, and liberative action are alike is that they all construct alternative worlds, nourishing themselves with imaginative visions. Different from ordinary life, they move in a kind of liminal space, at the edge of, or in the cracks between, the mapped regions of what we like to call "the real world." We shall have more to say later about liminality, a concept recently made prominent by anthropologist Victor Turner. Meanwhile, we may simply note that it is characteristic of activities that are liminal that they also may be regarded as performances. That is to say, there is something about them that is "put on."

The verb "to perform," like its shorter but not simpler cousin, "to act," is two-faced. On the one side, these words mean "to do," while on the other, they mean "to pretend." This ambiguity tells us much about the kind of actors human beings are.

If a child is drowning, a person may act to save it. But to act the rescuer is not necessarily to save anyone. I may perform the act of saving the child, and the child will be saved, but I may also perform the same act and no child is saved because I did it only for the movie camera. A surgeon may perform an operation with or without an audience. If the surgeon is any good, the performance is supposed to help the patient, who, being unconscious at the time, does not witness the performance; but there are occasions when the observers in what is called the "operating theater" are even more in the surgeon's mind than the patient.

A performance, then, may or may not have an intended effect unmediated by the response of an observer. If, in some play on the stage, I am supposed to sweep the floor, I may actually do it and get up the dirt; or I may just go through the motions as convincingly as possible, intending that whatever effect I produce will not be upon the floor but upon the spectator. An actor may actually sweep, or only pretend to do so, or, like a good mime, suggest sweeping through carefully chosen motions. Between these there is a great deal of aesthetic difference, but all three are performances.

Although to call something a performance ordinarily means that there is, or will be, an audience for whom the enactment is prepared, there are many situations in which the doer is her own spectator and makes the performance for herself, or for an ideal spectator who is not visible—God, perhaps, or one's deceased ancestor. "To observe" has an ambiguity parallel to that of "to perform" and "to act." To observe is to see, as in, "I observe the child playing"; yet to observe is also a certain kind of enactment, as in, "I observe the law," or, "At our house we observe the sabbath." Whereas an observation is something seen, an observance is something marked by a special kind of attention or faithfulness, and it has the connotation of something performed at the proper time and in the right way.

Performance, then, is a particular kind of doing. Although as a social, psychological, and moral phenomenon it is highly complex, it may be defined simply as that kind of doing in which the observation of the deed is an essential part of its doing, even if the observer be invisible or is the performer herself.

Animal ritualization is here elaborated upon in a particularly human way. In the animal world, behavior patterns become ritualizations when they come to be employed as signaling devices, either in addition to or in displacement of their more pragmatic functions. In human beings, this communicative function is not only made more efficient but is also deepened by the human capacity to pretend—that is, to create and project imaginary structures.

In the human being, the capacity to transcend an immediate situation, already present in the animal world by virtue of the acts of communication that go on there, is enhanced. Human beings not only act but know that they are acting: They observe themselves. They can deny that they are acting. They can do one thing while pretending another. In relation to the actual, they have great freedom. Yet such transcendence does not mean "getting away from" an immediate situation. A performance, being never purely mental nor entirely imaginary, is a material as well as a rational event. It takes place in an environment both physical and mental, both actual and imaginary, both immanent and transcendent. In performance the body that does is of no less importance than the mind that knows, for performance is the unity of doing and observing.

■

Performance in the ritual mode is, as I have already indicated, just one of at least three modes that performance may take. There is also a confessional mode, which has to do with personal identity, belief, and religious faith; and there is an ethical mode, which pertains to right ways of acting in relation to society. All that has been said about performance so far in this chapter has been broad enough to apply to all three modes. Now we shall spend the rest of the chapter focusing upon the ritual mode alone.

Performance in the ritual mode is theatrical, or quasi-theatrical: Something is "acted out" within a definite frame that sets the action apart as the kind of event that is, in the English language, usually called a "performance," whether it be a play on the stage, a game played on the playing field, a piece of music played in a concert hall, or a service attended in synagogue.

We are here in the realm of Aristotle's *poiesis*, or making, with a certain stress on "making up." Hence, when referring to the ritual mode, we refer to performances contrived for special occasions, including many kinds of play (certainly sporting events), play-acting (in theaters or elsewhere), and the performance of music and dance as well as religious and secular rituals. This broad grouping embraces what Milton Singer has spoken of as "cultural performances," a concept he came to while doing field work in the area of Madras in India, where he found, as he might have found in many other places, public performances recurring frequently and with considerable importance for the social lives of the people.[54] Such performances, he noted, included what

we in the West usually call by that name—for example, plays, concerts, and lectures. But they include also prayers, ritual readings and recitations, rites and ceremonies, festivals, and all those things which we usually classify under religion and ritual rather than with the cultural and artistic.[55]

Like Singer's "cultural performances," my "ritual mode of performance" deliberately lumps together types of performance that are both sacred and secular, that are religious, aesthetic, and recreational. I have a reason for this, over and above the theoretical point that all these types of performance have a certain phenomenological similarity: I believe that the revitalization of ritual in the churches in "modern" society requires a renewed appreciation of their theatricality. At present in most liberal churches, the theatricality of worship is like a dirty little secret that everyone knows but no one wants to talk about or affirm. Apparently fearing sensationalism and the trivializing of holy things, at the same time putting a premium on "sincerity," these churches avoid confronting the pretension, the artificiality, the contrivance, and the showmanship public worship entails. The result is not that the worship becomes any less theatrical but that it becomes theater of the worst kind, lacking zest, heart, and conviction.

Theatricality is not, of course, the whole of public worship. Liturgy cannot be reduced to theater without loss of its reason for being. But neither can it be purified of all theatrical elements. It is performance through and through; and if it refuses lovingly to embrace its kinship with theatrical performance, it will grow as ill as people who refuse to affirm and care for their own bodies.

We shall come presently to differentiate between ritual and its close kin in the performance family, but for the moment it is essential to note their resemblance. They all clearly stem from what we have previously discussed as ritualization. Besides, it is important to stress that creativity (often ignored in discussions of the subject) is as important to ritual as to the performing arts.

If the creativity of ritual is frequently not noticed, that is probably because people tend to identify ritual with repetitive patterns held steady by tradition. Rituals are influenced, however, not only by tradition but also by their affinities with other kinds of "cultural performances." Ritual creativity becomes evident when the great variety of rituals throughout the world is considered, and when one understands how frequently rituals change and how great is the role they play in social transformations, matters we shall take up at length in subsequent chapters.

In addition to its combining tradition with creativity, the ritual mode of performance is characterized by deliberate, disciplined use of the body. In this mode, "performance" is realized in the most literal way: Specific, finite, identifiable actions are carried out bodily at a definite time and place. Although a ritual includes pretending, the ritual performance itself is no pretense, but an actual, here and now doing. Similarly, an actress's portrayal of, let's say, Clytemnestra on the stage will entail a certain amount of make-believe; but as to the fact that the actress puts herself in front of the audience and, for better or worse, does the role, there is no pretense at all, as we can know from the experience of stage-fright. In the other performance modes, more emphasis is laid upon intentions, more has to do with the aims and ends. But in the ritual mode, as the saying goes, it is the performance that counts.

"As philosophers of religion and theologians push at the limits of religious language and belief," Ronald Grimes writes, "metaphors that once identified the sacred with height, depth, or inwardness seem to be giving way to ones that allow for a positive evaluation of surfaces, exteriority, and overt action." The new methods emphasize, he says, "the epistemological primacy of the body."[56]

"Savage religion," said anthropologist R. R. Marrett at the beginning of this century, "is something not so much thought out as danced out," with ideation remaining "relatively in abeyance."[57] We had best drop the condescending word "savage." Religion's being danced out, sung out, sat out in silence, or lined out liturgically, with ideation playing a secondary role, is not something confined to religion's early stages but is characteristic of religion as long as it is vital. This does not mean, of course, that ritual is mindless, nor anti-intellectual. It means that its form of intelligence is more similar to that of the arts than to conceptual theology, just as the intelligence of poetry is of a different order from that of philosophy or literary criticism. This is a truth too little appreciated in theological seminaries, leading to an almost unbridgeable gap between the theologically trained clergy with heads full of ideas and the practicing laity concentrated upon how religion is done.

As ritual does not simply embody or express preexistent ideas, so it does not merely flow from preexistent emotions. I agree with Richard Comstock that "there are no isolated emotions causing ritual behavior. . . . What must be stressed is the synchronic interaction of feeling, thought, and bodily movement in their concrete unity."[58]

Such unity is what I have in mind in speaking of a ritual mode of performance. Having the right thoughts and going through the motions does not qualify as ritual, any more than thinking, or even saying, the lines of *Hamlet* or "walking through" the role constitutes a performance of the play. That is because, although the body is of course present, it is not committed.

The *styles* of bodily commitment in ritual have great variety. In some traditions, for example in the black church in North America, exuberant displays of emotion are expected. In others, such as the way *sutras* are chanted in some Buddhist temples, or the offices read in some Anglican churches, the body is virtually still and the voice in monotone. No matter. In all these styles, it is possible, and necessary, for the body to be committed to its role. No good rituals are disembodied.

At the same time, there are no good rituals without spirit. Again, the spirits differ greatly from one occasion and one tradition to another, but they may not be absent. Perhaps the visiting spirits—gods, demons, ancestors, the spirit of the nation, the spirit of Beethoven's Ninth, the Christian Holy Spirit, or whatever spirit is invoked—may absent themselves for a long or short while; but the spirit that calls the spirits, the spirit of the performers, must be present and active, or else the performance falls short of itself.

This is to say that a ritual is a *process*, and is holistic. Although process has form, the form is not the process. One participates in the form of a ritual in order to take part in its process. In the measure in which the body is alienated—either by being discounted or else by being treated as a mere object that must hop, skip, and jump on cue—in that same measure will the ritual process be inhibited.

■

One of the most important aspects of performance in the ritual mode is display. We have noticed that a performance is an action meant to be observed, even if in some cases the observer is invisible or is the performer herself. We have also said that performance in the ritual mode requires commitment of the body, since such performance is a physical enactment. Taken together, these two aspects bring us to the matter of ritual display, which Richard Schechner calls "not simply a doing but a *showing of a doing*."[59] In the animal world, ritualized display is almost universal. It is no less common and no less important in the human.

It is helpful to divide ritualized display into two categories: simple and complex. In the simple forms, the motive is single, and the general rule is that the more eye-catching the display the better. Hence evolution has produced in some species amazing capacities for self-exhibition, such as the New Guinea bowerbird's elaborate courtship constructions or the spread of a peacock's tail. Displays of this kind are echoed culturally in human beings by the use of body decoration, costume, self-advertising dance and music, and panoplied ceremonial. In simple display, among humans and other animals alike, the aim is to call attention to the ritualizing individual or group, to vaunt certain skills or attributes, and in general to announce individual or group presence as convincingly as possible. We shall see later that this making of oneself strongly present has an important function in religious life.

In complex display, the motives are mixed, the exhibition being shot through with ambiguity and various degrees of dissembling. Take, for example, an animal's making its hair or feathers stand on end, enlarging its appearance and making a physical display of courage. Such an animal may, on a given occasion, be full of courage, or it may be mostly frightened. In the latter case, prompted by fear, the fur rises in a display of fear's opposite, courage, the better to frighten the adversary away. In this case there is a mixture of motives: The raising of the fur is intended to mask the fear and to avoid, if possible, the need for an actual fight. The occurrence of mixed motives, so familiar to us as human beings, is not always recognized in other animals. E. H. Gombrich writes:

What we mean by expression in human behaviour and particularly human art implies some kind of correspondence between inwardness and outward sign. How often have not religious leaders and reformers decried ritual when they found this correspondence wanting, how often have not critics done the same. In the study of animals I am sure this very distinction would be invalid. Professor Lorenz rightly insists that for the goose the friendship ritual *is* the friendship. We cannot separate the behaviour and its inwardness, as it were. Even in man [sic], I believe, that duality has its limits. There is surely much truth in the James-Lange theory which stresses the extent to which behaviour reacts back on the emotions. It may really be difficult to "smile and smile, and be a villain," or to feel sad while performing a gay dance; difficult, but it can be done.[60]

Gombrich is right to point out that there are limits to human dissembling, especially where body language is concerned. He is wrong to suppose that other animals are incapable of false faces. Since we lack access to the "inwardness" of Konrad Lorenz's famous geese, except through empathetic regard of their ritualizations, we do not know whether a goose might display friendship so as to pursue a different aim. Yet we do know that a fox can suddenly change course to throw its chasers off track, and (even more to the point) a chimpanzee that has been taught sign language is capable of prevarication. Maurice Temerlin, a psychotherapist, "adopted" into his family an infant chimpanzee, whom he named Lucy. She was taught American Sign Language (ASL) by a specialist named Roger Fouts. "Shortly before a language lesson, when no one was looking," Temerlin reports,

Lucy defecated in the middle of the living room floor. When Roger noticed the crime had occurred he turned to Lucy. Here is their verbatim conversation in ASL.

Roger: What's that?

Lucy: Lucy not know.

Roger: You do know. What's that?

Lucy: Dirty, dirty.

Roger: Whose dirty, dirty?

Lucy: Sue's.

Roger: It's not Sue's. Whose is it?

Lucy: Roger's!

Roger: No! It's not Roger's. Whose is it?

Lucy: Lucy dirty, dirty. Sorry Lucy.[61]

In her research at Gombe in Tanzania, Jane Goodall observed nonverbal acts of deceitfulness performed by a chimpanzee she called Figan, who gave misleading signals to other chimpanzees to induce them to leave a place where bananas were available, so that he could come back unobserved and eat them all by himself.[62] Anyone with a pet cat or dog is likely to have seen the animal engage in gestures, postures, and looks of the eye that communicate shame or the desire not to be punished. While such behavior may not clearly indicate, as did Lucy's and Figan's, a capacity to lie, it does show discomfort in the presence of a judging "other," in this case the human master.

In the ritual mode, human performance always requires some measure of display, the value and authenticity of which cannot be judged by simple criteria of "sincerity." Take, for example, the practice in some cultures of designating only certain people and not others to weep and wail at times of mourning. In Goroka, in the highlands of Papua New Guinea, I observed a certain extended family group who were walking about in the crowded marketplace. It took me a few minutes to notice that some but not all members of the group were in a visible state of mourning. They wrapped pieces of cloth around their heads and grasped them tightly below the chin. Their eyes showed grief, and some shed tears. Ever so often they would begin to weep, softly at first and then more loudly, until sobs passed into shrieks as their bodies swayed from side to side in a kind of keening, after which their noise would subside and they would move on with the rest of the family group to some other part of the market. All these mourners were women. The men in the family group were impassive, displaying no emotion at all. It became perfectly clear that the "work" of displaying grief had been delegated, no doubt by custom.

Gombrich, in the same passage cited above, mentions that "wailing women are . . . hired for the purpose of [mourning] rituals in the Middle East to increase the lament." I think the women mourners I saw in New Guinea were not hired but, as I say, delegated. Still, it is not a great difference. A person who accepts the role of weeping, whether for pay or not, is in a position similar to that of a priest who is ordained to perform rituals. Criteria of simple (rather than complex) display do not apply.

The crucial element of display in ritual performance moves the enactment toward a certain objectivity that will prove increasingly important as our analysis proceeds. At the same time, what I have spoken of as the commitment of the body remains crucial. Gombrich continues:

> The tearing of hair, the scattering of ashes, the mutilations of garments and even of the body, all these are the appropriate ritual that *not only expresses but produces the emotion.* I suppose a good wailing woman learns to experience the grief she is paid to express and so does the artist who perpetuates the wailing in stone. (Emphasis added.)[63]

In the New Guinea highlands, at the death of a man or boy, a close female relative will chop off a piece of a finger or even the whole finger. (This is not done, I think, at the death of a female.) In these instances and many others—think of circumcisions, scarifications, elaborate body decorations—the body is dedicated to the service of display. It is offered as the vehicle of communication, on account of which it may be irrevocably changed. Doing and showing are so wed that the display becomes a permanent part of the body.

Ritualized display is often directed inward as much as outward. Let us pause on this. A poem by Thomas Hardy illustrates something of the inward-outward complexity of display.

> "And now to God the Father," he ends,
> And his voice thrills up to the topmost tiles:
> Each listener chokes as he bows and bends,
> And emotion pervades the crowded aisles.
> Then the preacher glides to the vestry-door,
> And shuts it, and thinks he is seen no more.
> The door swings softly ajar meanwhile,
> And a pupil of his in the Bible class,
> Who adores him as one without gloss or guile,
> Sees her idol stand with a satisfied smile
> And re-enact at the vestry-glass
> Each pulpit gesture in deft dumb-show
> That had moved the congregation so.[64]

The girl in this poem (and Hardy as well?) is naive to suppose any ritualist is without gloss or guile. Ritual *is* gloss insofar as it is display, which is almost the whole of it; and it should go without saying that a sermon belongs to ritual and shares its ambiguities. Hardy depicts the preacher as vain, which his prototype no doubt was, but that does not prove him a charlatan. The scene in the vestry merely indicates that the performance of the ritualist is as much for his own benefit as for that of other spectators. We would see this instantly if the performer in question were a musician whose admirer had discovered him or her repeating with pleasure backstage what had already been done in front of the house. We would understand that in such cases rehearsal, even *after* the show, is anything but a mark of bad faith. It is a mistake to put the ritualist—even, or perhaps especially, the religious ritualist—in a different category. There is a religious as well as an aesthetic sense in which it must be said that the performance is what counts. My point, heaven knows, is not to rule out the possibility of fakery, certainly not in this age when shyster televangelists are everywhere on display, but rather to be clear that display is a good and necessary part of ritual that should not be evaluated according to a simple standard of sincerity but according to its moral results.

One July day during the annual pilgrimage at Saut d'Eau in Haiti, I sat near the foot of a tall tree, watching the comings and goings of the devout (and some not-so-devout) through a long, hot afternoon. The scene was so crowded, with so many details to occupy my eyes, that a woman standing not five feet away from me had begun to pray aloud before I became aware of her presence; but once having noticed her, it was impossible for me to divert my attention. Of me, she took no notice. Her gaze was directed upwards into the great tree, which had many votive candles at its foot and which, as her body language made clear, was either the locus or the symbol of the spirit to which she prayed. As I watched and listened, her prayer became more and more fervent. It turned, part of the time, into a litany, as I could tell from the cadence and the repetition of phrases, although I do not speak Creole and did not understand her words. She prayed for a long time, full of grief and imprecation, and then she stopped and moved out of sight on the other side of the tree.

Then Jean-Claude, my assistant and translator, made his way to my side, having observed all of this from some yards away. Would I like to know what she had said? Last year her son had been murdered. She had come here a year ago and prayed the spirit Damballah to take vengeance upon the killers. For twelve months she has waited. The months were recited, over and over (that was the litany), naming the times of her anguish. Now the ones who killed her son are trying to take away her land. Desperate, she asks not only for vengeance but also protection.

It moved me very much, and I asked Jean-Claude to go ask if I could greet her. She agreed, and we had a brief conversation through our interpreter. I gave her what I could, which was a bit of money and a prayer of benediction. Then, shameless as the researcher and photographer that I was, I asked if I might take her picture. I even asked if she would return to her place of prayer and let me photograph her in that attitude. A little to my surprise, she agreed. I would have been more surprised if I did not already know that Haitians are a remarkable blend of modesty and self-display. How they do it astonishes me, for I come from a cultural stream that prizes modesty and eschews all kinds of ostentation; but the Haitians, as one can see in the marketplace and elsewhere, know how to put themselves forward with great force of style when it matters, and how to withdraw and create an aura of privacy about them when it does not.

She came once again to her place of prayer before the tree, and I sat again where I had been, only this time I took the cap off the camera lens and prepared to shoot. She glanced at me to acknowledge what I was doing, and then she began for the second time to pray. At first she seemed a little stiff and self-conscious, but after I shot the first few frames I noticed a change: the ritual of her praying took possession. Soon she was committed, and the fervor of her original prayer returned. She seemed to forget about me and the camera. Her audience was once again in the tree, and the spirit there was made to hear again, in tones that would make a hard heart weep, the tale of her woe, the litany of failed expectations, and her deep-throated pleas, as cadenced as any biblical psalm, for deliverance from her enemies.

When she finished, some little while after I had stopped making pictures, she gathered herself and then turned to me. Now she had no shame, and her self-consciousness was gone. I touched her on both cheeks, thanked her, said a prayer for her in my own language, and departed.

This story of ritual display is of interest for three reasons. First, the display element was almost entirely created through gesture and vocal intonation, with minimal resort to colorful costume and none to music. In other words, the woman simply acted out, largely through narration, her self-on-display.

Second, the display was only incidentally created for the camera. During her first prayer, the audience (invisible to me) was in the tree, and during the second it became so again. Display belongs to all ritual and necessarily to prayer, since the petitioner must make herself and her thoughts known to the spirit. What happened in this case is that the display that was essential to the prayer became, at my request, available for the camera; and this is why the second prayer was so much like the first.

Finally, the thoughts and emotions of the prayer were so closely linked with its performance qualities that during the repetition, enacted at the request of a stranger, they came to her forcefully again and directed her attention once more to her sufferings and to the spirit whose aid she sought.

■

Performance, we have said, means both doing and showing. In the ritual mode, performance is done bodily and is shown through what we have called display. Let us look again at ritual as doing, for this is the side of the matter that is but slenderly understood in modern culture.[65]

To many minds, it seems plausible to understand ritual as symbolic display and hence to interpret it entirely in aesthetic, psychological, or semantic categories, the same as the other members of the ritual mode family: play, play-acting, dance, musical performance, and the like. I trust I have already made it clear that the aesthetic side of rituals is of great importance, yet it is not their only side. Rituals are not merely another form of art or play, although they are surely artful and playful. Rituals are perhaps the oldest, they are in many ways the oddest, members of the performance family. Their business in society is to effect transformations that cannot otherwise be brought about.[66]

Although rituals forge a link between bodily activity and symbol-making, and although ritualization is the earliest form of language, we do not well understand ritual unless we realize that within its frame of reference, action is primary and symbolism subordinate. It is necessary to take exception to interpretations of ritual that give primacy to its symbolic and mythic content.[67] For instance, Edmund Leach has said that "myth is a charter for ritual performance and . . . we can only understand what is being symbolized in the ritual if we take note of what is being 'said' in the mythology."[68] In *Secular Ritual*, Barbara Myerhoff considers ritual to be a kind of rhetoric, calling it a form of "persuasion" and remarking that "rituals are stylized because they must be convincing."[69] These comments seem too rationalistic even for the performing arts, let alone ritual. Is it better to say that the gesture of a dancer is stylized in order to be convincing, or that it is convincing because stylized? The closer dance is to ritual—think of the work of Martha Graham—the more the movement per se is the core of the matter. In this circumstance, the movement does not represent something (a story, a myth, an emotion) that already exists, but instead articulates something never said before, brings it into being. The act of shaping and forming (articulating) the movement is basic to any subsequent symbolic interpretation.

If we think of ritual as enacting a myth, or as a means of persuasion, we are looking at it from the rear. Rituals acquire mythical and symbolic interpretations in the course of time. Some rituals have numerous, often contradictory, mythological "explanations," just as the rite of Christian baptism, for instance, is subject to widely varying theological interpretations: One commentator will say that the rite is necessary to save the soul from damnation, another will regard it as a death to sin and rebirth into new life, while yet another will see it simply as a dedication of one's own life, or a child's, to God.

Like art, rituals are likely to bear more meanings than words can say. If we look at ritual from the front, from the point of view of its inception, we do not see clear rational meanings but instead the laying out of ways to act, prompted by felt needs, fears, joys, and aspirations.

Ludwig Wittgenstein expressed a view similar to this in some jottings posthumously published as *Remarks on Frazer's Golden Bough*. "What makes the character of ritual action," he said, "is not any view or opinion, either right or wrong, although an opinion—a belief—itself can be ritualistic, or belong to a rite."[70]

In other words, the action of the rite is primary; ideas may "belong to" it but are not its *raison d'être* or its explanation. Compare the following passage (pages 1–2):

When [Frazer] explains to us . . . that the king must be killed in his prime because, according to the notions of the savages, his soul would not be kept fresh otherwise, we can only say: where that practice and these views go together, the practice does not spring from the view, but both of them are here.

Wittgenstein carefully refrains from saying that the practice and the ideas are twin expressions of some underlying set of values or structures. He wisely stops with the descriptive observation that both the view and the practice "are here." This reticence shows a fine appreciation, evident especially in Wittgenstein's later writings, for the fact that the actions in which human beings engage cannot be reduced to some kind of surrogate for words.

When William Harman studied the rites celebrating the marriage of Shiva and Minaksi at the temple bearing her name in the city of Madurai in South India, he found great variety in the interpretation of the rites, among the priests as well as the people in the crowds. This is not surprising. His words in *The Sacred Marriage of a Hindu Goddess* are apt:

A person may participate in a ritual event, indeed many do, without knowing the mythology with which the ritual is associated. And s/he may find that ritual just as meaningful as someone who claims to know the mythology which the ritual involves. Ritual, once enacted, has a life of its own.[71]

Rituals are primarily instruments designed to change a situation: They are more like washing machines than books. A book may be *about* washing, but the machine takes in dirty clothes and, if all goes well, transforms them into cleaner ones.

Rites of passage, so named by Arnold Van Gennep in 1908, offer the clearest examples of rituals effecting change. Take marriage ceremonies, for instance. Common law marriage aside, there is no way in our society to get married except through a rite. The marriage license does not create a marriage but simply grants permission for a wedding ceremony to take place. The marriage does not exist until the ceremony, religious or civil, makes it so. The ceremony may be as elaborate as the Polish Catholic one that lasted all day and night in the movie *The Deer Hunter*, or it may be as brief as the one in the film version of *Out of Africa*, thrown together on the spot and finished in less than a minute; but the point is that it must be performed, else the couple do not pass from the unwed to the married state.

Similarly, there is no way to become President of the United States, or a judge, or the governor of a state, without a rite of induction. One may, in an emergency, temporarily act as such an officer without the ritual, but then one is not "really" in office. There is no way to become a priest of the church without a rite of ordination, and no way to become a member of most churches without having undergone baptism. Rites of passage are performed not simply to *mark* transitions but to *effect* them.

In Istanbul a post-office bureaucrat introduced himself to me and my wife on the street, the better to practice his English and pass a civil service exam. Learning of our interest in rituals, he invited us to what he called a "circumcision wedding" to be held in the central post office building the next night. Most of the building was dark when we got there, but at last we found a grand party in full swing in the cafeteria. A wan-looking boy of ten lay in a bed near the wall recovering from the surgical rite he had undergone an hour or so earlier in an adjoining room. He received gifts and greetings without much enthusiasm, while the dining and dancing he did not feel like taking part in filled the hall with gaiety. After enjoying ourselves for a while, dancing with people of four generations, we asked our host about his calling this event a "circumcision wedding," which curious name we supposed was an indication that his English did indeed need improvement. Seeing our

perplexity, he consulted his neighbors, who determined after lengthy
debate that it was the right choice of words. After we objected once
more, suggesting several alternative phrases, someone was sent to fetch
a Turkish-English dictionary, which was examined by several people, all
of whom agreed once more that what we had here was a circumcision
wedding and nothing else. At that I decided to leave semantics aside
and inquire into what the ritual was accomplishing.

"What has happened to this boy today?" I inquired, and was of
course told about his operation.

"Yes, I know," said I, "but what difference does it make in his life?"

The reply was immediate: "He has changed from a child into a boy."

"I see. And how long will he remain a boy?"

"Until he gets married."

"And what," I asked, "if he does not get married?"

The question was met with laughter. "Then," they informed me, "he
will never become a man."

The obligation to be wed in order to become a man is not, I hope,
universal; but the importance of rites of passage, in one context or
another, must be nearly so. Without ritual, certain important transitions
do not take place. It is often true, as in this example, that a ritual is not
the *sole* agent of a transition, but it is nonetheless a necessary one, or else
it loses its character as ritual. "In sacrifice," say Hubert and Mauss in
their famous essay on the subject,

the devotee who provides the victim which is the object of the consecration is
not, at the completion of the operation, the same as he [sic] was at the beginning.
He has acquired a religious character which he did not have before, or has rid
himself of an unfavourable character with which he was affected; he has raised
himself to a state of grace or has emerged from a state of sin. In either case he
has been religiously transformed.[72]

Rituals, let us say, are performative actions. Discussing the wide
range of types of performance in human society, Richard Schechner has
proposed that we think of all performances as existing within a
continuum that runs from a pole of *efficacy* on the one hand to that of
entertainment on the other.[73]

Theater, which has some of the qualities of ritual and is therefore
included in what I am calling the ritual mode of performance, is closer to
the entertainment end of Schechner's continuum, while ritual proper,
which has some of the qualities of theater, stands closer to the pole of
efficacy. This "efficacy/entertainment dyad," as Schechner calls it,
corresponds to the ambiguity of doing and showing that we have
already noted as belonging to all performance.

Without the quasi-theatricality of display, ritual could not exist: It would have, we might say, nothing to show for itself. Along with display, as we have seen, go ritual's communicative and symbolic functions. Yet these functions are, in ritual, subdominant ones, important but not primary. The dominant functions, the ones that constitute ritual as ritual, have to do with efficacy, with bringing about some change in an existing state of affairs. Hence Schechner coins the term "transformances," meaning performances that are "the means of transformation from one status, identity, or situation to another" (Schechner, page 71).

Let us look closer now at the kinds of transformation rituals effect. We have already taken note of rites of passage, in which there is a change of status and/or identity: the unwed become wed, the layperson becomes clerical, the citizen becomes President, an individual becomes charged with responsibility, and so on. There are many other kinds of transformance not usually thought of as rites of passage. They may occur repeatedly in a lifetime—rituals of spiritual and moral cleansing, for example, and, closely related to those, rituals of healing. We should think also of such regularly performed rites as, in the Christian tradition, the Eucharist and prayer.

According to Roman Catholic doctrine, the Mass accomplishes the transformation of bread and wine into the body and blood of Christ. It also repeats and perpetuates the efficacious sacrifice of Christ for the remission of sins. In some Lutheran and Anglican theologies, the efficacy of the Eucharist is retained, even without the doctrine of transubstantiation; but for most Protestants the rite is interpreted simply as a service of commemoration, its efficacy lost: Communion becomes solely an act of communication rather than a transformation. To the extent that this happens, the rite moves away from the pole of efficacy toward that of entertainment, even though it may be rather dull to watch or take part in. Although my Protestant theology does not include a doctrine of transubstantiation, and I do not hold to a hierarchical sacramentality, I believe that a rite that has lost its power to transform runs a strong risk of becoming mere show. We shall look at this again when we come to the possible rejuvenation of Christian sacraments toward the end of the book.

As for prayer, its character as transformance may be considered in two different ways. The most familiar version of "the efficacy of prayer" is the idea that the deity, prompted by prayer, grants the express wish of the petitioner: The prayer is "answered," prayer "works," and so on. There is another, perhaps less obvious, sense in which prayer may be understood to transform a situation. The act of prayer may establish, or reestablish, relationships—between the people or groups who pray, the deity *to* whom they pray, and the people or circumstances *for* which they pray. Like speech in general, prayer may on occasion have not only, and not mainly, the function of conveying information, but rather that of establishing or consolidating relationship through intensifying the "presence" of one being to another. Hence prayer may transform isolation into community, emptiness into fullness, despair into hope, and so on. I am suggesting that it is not the mere thought of deity that accomplishes this, but rather such thought in conjunction with the physical enactment of prayer in speech or body language—that is, in performance.

Standing at the kitchen stove early in the morning, looking past it through an open window, I feel sleepy, unfocused, fragmented, waiting for the coffee water to boil. An impulse to pray arises in me, but the thought of God remains as vague and unfocused as I feel myself to be at that moment. I am not in the mood for words. A few months ago I was in India, and now, without consciously thinking what to do, I find myself raising my hands in front of my face and putting palms together, the way Indians do in their gesture of respect. Quickly, my emotions change. I become aware of a stir of energy throughout my body. My hands, palms still together, move downward until they are in front of my navel. I feel centered for the first time since arising, and the tree leaves outside the window begin to sparkle. During this little rite, which I have never performed before, no words pass through my consciousness. Theologically, there is either nothing or everything to say about it. Some, including myself, will call it prayer, others not. In any case, it was a short and subtle ritual of transformation.

When we speak of the efficacy of ritual, we are not speaking of every conceivable instance of effective performance. For example, a traffic cop's gestures do not a ritual make. As Meyer Fortes has said, if "ritual is wholly subsumed within the category of 'communication' then the policeman on point duty is performing a very explicit and efficacious ritual."[74] The usual way of distinguishing ritual from the kind of action the traffic cop engages in is to say that the policeman performs in a secular context, whereas ritual requires a sacred one.[75]

I would like to suggest a way of thinking about the efficacy of rituals that does not require reference to supernatural agency or to "the sacred," and yet avoids regarding the traffic conductor as performing a ritual just because he gives a performance that has a clear effect. Why is the policeman's performance not a ritual? To put the question differently, why would calling it a ritual trivialize the subject?

The answer does not require reference to supernatural or sacred powers, but does require reference to the agency of otherwise *unseen* powers. A ritual is an efficacious performance that invokes the presence and action of powers which, without the ritual, would not be present or active at that time and place, or would be so in a different way. The most obvious examples of such powers, no doubt, are divinities, demons, ancestors, and other spirits that may be called "supernatural"; but they may also be certain powers of nature, of society, of the state, or of the psyche. The agencies with which ritual is concerned, then, are such that they must be represented symbolically if they are to be depicted at all. Here is the reason for the necessary and intimate relation between ritual and symbol.

But I have already said that rituals are not primarily symbolic. We must walk a fine line. I mean to say that in the first instance, and fundamentally, the ritual is not in service of the symbols, but the other way around. Rituals employ symbols so as to invoke, to address, to affect, even to manipulate, one or another unseen power. It is these actions—invoking, addressing, affecting, manipulating—that are primary. They are so much more fundamental than the symbols that we may even regard the symbols as having been generated through ritualization.

There is a profound sense, and I think not an impious one, in which the unseen powers, including deity, have been brought into being by the rituals that invoke them. Durkheim observed: ". . . if it is true that man [sic] depends upon his gods, this dependence is reciprocal. The gods also have need of man; without offerings and sacrifices they would die."[76]

Similarly, in scattered passages of their seminal work on sacrifice, most frequently in their chapter on "The Sacrifice of the God," Hubert and Mauss suggested that the ritual act itself gives birth to the religious ideas which ritual will later come to symbolize. For example, when discussing a ceremony at Jumieges in which "the part of the annual vegetation spirit was taken by a man," they report that "the ceremony did not have as its effect merely to embody the spirit of agriculture; the spirit was born in the sacrifice itself."[77]

Later they remark: ". . . not only is it in sacrifice that some gods are born, it is by sacrifice that all sustain their existence" (page 91).

Countering a view earlier put forward by William Robertson Smith,[78] Hubert and Mauss maintained that the victim is not sacrificed *because* of its religious nature but that "it is the sacrifice itself that confers this upon it" (page 97) and that "the rite sets in motion the whole complex of sacred things to which it is addressed" (page 98). The dependency of deity upon offerings and sacrifices is true, according to Durkheim, "even in the most idealistic religions."[79]

Religious rituals depend upon gods and spirits for their sense, but the gods and spirits are dependent upon ritual for their being. As the Haitians say, "It does not matter whether you believe in the *loa* as long as you serve them." Such bracketing of the ontological status of deity is an affront to many theologies, but in my theology it is fine, for I regard divinity as a kind of relationship, the kind Martin Buber had in mind when he wrote, "In the beginning is the relation." Apart from this relationship it makes no sense to speak of God. Without ritual, the divine-human relationship is broken, and in the break everything that can be truly identified as either divine or human perishes. The first verse of Genesis, which says, "In the beginning God . . ." comes from an ancient liturgy and "works" only within the context of ritual.

■

If there is any one thing that clearly distinguishes performance in the ritual mode from other kinds of events, it is that the performer assumes roles and relates to what is going on in an "as if" way not appropriate to the workaday world. As Victor Turner insisted, ritual realizes itself in the subjunctive mood. The so-called "sacred space" and "sacred time" of religious rituals are, above all, imaginative constructions, "rules of the game."

A creature with its nose always to the grindstone, with no opportunity or inclination toward spontaneous gesture, having no time to "kill" and no inventiveness to throw away—such a being, a stranger to play, could not ritualize, could at best take part in ritual only by doing exactly as told.

The playfulness of rituals, however, does not mean that they are nothing more than play-acting, much less that they cannot be efficacious. When a Christian priest lifts a chalice, or a New Guinea man greases a sacred stone, each really *does* what she or he is doing. Such a performer does not only pretend, as might an actor on a proscenium stage. In rituals, for the most part, there is no question of illusion. Gestures are actually performed, and these gestures have social, personal, and religious consequences. In short, rituals are a kind of playful work.

We may speak of ritual, then, as work done playfully. Wherever the spirit of play enters it, work starts to become ritualized. It develops routines that are multipurpose, serving to communicate, to entertain, and to invoke something or someone not otherwise present in the labor itself.

As work done playfully, ritual is different from art. What we know in complex societies as art, something that has become distinct from ritual, is play done workfully. Art departs from ritual in the measure in which it assumes that, as art, it can become a necessary work. To take the playfulness of creativity and turn it into serious work moves (we come to paradox again) in the direction of aestheticism, of art for art's sake, of an absolute creativity free from all social responsibility. Play done workfully risks turning in on itself and becoming empty, while work done playfully becomes charged with energies and meanings.

As work done playfully, ritual remains in touch with what is "other." Ritual is not about itself but about relation to not-self. Secular or religious, ritual is always concerned with powers that are understood to have their being outside the ritualizers, even though it is ritual that gives these powers their being, instantiating them within its circle of magic. Yet magic is a preposterous idea, and few, if any, minds are so "primitive" as to be unaware of this. People are almost always conscious of the absurdity, the contradiction lying within ritual pretension. As for the gods, we have to remember that, in ritual, sacrality and sacrilege are twins; and outside of ritual they vanish. The work of ritual cannot get done if no hands are dirty. The serious must play if ritual is to be capable of any lasting transformations. In Christian theological perspective, work done playfully is a sign of grace. That is, it cannot be accounted for rationally, for it is transformative work accomplished through play.

∎

Although I would like to write at length on grace and play, rejoicing in the freedom that can accompany the seriousness of ritual performance as the psalmist rejoiced to "dwell in the house of the Lord forever,"[80] we must not be lured into forgetting that in rituals all is not light. If rituals play, part of their playing is with fire; and their mode of renewing life requires them to be more than slightly in touch with death. Performance has a sinister side.

The fearsome side of ritual provided the basis for "The Lottery," a well-known story by Shirley Jackson. With strong literary effect, Jackson did not rationalize her story's association of ritual with violence. Instead, she described an entirely fictional, apparently benign, ritual occasion, withholding until the story's final paragraph her disclosure of the ritualized lottery's deadly outcome. In this way, she evoked her readers' dread of ritual as something which, however benign it may be on the surface, is at heart destructive. The story, I think, is not primarily about ritual but about the violence that lurks underneath human skin. Even so, it astutely suggests that ritual may lance that skin, providing an occasion for the violence beneath to erupt.[81]

The dangers of religious ritual are associated with sacredness and sacrifice. It is often said that gods and other sacred phenomena are a threat to human beings, requiring rituals to provide a safe approach to them; but we may be nearer the mark to suggest that the dangers inhere in performance itself, whence they are projected onto "the sacred."[82]

All performances in the ritual mode require limits. The performance must have limits that are preset, or else these must be generated during the performance itself, marking off spaces, times, gestures, words, and objects that it is necessary to avoid (to go around), and others that it is necessary *not* to avoid but obligatory to do, touch, or say. This delineation of what to do and not do is rooted in ritualization's being, as we have seen, a process of channeling and marking, of making pathways for behavior. In order to achieve definite form, ritualization encourages certain acts, reinforcing them with repetition and slight variation, while ruling others out. In short, ritual performance requires (and makes) rules of the game, whether these be known from previous usage or come to be elaborated upon the spot. This inner necessity or "logic" of ritual performance is, then, available for elaboration in the direction of a religious sensibility, where it will give rise to the notion of things taboo and things permitted. We can say that the profane becomes known from the fact that ritual allows us to walk upon it, the sacred from the "rule" that we may not.

"Do not come near," God said to Moses in the desert. "Take off your shoes, for the place where you stand is holy ground."[83] On its face, this seems to imply that the holiness of the ground is what makes ritually necessary the removal of shoes. Yet the core of this scene is not the holy ground, nor even the holiness of God as such, but rather the *encounter* between Moses and God, which first manifests itself as a double-bind injunction: while the unconsumed burning bush beckons Moses to move in for a closer look, the voice of God commands him to stay back. To "read" the scene, we must imagine the bodily actions of Moses on the spot, together with what these mean to him.

The sacred is ritually proscribed, as Durkheim saw; but we are closer to the mark if we suppose it to be sacred because it is off limits than if we think, as he did, that it is proscribed because of an a priori sacredness. In this connection, we should recall Van Gennep's fine sentence, "The magic circles pivot," which refers to the fact that "sacredness as an attribute is not absolute" but "brought into play by the nature of particular situations."[84] Jonathan Z. Smith phrases the matter this way:

. . . there is nothing that is inherently sacred or profane. These are not substantive categories, but rather situational or relational categories, mobile boundaries which shift according to the map being employed. There is nothing that is sacred in itself, only things sacred in relation.[85]

Smith speaks of a sacred place as "a focusing lens" and says that an ordinary object becomes sacred "by having our attention directed to it in a special way" (page 55). Well said, but it is not placement alone that achieves this. It is done by the ritual context, for it is ritual that delimits and defines the sacred territory and the objects that belong there.

As the division between sacred and profane arises out of ritual and represents the development of religious potentialities latent within performance, so also the presence of sacrificial victims and their destruction is best seen as elaboration upon other, potentially dangerous, performance dynamics. Constituted on one side by limit, order, and restraint, bringing form out of formlessness, on another side ritual drives beyond all limit, aspiring to make itself the vehicle of an absolute ecstasy. Nietzsche was right to see in tragedy, which is a cousin if not a direct descendant of ritual, a Dionysian as well as an Apollonian motif.[86] Ritualized performance may tend toward orgy, loss of self and consciousness, bursts of energy extreme and sometimes deadly.

The sacrificial victim, prior to all specific symbolization, is the target of ritual's own quest for an ultimate performance. Something of this sort was intuited earlier in this century by that herald of a ritualized "theater of cruelty," Antonin Artaud.[87] While he meant such a theater to include scenes of pain and death, these were not the sole exemplars of the cruelty he had in mind, for he thought that all acts were "cruel" if they were absolute—if they were performed for their own sake and, once done, never to be undone. There is something in ritual performance, the more so as its proximity to the pole of efficacy increases, which aims at irrevocable acts.[88] Among these are scarification of the body (used in many initiation ceremonies), sexual intercourse, and killing. When ritual performance engages in a killing, as it very frequently does in all parts of the world, and when the act is interpreted by religious sensibility, the victim becomes a "sacrifice."

Most theories concerning ritual sacrifice serve to rationalize it by proposing that its roots lie in some socially useful activity, whether in the killing of wild prey, the slaughter of domesticated animals, the redirection of violence onto a substitute victim, the propitiation of a god, or what not. I do not deny that such actions may have something to do with the origins of human or animal sacrifice, but I question whether any one of them, or all together, provide a sufficient explanation. There is something terrifying, because motiveless, in ritual sacrifice. That is, all the stated or supposed motives have about them the aura of rationalizations, which is why none ever seems satisfactory, and the scholarly quest for the origins of sacrifice appears unending. My suggestion is that one of the motives lies within performance itself, where it originally has nothing to do with any rational reason for killing but instead has to do, as I have said, with a desire to perform something absolute. Shakespeare expressed the impulse in Lear's pathetic lines:

> I will do such things,—
> What they are yet I know not, — but they shall be
> The terrors of the earth.
>> (*King Lear* 2.4.280–82)

Lear's case is particular, but the desire to shake the superflux is well-nigh universal. Perhaps there is no need to turn to psychology, theology, myth, or carnivorousness in hope of finding an "explanation" for the human urge to slaughter. Human beings observe the destruction of life in which nature regularly engages, and they are able to perform the same way in their own terrifying freedom. Once the act of killing is done for its own sake, it has begun to be ritualized.

In ritual slaying, the polarity in what Schechner calls the "efficacy/entertainment dyad" seems to collapse: The ultimate entertainment (the drama of killing) has also the greatest efficacity (that the victim is really and truly slain, an irrevocable act). This way of viewing the origins of ritual sacrifice is different from Durkheim, Hubert and Mauss, and the whole scholarly tradition (one thinks of both Rudolf Otto and Mircea Eliade) that interprets religious ritual as stemming from manifestations of the sacred. It differs also from two more recent points of view that have gained much attention, those of René Girard and Walter Burkert. Both scholars have wisely and courageously faced the very large role that violence plays in ritual and in human behavior generally, but I think they are mistaken about the cultural roots of sacrifice.

Girard's view of ritual sacrifice, set forth in *Violence and the Sacred,* [89] appears to have been suggested by his reading of Freud; but since he has considerably modified Freud's idea, we should call the stance neo-Freudian. In both cases, culture is seen as based upon a primordial act of group violence—the slaying of the father by the primal horde, according to Freud, and a group's killing of an innocent victim, according to Girard. In both theories, the original act has been removed from consciousness and can become known again only through the work of the psychoanalyst or the critic of culture and literature. This means, we may note, that these putative events must forever remain hypothetical. To the extent that they inform a total view of culture and the human situation, they are of a mythical rather than an empirical character.

Burton Mack offers a usefully brief synopsis of what he calls Girard's "scenario":

Humans have no braking mechanism for intraspecific aggression. This means that rivalries and conflicts, once unleashed, cannot stop short of manslaughter. Violence, therefore, is endemic. Since the only answer to murder is another murder, cycles of reciprocal retaliation create unending series of revenge killings. To bring the series to an end, a "final" killing is necessary. The final killing is achieved in the "mechanism of the surrogate victim." From within the group, one person is separated out as victim.[90]

Since the danger of repetition of the original killing is ever-present, ritual sacrifice is needed to deflect and contain the impulse, and to assist in keeping knowledge of the original event from consciousness.

Girard says that "Ritual is nothing more than the regular exercise of 'good' violence."[91] He proposes that the violence in sacrificial ritual takes the place of violent acts that would otherwise be committed against members of society.

. . . we have good reason to believe that the violence directed against the surrogate victim might well be radically generative in that, by putting an end to the vicious and destructive cycle of violence, it simultaneously initiates another and constructive cycle, that of the sacrificial rite—which protects the community from that same violence and allows culture to flourish. (page 93)

Girard's argument depends on the (unproven) assumption that the victim is a surrogate and that if it did not die a ritual death the amount of antisocial violence would be the greater. Let us remember that Girard argues not simply for *ritual's* being a social regulator of violence, which would be plausible, but that the regulating mechanism is specifically that of "the sacrificial process." What is the evidence for this assumption? I do not see it in the societies I know anything about.

One place I have witnessed animal sacrifice is Haiti, where it takes place regularly in the practice of *vodou*. The country is also Catholic, of course, and has Christ as surrogate victim in the Mass, in addition to the chickens, goats, and bulls put to death in *vodou*. Yet, sadly, Haiti is a land of agonizing social violence. I do not suggest that it is more violent than my own country, which has used atomic weapons, taught methods of torture in schools run by the CIA, and shows a high incidence of racist police brutality. I cite Haiti because it is one of the lands where animal sacrifice is common.

Until recently, most Haitian violence was monopolized by the government, through a reign of terror unhesitating in its use of murder and torture. There was then very little crime in the streets; but the practitioners of violence in the government were no strangers to animal sacrifice. Indeed, François Duvalier encouraged the sacrificial practices of *vodou*, hoping to bring the popular religion under his political control. With the downfall of the Duvalier dynasty in February 1986, violence spread into the streets, where much vengeance was taken on the formerly dreaded security squad, the *Tontons Macoutes*. In November 1987, on election day, some dozens of voters were massacred at polling places, and the provisional government, which may or may not have engineered these killings, called off the elections. It is difficult in Haiti to see any correlation between ritual sacrifice and the bringing of a "vicious and destructive cycle of violence" to an end.

I suspect, however, that specific examples do not have much to do with Girard's thesis, which has a largely mythical character. I mean that it is about an imaginary past (the "originary event") and describes what Girard thinks the function of ritual sacrifice ought to be. His thesis has been derived mainly from interpretation of literature (epics, novels, and dramas), far less from the study of rituals and the social circumstances of their performance.

More plausible is the suggestion of Walter Burkert that sacrificial killing is derived from the hunt.[92] Here at least the theory starts from ordinary behavior, attempting to trace the steps by which it became translated into performable ritual. It is plausible to consider that the hunt, its prey, and the kill became invested with many layers of meaning, and that hunters developed some identification with the prey they stalked, and hence were ambivalent about killing it. These attitudes could be acted out in ritual, and the ritual could serve a useful function to influence the time and manner of subsequent hunts, as well as to transmit necessary information and skills. In Burkert's thesis, the sacrificial victim stands for but does not replace the object of the hunt.

One difficulty with Burkert's hypothesis is that it does not seem to address human as well as animal sacrifice. Another, pointed out by Mack, is that there is little evidence for hunting (rather than gathering) during the Paleolithic period, when we do have evidence of ritual sacrifice.[93] Another difficulty is that rituals of destruction are associated with agricultural societies no less than with hunting societies. However, the main objection to Burkert's very interesting approach is that it does not take seriously enough the material from ethological studies that Burkert himself was among the first to recognize as essential in the interpretation of ritual. I am suggesting that ritual killing may emerge from the animal/human nexus of ritualization itself, without need of reference to the hunt.

How could this be? Very simple, I believe, yet terrifying. All we need is the recognition of two well-established facts concerning our species. First, we have developed ritualization to a very high level of elaboration, much higher than any other animal. Second, we lack a genetically coded inhibition against intraspecific violence. We humans are able to kill anything, even members of our own species, for sport. With us, killing is sometimes done for the sheer performative effect of it. Being killers, we have proceeded to ritualize killing, and for this there is no ulterior reason at all.

There is more to say. The presence of killings in ritual, once they have appeared there, actually contributes, pace Girard, to the spread of senseless killings in society. We can find a name for the process in a phrase that Girard has coined: "mimetic desire." Desire, he reminds us, is learned through imitation. Should we not speak of a desire for killing that is learned mimetically? There are important ways in which life imitates ritual. Is not killing one of these? This is not to say that without ritual we would not kill. It is rather to say that the sources of killing by humans are multiple, and that one of them is ritual itself. For ritual is not only reactive, not only imitative or compensatory in its functioning, but also generative. Not everything that it generates is good.

If there are circumstances in which ritual performance moderates or inhibits undesirable social behavior, as I think there are, these circumstances do not always obtain. Rituals are indeed necessary sources of limit, steering human behavior in socially desirable ways; but they are also inciters of extreme behavior, including murder. Prophetic voices, from the time of ancient Israel if not before, have warned that both religion and ritual are morally ambiguous. As they bring grace and provide protection from evil, so they may also bring falsity and the destruction of all that is humane. Rituals have made us human, to be sure; but part of what it means to be human is to lose by what you gain. In our age, ritual has been employed in totalitarian fashion by governments both fascist and Communist. It can be a powerful inciter to the frenzies of war.

My principal aim in this book is to show how necessary ritual is to human freedom and to social processes of liberation. The fact that ritual tends also toward senseless violence shows that any link we may find between ritual and liberation will not be a simple one. To see it rightly, without blinding ourselves to the destruction of life that rituals often pursue, we need to consider performance at greater depth by turning to its confessional and ethical modes.

6

Ritual's Two Siblings: Performance in the Confessional and the Ethical Modes

The condition of truth is to let suffering speak.

—CORNEL WEST[94]

Religion, like art, *lives* in so far as it is performed ...

—VICTOR TURNER[95]

Because the kind of performance done in theaters and concert halls has such a strong family resemblance to that done in rituals, I grouped all these together, in the previous chapter, within a single mode of performance, which I call the ritual mode. If we think of ritual as being related to artistic performances on one side, we may imagine that has it relatives on its other side, too. These belong to its existential and life-urgent lineage. I find it helpful to regard them as comprising two additional modes of performance, which I call the confessional and the ethical. If these are not kept in mind, it is easy to misunderstand or lose sight of the connection that rituals have to religious and ethical life. The sheer pleasure of doing rituals, or else the doing of them from a vague and general sense of duty, may take over, resulting in a fruitless attitude called ritualism.

Let us recall what is meant by performance. It is not simply the doing of something, although such a meaning of the word is to be found in the dictionary. In all three modes of performance that concern us in this book, doing is combined with showing—not show-and-tell, but do-and-show. We are accustomed to this in theater and in rituals, which are quasi-theatrical. In the confessional and ethical modes, we encounter do-

and-show outside the theater, beyond the temple, the church, the sacred grove, or the playing field, away from a sabbath or other "sacred time," in a world that exists beyond the boundaries that performance in the ritual mode always creates for itself. We ask: What is performance and what good is it when it does not have walls either sacred or aesthetic to protect it? What is the nature of performance when it deliberately exposes itself to life's risks and dangers, unprotected by the ritual mode's ability to dodge serious engagement by appealing to make believe?

The modes I call confessional and ethical are closely related and, in some respects, the same. However, there is a difference of emphasis between them that needs to be seen. Performances in the confessional mode, as we shall see, are primarily concerned with identity and self-disclosure. Since mystery and awesomeness accompany self-revelation, the confessional mode always has something of a religious quality, even though many specific instances of it have nothing overt to do with religious traditions. Nevertheless, many religious traditions include a clear call for personal confession, which on some occasions is highly ritualized and on others not.

In the ethical mode, performance has a different emphasis. Less focused upon the identity of the performer(s), it is oriented more toward affecting the world through direct social and political action.

Using terms familiar to Christian theology, we could say that the confessional mode has more to do with "faith," the ethical more to do with "works." This terminology should lead us to suppose that the connection between the confessional and the ethical modes of performance is both momentous and subtle, remembering that the relation between faith and works has been a challenge to Christian theology throughout its history. While I shall not review that history, I hope to cast a little light on the issue through the discussion of performance. The matter is not relevant solely to religion, since it has to do with the correlation in all human beings between self and world.

Two questions suggest themselves:

1. Does it make sense to speak of faith or confession as performance? Do not these have to do with heart, mind, and soul—things quite interior? Faith seems to be a certain point of view rather than the doing of anything, and its integrity may seem to be jeopardized when it becomes a matter of display.

2. In what sense is the doing of an ethical act a performance, especially when performance has already been defined as including the display of what is done? Once it has been decided that a certain course

of action is good, should not people aim to do it with the least show possible? Does not the display of good works corrupt them?

These complementary questions suggest that the confessional and the ethical modes of performance are two aspects of a single whole. These modes exist in some tension with each other, yet between them, as we shall see, is an intimate and necessary linkage. To expound them, we shall start with the confessional and find ourselves led into consideration of the ethical as we go along.

■

Confessional performance is highly personal and dramatic. Although it involves interior attitudes and feelings, it is marked by direct address, Job-like challenge and response, leaps of faith, existential commitments, daring, contemplation, lamentation, and praise. Because it is personal and dramatic, the confessional mode poses to its expositor a question of style. What style will do justice to Luther's "Here I stand!" To Job's "I know that my redeemer lives!" To Moses' challenge to the people of Israel: "I call heaven and earth to witness against you this day, that I have set before you life and death, blessing and curse; therefore choose life, that you and your descendants may live . . ."[96] The confessional mode needs a language capable of saying, "I believe. Help my unbelief."[97] Even so, I shall resist the temptation to dramatize my dramatic theme.

The confessional mode has to do with faith and belief. Not all religions emphasize these as much as the biblical and koranic traditions do, for the confessional mode is lifted into high relief by monotheism, especially when this is combined with a sacred, canonical text; but the act of confession—not so much confession of sin as confession of loyalty—is found in many religions. I turn once again to Haitian *vodou* for an example.

In *vodou* Almighty God (the Haitians say *Bon Dieu*) is somewhat eclipsed by the many *loa*—gods, or divine spirits. The Bible takes its place alongside oral traditions from Africa, from slave experience, and from Native American sources, so there is not much concern for canonical text, and anyway most *vodouissants* cannot read.

Because vodou mixes monotheism with polytheism and has neither creeds nor sacred text, it does not have as much invested in credal formulas as Roman Catholicism, which it has adapted to its own purposes, nor as much as Protestantism in Haiti, which utterly opposes *vodou* and asks for confessions that repudiate all service to the *loa*. When Haitians say, "It does not matter if you believe in the *loa* as long as you serve them," that mainly means "as long as you perform the *services* (ceremonious rituals) the *loa* expect." But there are subordinate meanings, too, present in the Haitian idea of "serving." Some Haitians go so far as to *marry* (in a service of holy matrimony) the *loa* who is most important to them. Many more go through a ceremony in which a certain loa is recognized as one's "master of the head" (*maît-tête*). Like most religions, *vodou* displays a great range of intensity in the devotion of its followers. The confessional mode of performance is not absent from *vodou* and is even of importance to it, but not in the exclusivist and credal way that characterizes so much of Christianity. Indeed, the possibility for confessional performance to be nonexclusive and noncredal, while remaining personal and dramatic, sheds an important light on what the confessional mode of performance is.

Wilfred Cantwell Smith has called attention to the difference between "faith" and "belief" in modern usage. Faith, he writes,

is an orientation of the personality, to oneself, to one's neighbour, to the universe; a total response; a way of seeing whatever one sees and of handling whatever one handles; a capacity to live at a more than mundane level; to see, to feel, to act in terms of, a transcendent dimension. Belief, on the other hand, is the holding of certain ideas.[98]

Smith urges that "belief" and "believe" be "dropped as religious terms, since they now no longer refer directly to anything of human ultimacy."[99] He demonstrates at length, however, that "belief" and "faith" originally had very similar meanings. "Believe," he says,

began its career in early Modern English meaning . . . to hold dear, to cherish. . . . To believe a person, or to believe "in," or "on," or for a time "to" or "of," a person, was to orient oneself towards him or her with a particular attitude or relationship, of esteem and affection, also trust—and more earnestly, of self-giving endearment. The noun "belief," whose development accompanied but later out paced that of the verb, similarly meant literally endearment, holding as beloved, and specifically then a giving of oneself to, clinging to, committing oneself, placing—or staking—one's confidence in.[100]

While Smith rightly points out that Western Christianity has put more emphasis than have most religious traditions upon theological orthodoxy, and hence upon belief in its modern sense of intellectual assent to doctrine, he does not dwell upon the fact that in this tradition "faith" has tended to become something private, interior, and invisible.

At the same time that "believing" was becoming a rational, intellectual matter, "faith" was becoming an attitude of the "inner" person. It is this turn that separates Western Christianity from most other religious traditions and makes trouble for Smith when he universalizes faith as the essence of all religious traditions throughout the world.

In order to understand why belief and faith are so important to the human condition, we must discern their connection with performance. In religious life, as in cultural life generally, one is concerned with realities that are unseen. All full-blown rituals, whether religious or not, make reference to realities not always visible to the physical eye. The word "belief" highlights a people's convictions about certain things they cannot see except in the mind's eye. If they act in relation to these with any degree of passion, they may be said to "believe." The sense of the verb should govern that of the noun: "Belief" is the abstract way of referring to the *act* of believing: To believe is to make and preserve a relationship of trust.

To confess, in this context, is to acknowledge that one is engaged in the act of believing. Hence, it is to reveal oneself, to expose the heart. Persons or groups who confess their believing become open to the gaze and the unpredictable reaction of others. For this reason, we should regard all confession made under duress as a form of obscenity. And yet confession within community, provided it is not compelled, is part of what it means to be human. It is essential, as we shall presently see, in the initiation of freedom movements.

To get a better grasp upon the confessional mode of performance, I want to back up a moment and take another look at the ritual mode. I want to consider the relation of ritual performance to religious belief, and vice versa. My purpose is to bring into view the way in which the confessional mode of performance arises out of the ritual mode and in turn gives rise to the ethical.

Believing, as I have said, is making and preserving relationships of trust. While beliefs involve ideas, they are not the same as ideas. When beliefs are taken simply as thoughts in people's heads, they are imagined as *not* performative but as requiring somehow to be translated *into* action. Rituals are then seen as the outer forms of religious ideas that exist independently. This is a view of beliefs and rituals born of a dualistic picture of the world, in which mind and body are separate entities. Beliefs are to actions, so it is thought, as mind is to body, with priority of value given to beliefs and mind, since the body, understood as mindless in itself, is assumed to have neither light nor orientation. If the earliest modern exponent of some such view as this was Edward B. Tylor,[101] who assumed, as Edmund Leach says, "the priority of belief over ritual,"[102] he has had many successors, for example J. R. Goody.[103] Even Durkheim saw religious rituals as media for the expression of religious ideas. "Religious phenomena," he wrote,

are naturally arranged in two fundamental categories: beliefs and rites. The first are states of opinion and consist in representations, the second are determined modes of action. Between these two classes of facts there is all the difference which separates thought from action.

He adds that "It is possible to define the rite only after we have defined the belief," explaining that the belief is the "object" of the rite.[104] Later he says:

If we stick closely to appearances, rites often give the effect of purely manual operations: they are anointings, washings, meals. . . . But these material manoeuvres are only the external envelope under which the mental operations are hidden.[105]

Here we notice the familiar vocabulary of outer and inner, husk and kernel, appearance and reality, which signals a dualistic analysis of human life. Actions, which constitute ritual, are reduced to the status of "material manoeuvres." This dualism obscures Durkheim's vision not only of rituals but of religious beliefs as well, for he does not seem to glimpse the rootage that all thought has in action, nor the actionful character of religious confession. This had been better grasped by Robertson Smith when he observed that "the study of ancient religion must begin, not with myth, but with ritual and traditional usage,"[106] an insight later pursued by the "Cambridge Anthropologists" (Jane Harrison, Francis Cornford, Gilbert Murray, and others) and echoed by Suzanne Langer in her sections about ritual in *Philosophy in a New Key*. [107]

Rituals are expressive of human agency, the power of human beings to act. It is misleading to suppose that rituals are undertaken out of weakness, as if they were a substitute for more effective actions that people cannot or will not do. That may sometimes be the case, but it is not, contrary to the Freudian view, always the case; and it is certainly not prototypical. Anyone who has spent time in ritually active communities knows that rituals mobilize human energy and focus it in collaborative action. However, this is sometimes hidden from the consciousness of those engaged in ritual activity, who may ascribe their ritualizing to tradition, to supernatural revelation, or to the will of religious or civil authorities. Hence there comes a time when people need, for the sake of moral development, to assume responsibility for their rituals, and it is this which brings them to the confessional mode of performance. The confessional mode transcends the ritual mode inasmuch as the performers recognize and speak out (confess) their moral responsibility for the rituals they perform.

The Bible contains a story about the absence, or betrayal, of the confessional mode. When Moses came down from encountering Yahweh on the mountain, he found his brother Aaron, who was a priest, presiding over a ritual in which the people were singing and dancing before the golden image of a calf. Moses, whose allegiance was to the liberator-God, Yahweh, and who was sworn to oppose all forms of idolatry, angrily challenged the goings-on. Aaron's reply denied responsibility: "I threw some gold into the fire, and there came out this calf."[108] At one level, this was true: When a ritual gets going, the results appear of themselves. It is natural to ritualize, and all manner of things can result from it. But Moses was concerned with another level of performance, the level on which it is both possible and necessary to make choices, and to acknowledge them for what they are.

The Hebrew Bible, with much ambivalence, depicts Yahweh as truly known in the performance of ritual, as positively requiring such performance, the rules for which are encoded as "law" (halakhah); yet Yahweh is also said to hate and despise feast days. Theology speaks of divine immanence and divine transcendence. The biblical God, who is immanent in ritual, also transcends it. In the image of God, human beings, who become human by way of ritual and need it in order to be humane, nevertheless will lose their humanity if they do not take moral responsibility for the rituals they perform. The ritual mode of performance gives rise to the confessional by the implicit question: "Who are you who do these ritual things, and what is your business in doing them?" When the moral identity of the ritualizers comes to be openly acknowledged by them, the confessional mode of performance begins.

∎

Although the confessional mode transcends the ritual mode, it is still performance. This point seems to be seldom understood, or seldom stated. To confess is to enact something, and to do it at risk, without the usual protections of the ritual mode. There are two senses in which confession is performance. I shall begin with the more metaphorical sense and proceed to the more literal, while remembering that the literal and the metaphoric are not as distinct in actuality and in ordinary speech as they are in intellectual analysis.

The first sense in which confession is performance is existential. Here confession means to position oneself in relation to the world. Confession answers the question, "Where do we stand? What is our situation?" As long as performance stays strictly within the ritual mode, it does not come to grips with this question. At best, it assumes some kind of answer. Rituals create make-believe worlds, just as works of art, dreams, and all other imaginative constructions exercise the genius of the human mind as a world-building instrument. As long as we remain strictly within the ritual mode of performance, any and all things are possible. We dream of them and play them out. It is true that rituals aspire to irrevocable acts, which we discussed in the previous chapter in connection with ritual killing, and it is true that a ritual is a public performance and not merely an event in one's psyche. And yet, as virtually all students of ritual observe, most notably perhaps Jonathan Z. Smith,[109] rituals have a kind of "ideal" character. They tidy up what is messy in ordinary life. They celebrate not the quotidian actual but the once-upon-a-time or the one-day-some-day potential. In the ritual mode, as in Scarlett O'Hara's fantasies, tomorrow is another day. The confessional mode of performance puts a stop to this by taking a stand. Being deeply existential, such performance has to be described with metaphors: To take a stand, to dig in one's heels, to raise the flag, or (in Jesus' startling reversal of imagery) to go into the closet and shut the door.[110] Nowadays, if we are to get the same start-effect, we have to speak of coming *out* of a closet, and this takes us to the second sense in which confession is performance.

To come out is to go public. In its second meaning, confession is to *demonstrate* where one stands, what one chooses to be, what the group is, where it stands. Confession is not only to take a stand subjectively but also to come out with it. Sometimes, perhaps most times, the coming out makes possible the subjective stand. There is a certain sense, an immensely important one, in which who we are waits upon who we say we are. When we perform ourselves, we do not simply express what we already are: We perform our becoming, and become our performing. There is fate in this, and freedom, too, and something of mystery.

The word "confess," as the dictionary tells, came into English from Latin by way of Old French. *Confessare* in Late Latin combined an intensifying prefix, *com*, with a verb, *fateri*, which in its infinitive form meant "to speak." This Latin verb is in turn traceable to an Indo-European root, *bha*, which apparently carried two rather different but perhaps associated meanings: "to speak," and also "to shine." Even today, "confession" refers to a kind of speaking which brings something hidden into the light. When *fateri* was prefixed with the intensive *com*, "to speak" acquired the connotation of speaking *out* or speaking *up*. This etymology reinforces much ordinary usage, suggesting that confession is a particular kind of display. What kind?

Confession almost always denotes disclosure of identity, or of something particularly important about an identity, something affecting it profoundly. If the term today often refers to confession of sin or confession of crime, its theological and existential import is acknowledgment of one's true state; and this is also the root of the matter when the reference is to confession of faith or confession of loyalty.

A clear and widely known instance of confessional performance today, outside of church and legal proceedings, is found in Alcoholics Anonymous (AA). One of the chief purposes of an AA meeting is not simply to know or realize that one is in the grip of alcoholism but to speak that truth out, to bring the shamefully hidden into the daylight of self- and communal recognition. A point is reached when the old, deceitful performance is no longer viable, and a more truthful one becomes necessary, provided the courage can be found to enact it. At the same time, an AA confession goes beyond admittance of the state of alcoholism to confession of dependence upon a higher power, that is, to a confession of "faith," and this with a minimum of credal entailment.

Another illustrative example of confessional performance is the "coming out" that many lesbian and gay persons have enacted in recent years, and which has profound social and political consequences, in addition to whatever it means psychologically and spiritually for individuals. As long as desire for someone of the same sex is experienced as "the sin that dare not speak its name," a person remains in what may be called a state of inhibited performance. Within the walls of the closet and ghetto, there may (or may not) be quite a lot of so-called "sexual performance," but it is limited in depth. The idea of going public with one's sexual identity is in most cases an explosive one, for the risk is high. It is not only the likelihood of being punished and shamed by society, friends, and family: It is also the risk of losing one's own present identity, losing self-esteem, giving up a known way of life without the reassuring experience of another. Persons who find themselves on the threshold of coming out are in the grip of a crisis concerning the self-world correlation. If they change, the world must change. If the world will not change, they cannot be who they are, save only in self-destructive ways.

To declare oneself sexually to society is a political act. That is as true for the heterosexual majority as for the homosexual minority, but only the latter's confessions make waves. The former's confessions increase their power, enabling them to perform their strength.

■

Discussing the public declaration of sexual identity, we have come upon the way in which the confessional mode of performance modulates into the ethical. The ethical is implicit in the confessional all along, for confession always changes the relation between self and world. The recognition of movement in the self enables, at a certain point, discernment of a dynamic in the world. In the awareness of a correlation between dynamic self and dynamic world, the ethical mode of performance is born.

It is helpful to recall the event that launched the gay rights movement, the riot at the Stonewall Inn in New York. The patrons of that gay bar decided one evening in June 1969 not to flee a police raid but to fight back with bottles, beer cans, and brick-bats. This unprecedented act of resistance was a performance in the confessional mode, yet also in the ethical. The opposition to the police, clearly a socio-political act, was at the same time a proclamation of identity. It is one thing to be accused of something, in this case faggotry, and another to accept the label and publicly perform that acceptance. At the same time, the resistance at the Stonewall Inn was aimed at changing public policy concerning the rights of homosexuals. The Gay Rights Activist Movement was born.

Confessional performance is an early, necessary step in the liberation of any oppressed people. I am speaking of acts in which people openly proclaim their identity as members of an oppressed group, and confess loyalty to the cause of liberation. The liberating power they call upon may or may not be divine. It may be a social movement, the solidarity of a people, an identified historical process, or indeed a divine will. In any case, it requires a manifestation of a people's loyalty, their willingness to suffer for the cause of freedom, and their expectation that deliverance will come. Two powerful aspects of the civil rights movement in the 1950s and 1960s were the confession that "Black is beautiful" and the singing of "We Shall Overcome," two acts in which faith and determination were blended. At the political level, Black Power was never very strong, because African-Americans (on the whole) are such

an impoverished minority in the North American population; but at the
moral and spiritual level Black Power was and is potent enough to put
racism on the defensive, because it is founded on a confession of
blackness as the identifying mark of a people more sinned against than
sinning.

A similar dynamic is at work in women's liberation. The
consciousness-raising groups in which many women participated
during the 1970s, and which at that time energized the women's
movement, were a striking instance of confessional performance. In
these groups, many women learned to tell their own stories in
performances that were difficult and painful, even though the groups
they spoke in were small. The women learned to distinguish between a
familiar but deceitful story of their lives easily accepted—nay,
fostered—by society, and a more shameful, disorienting, anger-
producing, yet more truthful story, the telling of which amounted to the
first stage of a conversion. Consciousness-raising groups became the
arena in which these confessions were performed, providing the support
necessary for their articulation and an audience in which the truth of
women's suffering under patriarchal systems could be recognized and
made meaningful within a liberative process. In Nelle Morton's words,
the women were "hearing each other to speech."[111]

Under patriarchy women have found it far from easy to perform
themselves. To do so has often been difficult to the point of horror. A
woman might rather be a madwoman in an attic, or dead on the floor,
than to be a real person in public, so strong was (is) the determination of
men to keep her from the ability to perform her will. Women are
learning slowly and painfully to display their own truth in public,
through a process of trying by increments to enact themselves. From
time to time, they have broken through to march in the streets, to picket,
lobby, run for office, make spectacles of themselves, risk ridicule. If this
is not performance, nothing is.

A similar confessional dynamic is at work today among Native
Americans coming awake to their history of exploitation, among
campesinos and residents of barrios in Latin America creating "base
communities" as forums in which to utter the truth of their suffering,
among black youths in South Africa to whom confessional performance
brings martyrdom, and in many other groups in the world who see the
necessary link between confession of identity and progress toward
freedom.

In the confessional mode, we are but little presented with formal
thinking, which tends in the direction of theoretical judgment

concerning truth, falsity, and the underlying causes of things. Formal analyses often *follow* from confessional performances, and they make enormous difference for deciding what remedial actions to undertake; but the confessional mode itself does not deal in theory. Its content is self-actualization through self-recognition, world-recognition, and self-proclamation.

In the confessional mode, selfhood is both personal and communal. It is *performance* that insures that the confession does not refer solely, or even mainly, to the individual self. As performance, the confession finds, or perhaps makes, its community, so that the situation of the individual comes to be seen as something the community shares, and the community is legitimated as the necessary complement of the individual. Every confession is aimed at dialogue. To perform confessionally is to place oneself in the presence of others, whether human or divine, making of one's very self a word of address inviting response. If, over time, confessional performance gets no response, or gets none that is commensurate with human dignity, then confession withers, grows silent, or perhaps lapses into purely credal statement, the graveyard of the confessional mode.

Confession bridges the gap, or what some people view as the gap, between institutional and personal religion. In *The Varieties of Religious Experience,* William James decided to "ignore the institutional branch" of religion. He would focus, he said, upon "personal religion," adding that "the acts to which this sort of religion prompts are personal not ritual acts."[112] This led to his working definition, often quoted:

Religion, therefore, . . . shall mean for us *the feelings, acts, and experiences of individual men* [sic] *in their solitude, so far as they apprehend themselves to stand in relation to whatever they may consider the divine.*[113] [emphasis in original]

James seemed to suppose that the self was most itself when in solitude, a view that has often been challenged. Attention to the confessional mode of performance reminds us that religion, even when most intensely personal, is public. Far from being an individualistic matter pertaining only to a soul's transactions with this or that god, religion is a communal matter pertaining to the way in which divinities and human beings all relate to each other within a single frame of reference. The disclosures these *persona* make to each other, and the actions they perform together, are at the heart of religious life.

It is true, as we had occasion to recall in the previous chapter, that human beings dissemble, a fact that lends great ambiguity to ritual life.

What one puts on display cannot be guaranteed to be truthful. History is full of false confessions using deceitful display, and the contemporary proliferation of communications media and media "hype" provides ever greater opportunity to substitute a contrived image for an authentic self-presentation. Religious fakery abounds. This is nothing new. Maybe the scale of it is new. There are at least two levels of fakery.

As religion and psychology both know, people frequently deceive themselves, masking the truth of their existence not only from others but from their own consciousness as well, so that the act of dissembling need not proceed from a conscious motive. Most often it proceeds from ideologies, those firmly held structures of belief that are biased in favor of one's social privileges, or perhaps rationalize one's victimization as inevitable.

Nothing in this chapter should be taken to mean that determinations of truth are easy, or that any truth is absolute. In speaking of truthful disclosure in confessional performance, I offer no talisman for judging truthfulness. I point out that the *question* of truthfulness (and relevance to life) sooner or later arises in connection with performance in the ritual mode. When it does, it presses toward a transcendence of that mode— not a leaving behind but a heightened level of awareness. The ritual mode is transcended by a more existential type of performance, to which I have applied the name "confessional," a mode in which members of human communities make known to each other, as best they can, the often veiled truths of their existence.

We are pressed to recognize here something even more intensive: The performance of confessional truth is not only its disclosure but also its formation. Confessional truth is not simply a known truth performed but also the transformation of a partial truth into a truth more fully formed. Prior to its confession, such truth is not entirely true, only potentially true. It becomes "true" in the act of disclosure. I am not what I am except insofar as I am what I say I am. If I do not mean what I say, I am less than what I am. If I do not mean to be what I do, I am less than nothing.

A traditional, perhaps now quaint, understanding of religion in the West is that religion is one's public confession. The profundity of this has been obscured by the split between "public" and "communal" that has opened up with the industrial revolution and the huge increases in population over the last two centuries. "Public" has come to suggest something massive and impersonal, "communal" something too intimately small to be relevant to the whole of society. This must be so, I think, unless, as in the examples mentioned above, the confessional mode of performance is linked to *issues* that are of large public consequence.

The coming-to-freedom of oppressed peoples in the world today is, if this needs saying, a matter of the largest public consequence. The confessional mode of performance, which is always a coming out from a closet, is today itself in the process of coming out. Long confined to the "confessional booth," the "mourner's bench," or the psychotherapist's clinic, it becomes insignificant if it does not assist human communities struggling to maintain their identity and cast off bonds of oppression. Arising from the ritual mode, the confessional mode of performance drives onward toward the ethical.

■

In the ethical mode, performance aims to affect society directly, through actions that are political. What matters in the ethical mode is the world—its well-being, its fate, and the justice that is possible within it. In this mode, then, performance does not primarily mean showing but rather doing or accomplishing. Its aim is to get things done, and this by political intervention, not by prayer, saying a Mass, or holding a rain dance. This preference of the ethical mode for direct political action is reflected in all ethical critique of ritualism. To show identity is not enough for the ethical mode, for which "ought" carries more weight than "is." In the ethical mode, performance attempts to make a fresh clearing in the woods. Forging ahead, transforming what is now the case into what ought to be—this is the way of ethical performance; and since this cannot be done secretly, an ethical act is performative in both senses of the word we have identified, as doing and also as showing, even though, in the ethical mode, the doing is primary.

A problem arises here, one that is particularly acute within Christian tradition, where there has been a strong tendency to regard virtue as self-effacing. Any suggestion that an ethical act is done for show runs counter to much Christian teaching, including some words of Jesus himself. To call ethical action performative, therefore, is to make a statement not everywhere agreed to. Jesus says:

> Beware of practicing your piety before others in order to be seen by them; for you will have no reward from your parent who is in heaven.
>
> Thus, when you give alms, sound no trumpet before you, as the hypocrites do in the synagogues and in the streets, that they may be praised by others.

Truly, I say to you, they have their reward. But when you give alms, do not let your left hand know what your right hand is doing, so that your alms may be in secret; and your parent who sees in secret will reward you.

And when you pray, you must not be like the hypocrites; for they love to stand and pray in the synagogues and at the street corners, that they may be seen by others. Truly, I say to you, they have their reward. But when you pray, go into your room and shut the door and pray to your parent who is in secret; and your parent who sees in secret will reward you.

And in praying do not heap up empty phrases as the Gentiles do; for they think that they will be heard for their many words.[114]

Hannah Arendt had this passage in mind when, in *The Human Condition*, she drew a sharp contrast between "goodness," as she thought Jesus and Christian tradition have understood it, and human action in the public sphere. The latter was the main concern of her book. "No matter is more alien to us," she quotes the second-century Christian apologist Tertullian as saying, "than what matters publicly."[115] Such "antagonism between early Christianity and the *res publica*" she sees as being partly a consequence of eschatological expectations in the early church, but she thinks there is another root in the teachings of Jesus.

The one activity taught by Jesus in word and deed is the activity of goodness, and goodness obviously harbors a tendency to hide from being seen or heard. Christian hostility toward the public realm, the tendency at least of early Christians to lead a life as far removed from the public realm as possible, can . . . be understood as a self-evident consequence of devotion to good works, independent of all beliefs and expectations. For it is manifest that the moment a good work becomes known and public, it loses its specific character of goodness, of being done for nothing but goodness' sake. When goodness appears openly, it is no longer goodness, though it may still be useful as organized charity or an act of solidarity. Therefore: "Take heed that ye do not your alms before men, to be seen of them." Goodness can exist only when it is not perceived, not even by its author; whoever sees himself performing a good work is no longer good, but at best a useful member of society or a dutiful member of a church. Therefore: "Let not thy left hand know what thy right hand doeth."[116]

Arendt's writings are always worth pondering, but in this view of Jesus' and Christianity's relation to "the public realm" I think she was too much under the sway of Kierkegaard and the neo-orthodox atmosphere at the time she wrote. Too bad, because her book's major concern is to advocate ethical activity in the public sphere, and that is close to what I have in mind as performance in the ethical mode.

Arendt thinks that Christianity is otherworldly, which is true of certain periods and some streams in Christian tradition, but is very far from the whole truth of the tradition. As for Jesus, "otherworldly" is about the last thing to say of a man who prayed, "Thy kingdom come, thy will be done, on earth as it is in heaven." When Jesus said, confronting Pontius Pilate, "My kingdom is not of this world," the last thing on his mind was that this world did not matter. Allowing for the obvious irony in his sentence, we have to hear his words as closer to revolutionism than to otherworldliness.

Jesus, after all, died for public (that is, political) reasons. The Herodian and the Roman governments both had political cause for wanting him executed, and the Romans ended up putting him to death in one of their most public ways, by crucifixion. It took place on a hill, in full daylight, alongside two other criminals, with a crowd watching. The "secrecy" in Jesus' counsels is not necessarily the "secret" of his ethic. If an itinerant preacher, drawing crowds wherever he goes, and stirring up opposition in high places, speaks of "secrecy," we should at least imagine that he has more on his mind than a Kierkegaardian "purity of heart." Jesus should never be imagined as having prescinded from declarations that affront the powers that be.

Hannah Arendt did not mention another utterance of Jesus also found in the "Sermon on the Mount," where Jesus tells his listeners not to hide their light under a bushel: "Let your light so shine before all that they may see your good works and give glory to your Father who is in heaven."[117] Even if one could argue, mistakenly as I think, that "the one activity taught by Jesus . . . is the activity of goodness, and goodness . . . harbors a tendency to hide from being seen or heard,"[118] one has to reckon with the fact that Jesus became, willy-nilly, a public figure. So did his followers. There is no way to be a Christian in secret—*pace* Kierkegaard and his "knight of faith"—except perhaps temporarily under conditions of persecution when to be a Christian in public is suicidal. That is: Any reason for secrecy in a Christian's performance of ethical acts must be a *political* reason and carry the burden of proof.

Clearly, Jesus was offended by hypocritical ostentation, which seems to have been as plentiful in his time as it is now; but his warnings against the public show of virtue probably had another motive, too. The transformation of the world that Jesus envisioned was so radical that it had no chance of entering the imagination of any large part of the public. The gap between the kingdoms of this world and the "kingdom of God" was too great. The immediate task, then, was to create a smaller "public," a community of persons who would live in expectation of God's will being done "upon earth as it is in heaven." Hence, the emphasis in the Gospels upon communications more or less confined to the company of Jesus' followers.

In addition, Jesus, and not just Tertullian and other early Christians after Jesus, believed that the known world had not long to live. As Albert Schweitzer argued, it is most likely true that Jesus believed the present age, the "world," was in its last days. It was to end by divine intervention, which would not totally destroy the world but transform it utterly. Jesus' radical eschatology has long constituted a problem for Christian social ethicists, who do not (and should not) share that particular eschatological myth. But Jesus and his eschatology are not one and the same. Even if he believed the known world would soon end, he nevertheless committed himself to action *in* the world. One is hard pressed to find in all history a more public figure. His life and death were performed openly.

There is a division, which we can notice in all of Jesus' ministry, between the present world and the age to come. The counsel to pray in secret and not to put one's good works on display powerfully reinforces the idea that the present world, being but temporary and not of God, makes a poor audience for virtue, though it serves hypocrites well enough. Jesus suggests that in the present age the only adequate audience for goodness is God, who "sees in secret." But this means, on Jesus' own terms, that ethical performance includes a certain kind of display. God sees, and God rewards. The performances put on by hypocrites are perversions of more genuine performance, which acknowledges God (and the neighbor) as the proper witness and judge of virtuous acts.

We should notice also that the Gospels portray Jesus' entire life, ministry, and passion as a *display* of the liberative action of God. Whether Jesus ever saw his own life in this way is a question I shall not debate. It is enough to point out that his life *became* a display. In my opinion, historical Christianity has erred in putting Jesus too much on show, emphasizing him so exclusively as the way of salvation that his figure obscures the divine end, which is the freedom and health (salvation) of all humankind. But it would be a naive error to think that if Jesus be any part, let alone the chief part, of the means God has used to work for human liberation, the means should not be visible. A liberative act of God does not achieve its end if it is not seen for what it is. A divine work must somehow show itself, not because God is eager to get proper credit but because part of what it means for something to be good is that the act which brings it about is seen as good. "Doing the good" has a twofold meaning: to achieve a good end, and to achieve it well. Certainly, if ethical performance comes to be dominated by doing-for-show, then it is fouled. But if it imagines that the good may be done with no show at all—or that the only show is at the very end when the cloth is lifted and the good result pops out of the box giving total surprise—then ethical performance is perverted as surely as if it had been done all for show from the start.

An ethical act is one that is willing to be seen. It is the exact opposite of a covert operation. Since it is willing to be seen, it *wills* to be seen: It shows itself. Yet this willing is held under a certain restraint: The ethical act wills to be seen (and judged) as the means proper to the achievement of the ethical end. The crucial factor here is judgment, and it is this which gives to ethical action its most incisive meaning as performance.

We have said that an ethical act is mainly concerned with results, for its aim is to alleviate suffering and to increase every person's measure of dignity and justice. Yet if results were all that mattered in ethics, we would come to the cynical affirmation that the most ethical act is the most efficient. The ends would justify the means; or the means, by their efficiency, would determine the ends, something that does occur only too often. Ethical action requires a concern for the appropriateness of the means. In other words, to act ethically is not only to do the right thing but to do it *in the right way;* and this means that an ethical act has an eye to how things look, conjoining the pursuit of good ends with display of right ways of acting.

Display, of course, is itself an action, and its ends and means, on any given occasion, are to be evaluated. The end toward which ethical performance aims in displaying itself is not to receive credit but to be open to judgment. In order to be ethical, an action must be "right" according to some standard of judgment transcending the self-interest of those who perform it. One might even say that the ethical act is constituted by the opening of itself to critique. An ethical act requires observers who evaluate, who may on occasion be the doers observing themselves, but who in principle are other judges, human or divine. An ethical act is never merely executed: It is performed.

By the same token, the ethical act is inherently communal, requiring some consensus of value among doers and evaluators. It is not solitary but implies a community of value and the shared joy of participating in a type of performance that has its justification not only in the welfare of the human race but in mutual acknowledgment of goodness. That is why ethical action so often is preceded and followed by ritual celebration. The ritual is the home and the matrix of the shared values, and it shelters the fellowship that ethical action both requires and produces.

I am saying that ethical action is performative insofar as it wills to achieve its end and at the same time is willing to be seen and evaluated. Conversely, if an action is *unwilling* to be judged by its appearance alongside its results, it does not deserve the name "ethical." An ethical act aims to unite what is, what seems, and what should be.

In its concern for witnessing and witnesses, the ethical act reveals its affinity with religion. It can be argued that religion is performance in the sight of unseen powers. Religion has it that some, if not all, our actions are observed by a realm of unseen, or usually unseen, watchers and listeners. These are gods, spirits, demons, angels, ancestors, bodhisattvas or what-you-will. Unreligion supposes that there are no such unseen powers, certainly none that could pay attention to us or intentionally influence our lives, and so humanity has no audience except itself. Whereas for the unreligious we live, as Wallace Stevens phrased it, "in an old chaos of the sun . . . or island solitude, unsponsored, free," for the religious we are surrounded by what the Epistle to the Hebrews called "so great a cloud of witnesses."[119] In this sense, religion is fundamentally the understanding of life as performance. Richard Schechner wisely asks: ". . . has this not been religion's project from the very beginning of human history? To locate, establish, and keep contact with non-human beings?"[120]

When St. Paul appealed to the Romans to "present your bodies as a living sacrifice, holy and acceptable to God,"[121] he conjoined the ethical with the religious, choosing as metaphor the practice of animal sacrifice in the Jerusalem temple, and perhaps alluding also to the so-called "sacred prostitution" of other temples. The appeal to present one's body as living sacrifice unites religion and ethics in a summons to a kind performance that includes but cannot be limited to ritual. The same conjunction had been made earlier by Jesus: ". . . as you did it to one of the least of these, . . . you did it to me."[122]

Because ethical acts are public and not covert, because they address themselves to communal values and often seek either to change or to recall these, ethical acts frequently become public demonstrations. People will march *en masse* to Selma, Alabama, while those of a different ethic will jeer and threaten them, the police standing by in uniform. An ethical act may be to go to the underground nuclear testing site in Nevada, in the company of hundreds of demonstrators headed by the actor Martin Sheen, and there publicly to cross a no-trespass line in witness to certain values dear to humanity that the government itself is trespassing. Civil disobedience is not *mere* demonstration. It demonstrates by way of a real action carrying real consequences—arrest, arraignment, court trial, penalties, perhaps jail.

When it takes the form of civil disobedience and other public demonstrations, the ethical mode of performance reaches out to embrace the confessional and ritual modes. To "step over the line" in civil disobedience, or even to go into the streets in a legal demonstration, is often a self-declaration and a witness of identity in the confessional mode, just as much as it is an ethical act aimed at changing society. It is also an act of ritualizing, because these occasions take on many ceremonious features. We can say that the ethical mode becomes ritualized, or that the ritual mode is politicized. These transformations are possible because each of the performance modes is latent in the others. On a given occasion, any of them may be ascendant. The ritual, confessional, and ethical modes of performance are not always different *acts* but different ways of doing the same or a similar act. As in music a change of mode does not always require a change in melodic structure, so in human performance different modalities do not necessarily mean total changes in the script. The modes make sense in relation to each other, and we recognize them all as ways of acting in the world. A musical analogy is better here than a visual one. We do not so much *see* differences between the ethical, confessional, and ritual modes as *hear* them. As with music, such hearing has little to do with being told something. Without explanation, you hear what the performance is about.

■

My own ethical convictions, as may be clear from the foregoing discussion, are less deontological than teleological. In ethical theory, deontology refers to the performance of *duties*, as they may be known through law, tradition, custom, and perhaps divine revelation. Teleology refers to performance of acts that are *goal-oriented*, attempting to realize a state of affairs not yet in existence. From my point of view, an ethic that is primarily deontological must emphasize too much the sense in which an ethical act is pro forma. It tends toward legalism and ritualism.

For me, the *teloi* of ethical activity are determined partly by reflection upon life processes, partly by the great *need* of people to live in conditions of dignity and justice (the combination of which is freedom), and partly by the Christian eschatology symbolized in Jesus' proclamation of the world of God. Eschatology points to a divine intention concerning "the end of time," which I take to mean not the cessation of time but its fulfillment in justice. Such a perspective suggests that one should act "as if" the world of God will one day come to be. This "as if" ought not be confined to play-acting, nor even to the bracketed times and places of ritual enactment. Ethical performance is political, charitable, and goal-oriented action in the world, played out in the sight of God, in full public view, and before one's very own eyes.

Having looked briefly at confessional and ethical action as modes of performance in the world, we shall in the next chapter turn our attention again to rituals. We are ready now to look at their most important social functions, which are in some respects conservative and in others innovative and radical.

PART III

*Ritual's
Social Gifts*

7

Order

Through rites Heaven and earth join in harmony, the sun and moon
shine, the four seasons proceed in order, the stars and constellations
march, the rivers flow, and all things flourish.
. . . Through them the root and the branch are put in proper order. . .

—HSÜN TZU, *ancient Confucian text*[123]

In Part I of this book, I spoke frequently of rituals as pathways, and of
ritualizing as the making of these paths for behavior to follow. In Part II,
the focus shifted: I spoke of ritual primarily as performance, as a way
not only of behaving but of *acting* in the world. This led us to consider
the need to assume moral responsibility for our acting, a dimension of
the subject that is reflected in modalities of performance that I called
confessional and ethical. Although I have stressed that rituals are playful
work, still they are serious business, in the sense that they have, in the
aggregate, momentous consequences for human life. In Part III, these
consequences are to be my subject. I speak of them as ritual's social gifts.

If we set out to catalog all the functions that rituals serve, taking into
account every sort of culture and all variety of social circumstance, we
should no doubt find that the tasks of ritual are numberless. I shall not,
therefore, attempt a catalog of functions but instead propose that there
are three major gifts that rituals bestow upon society. Devoting a chapter
to each, I shall call them order, community, and transformation.

The present chapter will be devoted to the contribution rituals make
to establishing and maintaining various kinds of social, and even
cosmic, order. Although ritual ordering has important psychological
dimensions, contributing in many ways to the organization of
individuals' conscious and unconscious life, I shall not address the topic
at the psychological level, leaving that to more expert witnesses and
thinking in any case that the human psyche is shaped primarily by its
social milieu.

The reinforcement, if not the actual creation, of social order is perhaps the most obvious of ritual's functions. To many minds, it is the only one, yet this is surely far from the case. The succeeding chapter will look at the way in which rituals create and preserve not only social order but also community, by helping to unite individuals in bonds of human affection. As closely related as communal life and social order may be, the one is not the automatic result of the other. People may be organized into social collectives without finding themselves in any significant sense belonging to communities. There is something about ritual that pushes beyond the concern for social order as mere form, reaching out toward substance, soul, life-feel, and the love of participation.

Discussion of community will bring us to a vantage point from which, in a third chapter, we may best see the numerous ways in which rituals often become agents of transformation. If we say that rituals have an ordering function, we should recognize that they have also an opposite one—to disorder and refashion the way life is lived. On occasion rituals serve the purposes of revolution, just as they may also assist reactionary causes.

Order, community, and transformation do not amount to a simple listing of ritual's effects. One part order plus one part transformation plus communal seasoning to taste would produce a bland dish. We shall need to show that these gifts of ritual form an energetic whole, a dynamic in human life having its own logic and utility, such that the working of rituals in society can be seen as a vehicle of grace, without our coming to the simplistic idea that rituals always result in the common good. It must not be forgotten that rituals can be devoted to destructive violence as well as to peace and freedom.

My discussion of the social gifts of ritual—order, community, and transformation—will move in an ascending progression of theological value. Social order is not an end in itself but is necessary to make possible the benefits of communal love. But even love is not an end in itself unless, allied with justice, it is devoted to freeing individuals and groups from the forces that oppress them. Static love is never enough, and genuine love reaches out to invoke powers and techniques of liberative transformation.

Our order of discussion begins with a discussion of order.

■

It is well to remind ourselves that for many persons the entire value of religious ritual is that it brings order and solace. The point has been well made by Penelope Lively in her novel, *Judgment Day*, through a character called Sydney, a widower living alone whose wife and children perished in an air raid long ago during World War II. For years Sydney has been the church warden, faithful in his duties, regular as the clock. This is how the authorial narrator describes Sydney's mind:

The padre talked of faith and the comfort of prayer and the love of God; he talked to Sydney as one believer to another. What he didn't know, what could never have been explained, was that it was order Sydney sought, and found, in the Church, rather than any of that. The order of things said and done each time in the same way, the order of knowing that nothing could interfere with how these things were said and done, the knowledge that this order had gone before and would go on after, that it survived the chaos of everything else.[124]

Desire for invariant ritual order is a strong force within society. Later I will try to show that this desire is not, by itself, adequate to the human situation; nor is order the most important social gift of ritual. Meanwhile, we must take it seriously. From Sydney, the lonely Anglican in need of an ordered life, I turn to Roy Rappaport's anthropological investigation, which began in Papua New Guinea.

Rappaport's field research in the New Guinea highlands was extensively analyzed in his book *Pigs for the Ancestors*.[125] In a later essay, "The Obvious Aspects of Ritual," published in his *Ecology, Meaning, and Religion*, he discusses what he calls "liturgical order." After indicating that the term, as he uses it, refers both to single rituals and to ritual cycles many years long, such as he encountered in his fieldwork, he says that

these series of events constitute orders in several senses beyond the obvious one of sequence. They are also orders in the sense of organization, form, or regularity (synonymous with the meaning of "order" in such phrases as "the social order"). As such they constitute order, or maintain orderliness, in contrast to disorder, entropy, or chaos. They are, further, orders in that they are in some sense imperatives or directives.[126]

Later in the essay, Rappaport goes further, declaring that the performance of a liturgical order "does more than *remind* individuals of an underlying [cosmic] order. It *establishes* that order."[127]

In other words, rituals of a particular kind, here called liturgical, are not only ordered patterns in themselves, and do not only reflect the way the world is ordered, but actually serve to put that order in place. It is a very large claim to make for ritual. Can it be defended rationally? I think so, but let us back up and approach it by stages, the first of which is the value and significance of going round and round.

Events that human beings cause to recur intentionally become *repetitions*. "The dialectic of repetition," said Kierkegaard, "is easy: for what is repeated has been, otherwise it could not be repeated, but precisely the fact that it has been gives to repetition the character of novelty."[128]

I once asked a friend if she had seen a certain movie, whereupon she exclaimed, "Oh yes! Last week I went to see it again for the first time," reminding me that Heraclitus was not the last to perceive that there is something contradictory about stepping twice into the same river.

We shall return to the interaction between doing things repeatedly and doing new things, but for the moment we want to consider the value of going, as the poet Edwin Muir expressed it, "twice in the self-same track."[129]

In an earlier chapter, we spoke of ritualizing as creating pathways or channels along which human behavior may move without always having to redesign its course. Ritualization introduces an economy into behavior, setting up routines that become part of a whole repertoire of "motions and gestures through which we regularly go."[130] These in their aggregate constitute a great part of culture: Think of body language, rites of daily greeting, and the little ways in which individuals habitually present themselves to one another.[131] Think also of rites so familiar that they are mostly taken for granted—how to decorate and present a birthday cake, what sort of thing to wear to a wedding, how to behave at a baseball game, and so on.

Ritual's ordering function extends, as we know, far beyond such common-knowledge patterns that regulate and punctuate our lives. Ritual's power to order life reaches into social systems that are formal, institutionalized, and governed by explicit rules and laws. René Girard does not exaggerate when he says, in a discussion of ritual and social order, that

all the great institutions of mankind [sic], both secular and religious, spring from ritual. Such is the case ... with political power, legal institutions, medicine, the theater, philosophy and anthropology itself.[132]

A similar point was made earlier by Johan Huizinga in *Homo Ludens: A Study of the Play-Element in Culture.*[133]

Julian Huxley viewed ritualization as the means whereby culture and society impose the kind of order necessary for the creation of shared worlds. He was aware that ritualization, which patterns behavior, affects the very way we see things, even such mundane things as tables and chairs. "We normally impose on the process of perception," he wrote, "a customary or 'normal' framework derived from conscious or unconscious learning from experience."[134]

In other words, through ritualization we make routine a certain way of seeing, hearing, touching, and otherwise perceiving the environment. Huxley pointed out that "the powerful formalizing effect of this ritualization of thought and feeling, even when unconscious, is revealed by our various escapes from it—into the fantasy-organized world of our dreams."[135] Hallucinogens such as LSD, he said, "seem to exert their effects by interfering with the 'normal' ritualization of the perception-building process."[136] He noted that this kind of interference can occur for other reasons as well:

In schizophrenia this is effected endogenously, by a genetic error of metabolism; the resultant lack of stable, adaptively formalized "standard" percepts and concepts leads to a progressive failure of communication with others, and thus to eventual withdrawal into the abnormal "unrealistic" but sometimes rewarding private world which is all the schizophrenic has been able to construct. . . . This is a reversal of adaptive ritualization, as it increases ambiguity and impedes communication.[137]

Following Edmund Leach and others, I have already suggested that human speech itself depends upon ritualized behaviors. Unless we have studied voice production, we scarcely know how we perform all the consonantal and vowel sounds that make up our speaking, but from repetition we know routinely—by "second nature"—how to do this. Hence, there is always open to us the possibility to do it more consciously, or better, or to gain a special rhetorical effect, or to play with speaking for the sheer fun of it, like a baby whose ritualizations of mouth-noise are still in the formative stages. The babblings (capricious word-plays) of comedians, parlor wits, shamans, and poets are, as Kierkegaard would say, not mere *recollections* of the child's first speaking but are *repetitions* done in the adult's time for grown-up purpose.

Suzanne Langer has imagined the way in which ritualizations that are nothing more than routine behaviors can be transformed into socially significant usages:

Just as one person develops personal "ways," so a tribe develops tribal "ways," which are handed down as unconscious mannerisms, until some breach in the usual pattern makes people aware of them, and they are deliberately practiced as "correct forms." As soon as they are thus abstracted, these proper gestures acquire tribal importance; someone sees a secondary meaning in an act which has attained such a formal unity and style. It seems to have a symbolic as well as a practical function; a new, emotional importance attaches to it.[138]

Out of the shared perceptions and ritualized "ways" of a people, as these gradually take on symbolic functions, there comes into existence a shared "world." Earlier I have pointed out that ritualization and performance include an element of "making something up." Now I point out that connections of an especially strong kind exist between ritual and life-world, because a ritual is a synecdoche granting its participants the glimpse, touch, and taste of an imagined universe. Conversely, a life-world depends upon ritual for its instantiation. In its ordering function, ritual performs the world, bringing it from chaos and the limbo of potentiality into actualized (actionful) form. It is not as if there were first a world and then someone thought of representing it ritually. It is rather that the perceived and imagined world is an extension, a projection, of the ritual forms a people practice. This is the sense in which it can be said that through rituals "the rivers flow, and all things flourish."

Because people often feel that all their known world and their whole way of life is somehow dependent upon rituals, these are often fenced around by rubrics designed to make their performance as invariant as possible, so as to protect the order and meaning that is present in them. There is a feeling, not entirely without rational basis, that if the rituals disintegrated the rivers would not flow nor things flourish. And rituals can easily disintegrate, not only from neglect but also from their tendency to change. Thomas Peterson says:

Precisely because ritual is so rich in possibilities for metaphorical activity, extreme care must be taken to maintain a precise ordering of activity in order to prevent the hilarity and confusion of an Alice-in-Wonderland world.[139]

The point is well taken, but there are many exceptions, many occasions on which rituals are employed more to foster than to prevent "hilarity and confusion." At carnival, for instance, or in the worship of trickster deities, the experience of an Alice-in-Wonderland world may be exactly what is desired. Even so, careful observers will note the presence of order in the ritually invoked disorder.

Victor Turner quotes from Sally Falk Moore's *Law as Process:*

Rituals, rigid procedures, regular formalities, symbolic repetitions of all kinds, as well as explicit laws, principles, rules, symbols, and categories are cultural representations of fixed social reality, or continuity. They present stability and continuity acted out and re-enacted; visible continuity. By dint of repetition they deny the passage of time, the nature of change, and the implicit extent of potential indeterminacy in social relations. Whether these processes of regularization are sustained by tradition or legitimated by revolutionary edict and force, they act to provide daily regenerated frames, social constructions of reality, within which the attempt is made to fix social life, to keep it from slipping into the sea of indeterminacy.[140]

The ordering function of ritual seems necessary not only to "fix social life" in the first place but also to restore order when it has been lost. This has been emphasized by Turner in connection with what he calls "social dramas," which take place from time to time in all societies.[141] He describes a social drama as moving through four phases:

1. The social drama is initiated by some *breach* of social custom, law, or ritual propriety (an act of theft, murder, conspicuous adultery, or offense against courtesy, let us say).
2. Because the breach has shown that society's ritual self-ordering has been incapable of maintaining order, a *crisis* ensues, usually characterized by hostility and feuding.
3. This is followed by the application of procedures designed to *redress* the situation.
4. Finally, the drama is resolved, either through the *reintegration* of the contending parties into society or in a public recognition and legitimation of an irreparable *schism* between them.

It is important to note that the procedures employed in phase three of the Turnerian drama are characteristically those of ritual. In some cases, healing rites are employed; in others exorcisms; in others ceremonies of prayer. In modern societies, the redressive rituals are most likely to belong to the judicial system, whether in a court of law, a Congressional inquiry, or what not. Likewise, the state of affairs that comes to be accepted in the fourth phase of the social drama, be it reintegration or schism, is likely to be publicly ratified in ceremony: the smoking of a pipe, the signing of a treaty, a declaration of banishment, exile, or prison sentence. Turner's "social drama" pattern highlights the use of ritual in defining order, maintaining it, and restoring it after it is breached.

Social order is not only a matter of convenience or biological necessity. We must think beyond the sheer necessity and utility of ritual ordering to a matter more deep, close to the root of human existence. Roy Rappaport and many others since Durkheim have seen that there is a link between the social functions of ritual and the idea (or experience) of sacredness.[142] The performance of certain rituals, following specified orders of procedure, is often regarded as a sacred duty, or else a sacred opportunity, the ritual providing the occasion for a numinous encounter. In the Eastern world, the holding to ritual as an order that should be followed out of sacred duty is most prominent, perhaps, in Brahmanic Hinduism. In the Western world, the oldest and arguably most faithful witness to it has been borne by Judaism.

A reader who casts an eye upon the ritual laws recorded at length, with so much repetition, in the Pentateuch must be struck with a certain precision of voice that lends to the texts themselves some of the quality of ritual. These are texts generated by ritual performances, preserved by ritual recitation over many generations, eventually encoded in writing (after which they have continued to be read aloud ritually), having as their subject certain acts that should be ritually performed and others to be ritually avoided.

Let us look at one example of this ancient Hebrew ordering, devoted to instructions for building a place of worship and ordaining a priesthood. I quote at length because length is an important part of this text's ritual quality. The reader should notice how the words describe actions, as if someone is telling how these things have usually been done, and also how the recitation of the words becomes itself an action. The sense of this can best be felt when the text is read aloud, which the reader is encouraged to do, the better to grasp how this passage, which describes and prescribes some articles used in ritual, has itself become a ritual text. One may note also that not a word is said about any words that are to be spoken in the ceremony the speaker has in mind.

Now this is what you shall do to them to consecrate them, that they may serve me as priests. Take one young bull and two rams without blemish, and unleavened bread, unleavened cakes mixed with oil, and unleavened wafers spread with oil. You shall make them of fine wheat flour. And you shall put them in one basket and bring them in the basket, and bring the bull and the two rams. You shall bring Aaron and his sons to the door of the tent of meeting, and wash them with water. And you shall take the garments, and put on Aaron the coat and the robe of the ephod [a kind of apron], and the ephod, and the breastpiece, and gird him with the skillfully woven band of the ephod; and you shall set the turban on his head, and put the holy crown upon the turban. And you shall take the anointing oil, and pour it on his head and anoint him. Then you shall bring his sons, and put coats on them, and you shall gird them with girdles and bind caps on them; and the priesthood shall be theirs by a perpetual statute. Thus you shall ordain Aaron and his sons.

Then you shall bring the bull before the tent of meeting. Aaron and his sons shall lay their hands upon the head of the bull, and you shall kill the bull before the Lord, at the door of the tent of meeting, and shall take part of the blood of the bull and put it upon the horns of the altar with your finger, and the rest of the blood you shall pour out at the base of the altar. And you shall take all the fat that covers the entrails, and the appendage of the liver, and the two kidneys with the fat that is on them, and burn them upon the altar. But the flesh of the bull, and its skin, and its dung, you shall burn with fire outside the camp; it is a sin offering.

Then you shall take one of the rams, and Aaron and his sons shall lay their hands upon the head of the ram, and you shall slaughter the ram, and shall take its blood and throw it against the altar round about. Then you shall cut the ram into pieces, and wash its entrails and its legs, and put them with its pieces and its head, and burn the whole ram upon the altar; it is a burnt offering to the Lord; it is a pleasing odor, an offering by fire to the Lord. (Exodus 29:1–15 RSV) . . . Now this is what you shall offer upon the altar: two lambs a year old day by day continually. One lamb you shall offer in the morning, and the other lamb you shall offer in the evening; and with the first lamb a tenth measure of fine flour mingled with a fourth of a hin of beaten oil, and a fourth of a hin of wine for a libation. And the other lamb you shall offer in the evening, and shall offer with it a cereal offering and its libation, as in the morning, for a pleasing odor, an offering by fire to the Lord. It shall be a continual burnt offering throughout your generations at the door of the tent of meeting before the Lord, where I will meet with you to speak there to you. There I will meet with the people of Israel, and it shall be sanctified by my glory. I will consecrate the tent of meeting and the altar; Aaron also and his sons I will consecrate, to serve me as priests. And I will dwell among the people of Israel, and will be their God. And they shall know that I am the Lord their God, who brought them forth out of the land of Egypt that I might dwell among them; I am the Lord their God. (Exodus 29:38–46 RSV)

The rich symbolism in this passage—meanings associated with resplendent costumes, burnt offerings, oils, anointings, blood, earth, fire, water, and so on—we shall leave aside, the better to concern ourselves with the question of ritual order, which may also be called liturgical prescription. These words from the so-called Priestly Code, meant to fall upon the ear in wave-like repetition, state exactly what is to be done, and in what manner. Much is specified. A great deal is not. Weather is not mentioned, nor the mood of the participants, nor their number, etc. Room enough is left for *midrash* and numerous decisions a ritual performer would need to make on the spot. There is latitude, yet the form is clear, and it comes with the voice of injunction: "You shall . . . " It is magnificent.

Ritual ordering is not, however, an unmitigated blessing. It does not

always motivate people toward freedom, even if, as in this case, the
ritual memorializes a liberating event, the deliverance of the Israelites
from Egypt. Jewish ritual law has not been as liberating to women as to
men: It prescribes, as is the case in many other religions, an inferior
status for women, which—precisely because it is ritualized—is
extremely difficult to overcome. There is a problem here to which we
shall have to return, yet our purpose at the moment is to see ritual order
not as enemy but as friend. We can state the point simply by saying that
ritual order is a blazed trail. It is a people's friend inasmuch as they (we)
need to know a path to follow. There may be something wrong about a
particular path, even though it is well trodden, in which case the rituals
themselves are in need of transformation, as is manifestly the situation
today in both Judaism and Christianity; but when a terrain is
experienced as wilderness, or when the surrounding area is thought to
be full of hazards, a cleared path is welcome. More than that: The path
which, if followed, will protect a people from harm is regarded as
sacred, and the following of it a sacred duty. "Judaism," Jacob Neusner
has written,

transforms the ordinary into the holy . . ., and the rite on the remarkable
occasion takes second place behind the ritualization of the everyday and
commonplace—that is to say, the sanctification of the ordinary.[143]

In this sensibility, doing things rightly, in the way the ritual order
prescribes, is to walk in God's way, to partake of holiness. Scholars
speak of one part of the ritual laws in the Pentateuch (Leviticus 17–26) as
the "Holiness Code." Neusner continues:

The word *halakhah* is normally translated as "law," for the *halakhah* is full of
normative, prescriptive rules about what one must do and refrain from doing in
every situation of life and at every moment of the day. But since *halakhah* derives
from the root *halakh*, which means "go," a better translation would be "way."
The *halakhah* is the "way" . . .

With the destruction of the temple at Jerusalem in 70 C.E., Judaism's
animal sacrifices ceased; but the sense that ritual is a sacred obligation
did not. Neusner argues that synagogue prayers are obligatory offerings
of the entire Jewish people, made in lieu of the whole (animal) offerings
which used to be made in the temple. He thinks this understanding of
synagogue prayer is ancient, dating from the time of the destruction of
the temple, and perhaps before:

Since what the community owed, which the individual did not, were regular and
routine public offerings, public prayer—in the aftermath of the destruction of the

Temple—took the place of these offerings and was owing from the community just as offerings were. (That is not to suggest that, prior to the end of the animal sacrifices with the destruction of the Temple in Jerusalem in 70, such a conception did not characterize public worship. . . .) One example of that prevailing conception derives from the debates in the Talmud about whether the recitation of a certain prayer is valid even when done mechanically and not devoutly.[144]

Neusner decides that even under such circumstances, the saying of the prayers is obligatory and valid. He regards the act itself, not the feelings and thoughts of the performers, as a sacred duty. The ritual itself, since its performance is required by God, takes precedence over the subjective piety of those who perform it. I think of an analogy not offered by Neusner: The sailor's chart, and the movements it requires one to make with the rig and the wheel under this condition or that, matter far more than what the sailor feels, hopes, and wishes. More precisely, the sailor's subjectivity, if not in line with what the seas, the weather, and the chart require, is better left out of account. "The prayer, the recitation of the *Shema*," says Neusner, "does not contain personal requests but reviews certain passages of Scripture."[145]

Judaism has a world defined by the sense of God as creator, bound in covenant to the Jewish people, to whom God has promised redemption. This world is not grounded primarily in theology, nor even in Scripture, Neusner is saying, but in ritual. It is a world held in being not by ideas so much as by a people's obedient following of "the way." When the Jerusalem temple was destroyed, the people's collective prayers in synagogue took on added ritual importance. Others have suggested that scripture also took on an increasingly ritualized role once the sacrifices in the temple were made no more. The point is not that scripture took the place of ritual, as some might imagine, but that ritual was modified so as to embrace the Torah texts and exalt them as sacred.

William Scott Green, for example, denies "that halakic observance was determined by Bible-study," saying that "if the Mishnah can be said to have a major focus, it is the temple, not the Bible." He adds that "rabbinism's initial catalyst"

was neither the canonization of the Hebrew Bible nor readerly research of scripture but the demise of the second temple and its divinely-ordained cult, the rites of which guaranteed God's presence in Israel's midst. The loss of the Holy of Holies—the principal locus of Israel's invisible and silent God—meant the absence of a stable cultural center and generated an acute religious crisis, primarily in the realm of behavior.[146]

Green maintains that the sanctity of scripture in Judaism grew out of the need for ritual order rather than the other way around:

... particularly after the Bar Kochba debacle in 132–35, rabbis must have known
that the temple was gone for good. To compensate for that loss and to preserve
the sacred center required by their piety, rabbinic Judaism developed a
distinctive theory of the sanctity of scripture.[147]

The need for ritual order found expression in the way in which the
scrolls were to be produced and handled:

The talmud's elaborate rules for the scroll's production and treatment decisively
distinguish its content from ordinary writing. The *sefer Torah* [the scroll of the
Hebrew Pentateuch] was used in synagogue worship and was written without
vocalization. It had to be transcribed on specially prepared parchment marked
with lines . . ., in a particular script . . ., and with orthographic uniformity. . . . In
the scroll, seven Hebrew letters, each time they appeared, were to be drawn with
tagin, three-stroke decorative crowns or tittles at the top of the letter. . . . A sheet
that contained four errors was to be buried, not corrected . . ., but scrolls
produced by Jews deemed heretics or sectarians were to be burned. . . .
Worshipers were expected to rise in the presence of the Torah scroll . . ., and no
other type of scroll could be placed on top of it. . . . To touch the parchment of a
Torah scroll with bare hands was judged an outrage.[148]

One might say of this that scripture is being defined by the rules of
performance concerning it. The behavioral rules go a long way, then,
toward determining how the texts will be read and interpreted. Ritual
guides hermeneutics. In Judaism and many other religions, certain
rituals contextualize the text and secure its place within the ordered
world. Failure to appreciate the relation of sacred text to sacred ritual
results, says Green, in "the popular notion, promulgated equally by
Jews and Christians, that Judaism is a 'religion of the book.' " This, he
adds, "simply recasts, and inaccurately, Judaism as a kind of
Protestantism. It is as if the most important thing Jews and Christians
ever did was to read the Bible and think about it."[149]

Although I would not want to suggest that the ritual sensibilities of
Protestantism are the same as those of Judaism, I would certainly argue
that Protestantism, even fundamentalist Protestantism, is no closer to
being a "religion of the book" than is Judaism. Among Protestants also,
the scriptures are defined by the protocols (mostly unwritten and passed
along by tradition) concerning their use. It is these protocols, not the
scriptural words per se, that order Protestant life and give it the
character that it has. It is not difficult to give a well-received sermon that
contains a radically new twist on some passage of scripture and is soon
forgotten, but it is very difficult to tamper with an order of service in the

average congregation, or even to change the tempi of the hymns.

Let us take another example of ritual order, this time from Haitian culture. Medical anthropologist Paul Farmer, while conducting research on indigenous medicine in the village of Do Kay on Haiti's Plateau Central, interviewed a certain Mme. Victor, a healer known for her ability to treat *move san* (bad blood), an ailment that Haitians often diagnose in women whose pregnancies are difficult. Here is Mme. Victor's description of how to make a remedy for *move san:*

To make the remedy, you soak the roots of *bwa let*, the roots of *kayimit, bwa jon*, and coconut, and the leaves of *sorosi* and *fey sezi*. If the person with *move san* is a woman with a nursing baby and her milk has gone bad, you need to add the leaves and roots of *bwa let* and also to add one small spoonful of the spoiled milk to the bottle [that contains the remedy]. This is for the person to drink, and will separate the blood from the milk. . . . But there's more to it than that: you must buy a piece of white soap and a coconut, a bit of coffee, a measure of black beans, and then you bring down the blood *(fe let la desann)*. You grill the coffee together with the black beans and seven grains of salt. When you've finished grilling, you grind it up in a mortar and put it in a pan, add water, and mix it up. From this you make a compress for both the brow and the back of the head, and keep it moist with the concoction all day long. . . . You can also place an empty shallow basket on the person's head, and pour the medicine in the basket; it will run down over the head and body. Each time you dampen the compress also rub down her arms and legs with the medicine. Do this for a week or so. Also put a grain of virgin salt [i.e., from a fresh box not yet used for cooking] in the palm of each hand. Place a grain of salt under each of [the patient's] feet and stand on a palm leaf. She must stand still. This will make the milk return to its rightful place.[150]

Farmer aptly calls this "a precise and somewhat ritualized regimen." Here, as we noticed in the passage from the Pentateuch, much is specified while much is not. The roots are to be soaked, presumably in water. Where to get the water and what kind of a container to do the soaking in are left to the discretion of the practitioner. White soap is called for, but the brand is not named, and indeed the use of the soap is not specifically indicated. All in all, one gets a vivid picture of the actions to be performed, which are no less important (perhaps more?) than the medicaments themselves. The prescription ends with instructions to the patient to stand in a certain way on a palm leaf with a grain of salt under each foot.

In Judaism and other so-called "high" religions, the following of ritual order is, as I have indicated, understood as sacred obligation. In the case of Haitian and other folk cultures, the word often used is "magic," but the two concepts are not as far apart as is sometimes thought. Both have to do with following a right way in order to stay or get out of harm's way. From the standpoint of empirical rationalism, there is not much difference between being told to daub an altar with the blood of a slain animal and being told to stand still on a palm leaf with a grain of salt under each foot. If the one duty has been prescribed by God and the other by a local healer transmitting folk tradition, nevertheless both are precisely structured *methods*, charged with symbolism, for communicating with invisible powers and affecting their behavior.

Concerning a magical cure described in Frazer's *The Golden Bough*, Wittgenstein once remarked:

> In magical healing one *indicates* to an illness that it should leave the patient.
> After the description of any such magical cure we'd like to add: If the illness doesn't understand *that*, then I don't know *how* one ought to say it.[151]

This witty comment reminds us that the oddities of ritual are not greater than the peculiarities of language because, at one level, ritual *is* language. But Wittgenstein's remark misses the sense of ritual as obligatory, the sense that if you are going to obey a particular God or to heal a certain disease, you must do it in a prescribed way. In short, ritual is not only language but also technique.

Within a ritual's form, there is often much latitude. If we ask, why must the thing be done this way and not that way, sometimes the answer is, "Oh, that can be changed. That part doesn't have to be done any particular way." But sometimes the answer is, "You may not change it, because . . ." And this answer, when it appeals to invisible powers—to gods, spirits, dead ancestors, revelations, time-hallowed traditions, unbreachable custom, or the authority of Scripture—exposes the sacred character of ritual order: The right way is the right way is the right way, and any other way leads to disaster. When Sigmund Freud saw in this the pattern of neurosis, he was not entirely mistaken, but he was certainly reductionist. No community can exist without some absolutes of behavior—that is, things that are supposed to be done out of moral necessity even when the community itself can give for that necessity no compelling practical reason. This is the germ of truth that resides in deontological (obedience-oriented) ethics. Communities are based, we might say, upon irrational consensus about certain behaviors that should and should not be performed. This truth about human life constitutes no argument against subjecting a people's conventions and sacred duties to rational critique, but it does indicate that such critiques cannot be total. A people cannot entirely know its own foundations, and if a community tried rationally—that is, in purely secular terms—to account for all its mores, it would either disintegrate or fall captive to tyrannical powers.

■

We may return now to Roy Rappaport's discussion of these issues. There are two senses in which he understands rituals to create and maintain order. He begins with their ability to mark times and spaces, to symbolize realities, and thus to represent a structured world. He says:

Annual rounds of festivals surely distinguish the seasons from each other more clearly than the weather, and reference to them may order the lives of [people] more effectively than the growth of plants or changes in temperature. The clarity of ritual occurrence combined with its general formality and nonutility suit ritual ideally for service in what Bateson [in *Steps to an Ecology of Mind*] calls "context-marking."[152]

The second sense in which rituals create and maintain order is more utilitarian. Rappaport speaks of rituals as sometimes being "factitive," meaning that they cause things to happen. Schechner and others speak similarly of ritual's "efficacity." Rappaport has been particularly interested in the way some rituals serve to regulate a society's means of material production and to guide the distribution and consumption of goods and services. In New Guinea, he paid special attention to the long ritual cycle of pig exchanges that the Maring, like other New Guinea highlanders, perform. Rappaport saw the cycle as

a sacred structure within which productive and reproductive activities (ecological, biological, and social) proceed and in terms of which social, political, and ecological relations are defined and given meaning.[153]

As an outsider making use of analytic concepts known to Western science, Rappaport was able to discern, in ways the Maring themselves did not articulate, the rational utility of the ritual cycle in the maintenance of the ecological system:

. . . the operation of ritual among the Tsembuga and other Maring helps to maintain an undegraded environment, limits fighting to frequencies which do not endanger the existence of the regional population, adjusts [people]-land ratios, facilitates trade, distributes local surpluses of pig throughout the regional population in the form of pork, and assures people of high quality protein when they are most in need of it.[154]

The use and renewal of the available land in the rugged mountains, the maintenance of the human and the pig populations at optimal levels, the distribution of a limited protein supply, the making of alliances among warrior groups, marriage agreements, and numerous other matters essential to the survival of the Maring, could be seen to be governed not by directly stated rules and laws but by performance of the ritual cycle in its numerous phases. Understandings about when, where, and how to perform the rituals led, when put into practice, to very practical benefits for the maintenance of the Maring way of life, both culturally and materially. Hence Rappaport holds that the power of ritual is greater than merely to symbolize relationships and stamp approval upon them. It "would not be improper," he says,

to refer to the Tsembaga and the other entities with which they share their territory as a "ritually regulated ecosystem," and to the Tsembaga and their human neighbors as a "ritually regulated population."[155]

Later he adds:

It may be suggested that ritually regulated societies comprise a mode of production commensurable with feudalism, capitalism, and oriental despotism. Because the operation of ritually regulated societies does not entail social stratification or even ranking, ritual itself may constitute a very old if not the primordial mode of production.[156]

To see the Maring and a number of other peoples as having "ritually regulated" ecosystems does not lead Rappaport to the untenable conclusion that all rituals in all societies are ecologically sound. Far from supposing that the cultural and the material aspects of society are always in harmony, he regards some measure of contradiction between them as inevitable. His thesis is simply that ritual and ecology affect each other profoundly, sometimes in ways that produce very viable systems, as in the New Guinea highlands prior to colonization, and sometimes not. An ecologically aware anthropology does not, according to Rappaport, "attempt to account for all of culture in ecological terms."[157]

It does, however, attempt to highlight those aspects of culture that bear upon the ecosystem and that may be interpreted as helping to regulate society's relation to it.

Upon this foundation, Rappaport approaches the subject of ritual order and sacrality. His insights concerning it might conceivably have been arrived at from a different starting point but, in any case, they are dependent upon one's asking what role ritual plays in forming and preserving social life.

The processes through which ritual regulates the life of a society, perhaps especially when these have significance for the maintenance of the biological life-system, are mostly hidden from consciousness. For example, incest or dietary taboos may be encoded ritually without any cultural awareness of the biological benefits they provide. In such situations and other analogous ones (which are not limited, by the way, to pre-industrial societies but are to be found at every level of social development), where a clear understanding of the rituals' utility is lacking, we find a vague sense that the perpetuation of a given ritual order is somehow necessary. This sense of "necessity" will be felt as the ritual's sacredness.

Rappaport thinks that sacrality is not projected upon ritual from without but is implicit within it. This, apparently, is because ritual life is fundamental to all other forms of social awareness and relationship:

I take ritual to be *the* basic social act. I will argue, in fact, that social contract, morality, the concept of the sacred, the notion of the divine, and even a paradigm of creation are intrinsic to ritual's structure.[158]

It is ritual, then, which teaches us to seek a created order in the world, and in so far as we find it, we have ritual to thank. This means that liturgical orders stand in a relation of some transcendence to the particular behaviors and norms they inculcate. Rappaport calls them *meta*-orders—performances that establish the propriety and obligatory character of any number of discrete acts.

Ritual performance is not in itself merely, nor even necessarily, factitive. It is not always performative in a simple way, merely bringing into being conventional states of affairs through conventional actions. It is, rather, *meta*-performative and *meta*-factitive, for it *establishes*, that is, it stipulates and accepts, the conventions in respect to which conventional states of affairs are defined and realized.[159]

The suggestion is that societies rest upon shared understandings of world and reality that are constituted ritually, through shared performance, long before they come to be expressed conceptually in words. It is as if Rappaport were to say, "In the beginning is the ritual act, for by it a people's cosmos is formed." His thought leads to a daring hypothesis:

It may be suggested that as the reality lying behind notions of the magical power of words is simple performativeness mystified, so may the reality lying behind the creative power of The Word—the Eternal Word—be meta-performativeness mystified—the establishment of conventions through participation in invariant liturgical orders.[160]

Rappaport's essay "The Obvious Aspects of Ritual," from which this passage comes, is notable for the way in which its anthropological starting point leads toward theological speculation. For our present line of thought, it is important to notice that Rappaport proposes to ground the theological concept of Eternal Word not in a paradigm drawn from ordinary language usage in the workaday world, nor from the literary use of words, let alone any use of language in schools, but rather from the performative and ordering character of ritual. The creative power of the divine Word is interpreted as an idea arising from the order-establishing power of ritual performance, which he calls liturgy.

Part, though not the whole, of what is meant by ritual's establishment of order is the acceptance of that order by those who participate in it. With this thought, Rappaport touches upon that aspect of performance I have earlier called its "confessional mode":

Liturgical orders are public, and participation in them constitutes a public acceptance of a public order, regardless of the private state of belief. Acceptance is, thus, a fundamental social act, and it forms a basis for public orders, which unknowable and volatile belief or conviction cannot.[159]

The distinction between "acceptance" and "belief" is important.

It is the visible, explicit, public act of acceptance, and not the invisible, ambiguous, private sentiment that is socially and morally binding. . . . We all know that a man may participate in a liturgy in which commandments against adultery and thieving are pronounced, then pilfer from the poor box on his way out of church, or depart from communion to tryst with his neighbor's wife. But such behavior does not render his acceptance meaningless or empty. It is an entailment of liturgical performances to establish conventional understandings, rules, and norms in accordance with which everyday behavior is supposed to proceed, not to control that behavior directly.[162]

In this line of thinking, a crucial difference appears between what ritual does and what conceptual language does, and this difference has much to do with the sacred dimension of ritual. The work of language is to divide:

The distinctions of language cut the world into bits—into categories, classes, oppositions, and contrasts. It is in the nature of language to search out all differences and to turn them into distinctions which then provide bases for boundaries and barriers.[163]

The work of ritual is quite different:

It is . . . in the nature of liturgical orders to unite, or reunite, the psychic, social, natural, and cosmic orders which language and the exigencies of life pull apart. It is of importance in this regard that representations in ritual are often multi-modal, employing at one and the same time words, music, noise, odors, objects, and substances.[164]

The contrast drawn here between language and liturgy is the same as may be drawn between discursive prose and poetry, between the mind's analytic operations and its synthetic ones, between the activities of the left brain and the right.

   In Rappaport's view, ritual expresses sacrality insofar as it serves to establish transcendent order. Rituals often contain within themselves a great deal of mockery and irreverence toward many temporal orders, but their net effect is to reinforce the power of order at a more transcendent level. As he says,

The denials of order in ritual are seldom if ever absolute, and while they may be denials of this world's order, liturgical orders are usually concerned with more than the order of the world of here and now. They also proclaim an order that transcends time, an ultimate or absolute order of which the temporal order is merely a contingent part. . . . Liturgy's challenges to the temporal are in the service of the ultimate, for they keep the conventions of time and place in their places by demonstrating that they are not ultimately sacred, but only sanctified by the ultimately sacred. They are also thereby in the service of evolution, for they make it easier to discard temporal conventions when times and places change.[165]

   "The Obvious Aspects of Ritual"is as brilliant an essay about ritual theory as any to be found. The astonishing scope of its argument is presented with a fine attention both to logic and to ritual's somatic and performative nature. I have quoted Rappaport at length because he speaks more powerfully than most researchers about the work of ritual in establishing both social and cosmic order. His is a vision, we might say, of the entire world, as it is understood by human beings, having been brought from chaos into conceptual and moral form through the performance of rituals. The path-making character of ritual performance has here become world-making. We glimpse ourselves as the inhabitants of a cosmos that is put in place and held firm around us through ritual performance.

   In his own way, through a method that began with investigation of how rituals helped some New Guinea societies maintain a balanced ecological system, Rappaport arrived at a vision similar to that of ancient Confucians, who declared that through rituals "Heaven and earth join in harmony, the sun and moon shine, the four seasons proceed in order, the stars and constellations march, the rivers flow, and all things flourish."

The ordering function of ritual is important, indeed basic. I have argued this since early in the book by speaking of rituals as pathways; and the argument has been expanded in this chapter by reference to the liturgical or world-making dimension of rituals that in many societies have a foundational character. In Western, pluralistic societies it may be hard to find such fundamental rituals, unless they are those that express the spirit of nationalism; but it is easy to find them for subgroups and religious communities within modern societies. The Mass, the Seder, the Order of Service, the *salat* (the prayers that Muslims make five times daily kneeling toward Mecca)—all these and more serve to make and sustain the felt worlds that give meaning to vast numbers of people. Among those for whom such rituals have lost all power, there is often to be found a pervasive sense of anomie, a directionlessness that haunts modern life and carries with it a threat of doom. This is the lesson that our century's social experiments with religionless communism have made entirely clear. It is a lesson that applies equally to capitalism in so far as the latter is a secular ideology that fails to unite social justice with liturgical order.

In the end, however, it is possible, as in the case of Rappaport, to put rather too much emphasis upon the presumed "invariance"of liturgical orders. Attention should also be paid to the ways in which liturgies are changed and sometimes abandoned in response to altered historical conditions. It is a mistake to assume that Truth and the Holy are, in principle, changeless. In an essay called "Sanctity and Lies in Evolution," Rappaport overstates his case by arguing that sacred postulates are wholly devoid of empirical reference:

The ultimately sacred, and thus absolutely unquestionable, is in an orderly adaptive system, confined to certain postulates expressed in the most invariant portions of liturgies. A feature typical of ultimate sacred postulates is of great significance here. I refer to their material and social vacuity.[166]

We should retain Rappaport's important insight concerning the transcendence of liturgical orders without committing ourselves to his assumption of invariance. To do this, the first step is to pay close attention to the role rituals play in making not only order but also something that is greater than order and deeper than society—namely—communities of love. If order is the first and most basic gift that ritual confers upon the social life of human beings, it is neither ritual's final nor greatest benefit. Through its ability to challenge social order with communal love, ritual provides a gift that surpasses order. To this aspect of our topic we now turn.

8

Community

In many rituals strong emotions are engendered and consciousness altered. Not infrequently there is a feeling of "loss of self"—that is, a loss of the sense of separation—and a feeling of union with the other members of the congregation and even more embracing entities.

—ROY RAPPAPORT[167]

One obvious aspect of ritual is that it not only brings people together in physical assembly but also tends to unite them emotionally. It bonds them in even deeper ways also, as we shall see. This aspect of our subject must be approached by drawing attention to what anthropologists have come to call "liminality."

Colin Turnbull has related his experience of the *molimo*, a ritual with music performed at times of crisis by the Mbuti, the pygmy hunter/gatherers in Zaire with whom he lived on three separate occasions. At his first "hearing the *molimo*" he was not yet trained as an anthropologist but had studied musicology. For the *molimo*, the Mbuti went away from their village dwellings to a hunting camp deep in the forest, which they think of as going to a separate world.

"My responses to the first *molimo* song I heard were immediate," Turnbull reports. The singing was done at night with "a felt need for . . . the curing power of the song, for it was sung from the very outset with great intensity, all the more intense because to begin with it was so quiet."[168] The singers employed a technique known to musicologists as *hoquet*, in which "the individual notes of any melodic line are ascribed to individual singers, so that no one singer carries the entire melody but each carries an essential part of it and all are therefore equally necessary."[169]

Turnbull noticed a sharp contrast between the intensity and complexity of the song, on the one hand, and on the other, the relaxed air of the performers' body positions and their casual movements around the fire to avoid smoke or to stretch their legs. When he mentioned this the next day to his hosts, who had asked what he thought of the music, they replied "that it was all the same: it was all dance, it was all song, it was all work, and it was all play."[170] At his next hearing of the *molimo*, he experienced the same contrast between intensity and relaxation, only this time it was the body movements that seemed intense, the music relaxed. Both times he felt the contrast between the two simultaneous moods so sharply that they seemed to him "two different, almost opposed states of being." Later he heard the *molimo* a third time, describing it in these words:

No longer afraid that I was going to miss anything, and no longer looking for any explanation, just intent on enjoying myself, I closed my eyes. . . . I felt free to let my own body move as though, not being able to see myself nobody else would be able to see me. And by the same illogic I felt free to join in the singing. And in an instant it all came together: there was no longer any lack of congruence, and it seemed as though the song was being sung by a single singer, the dance danced by a single dancer. Then I made the mistake of opening my eyes and saw that while all the others had their eyes open too, their gaze was vacant. . . . There were so many bodies sitting around, singing away, but I was the only person there, the only individual consciousness; all the other bodies were empty. Something had been added to the importance of sound, another mode of perception that, while it in no way negated the aural or visual modes of observation, none the less went far beyond them.[171]

In this beautiful account, we can notice the importance of communal gathering (intensified by going into the forest, singing at night, sitting by campfire), performative cooperation (very close and interdependent when using *hoquet* technique), and some kind of mystical participation, in which the various members, although interacting with each other only in the singing and not with eyes, spoken words, or physical touch, were yet as much united as it is possible for human beings to be.

Modern society offers few opportunities for this level of mutual participation. Some readers of this book have no doubt had experiences analogous to the one Colin Turnbull describes. Some others have not but may long to. Still others may find such loss of self through communal and mystical participation a frightening prospect. I myself have had experiences with just enough similarity to Turnbull's to make me wish for more.

■

"Anthropology," Rappaport reminds us, "has known since Durkheim's time that rituals establish or enhance solidarity among those joining in their performance," adding that "an awareness of this has no doubt been part of general common sense since time immemorial."[172] Huxley points out that while some rituals, like meditation and prayer, are done in solitude, "most of them, like collective worship or tribal dancing, have a social function," which he defines as "to ensure individual participation in a group activity," and to channel and intensify "the group's mood."[173]

What needs stressing, however, is not just that the greatest quantity of rituals are social but that ritual activity is interactive and social by nature. If, as Huxley and others have argued, the development of ritual is fundamental to the growth of communication systems in human and other species, and if, as Rappaport says, ritual is *the* basic social act," then we may say that performing *together* is a feature of ritual in its paradigmatic form.[174]

Although it is true that some rituals may be performed by individuals in private, these instances are unintelligible except as offshoots or imitations of collective rituals. We have already touched upon this in our analysis of performance, when we saw that performance is a "showing" that always requires an audience, even if the spectator is physically invisible or is an aspect of the performer's own self. In other words, ritual assumes community and must provide itself with an imaginary one if no other is present.

We should not suppose that the coming together of human beings for an occasion of ritual performance is a matter to be taken lightly, as if it posed no dangers. On the contrary, and in spite of the peace that fills experiences like Turnbull's cited above, collective performance always involves some peril because the aggressive impulses in human beings are accompanied by very few restraints, perhaps none at all except those maintained by culture. Ritual occasions are always fraught with the possibility that aggressions usually held in check by social pressure may come free.

"Aggressive" is used here in its literal sense, to refer to an inclination to move *toward* other persons instead of avoiding or fleeing them. This inclination is not always hostile, but it is always perilous. When it takes a hostile form, it leads toward conflict, abuse, or destruction; yet aggressiveness may also take a loving form, in which case the inclination to move toward other persons becomes a desire for intimacy. In the *molimo,* as Turnbull describes it, the intimacy seems ethereal and benign;

but there are times when intimacy can be threatening. Often aggression is doubly motivated by love and hostility at once, producing a situation of volatile ambivalence, as can sometimes be experienced during carnival and other festivals that countenance the flow of high libidinal energy.

One of the functions of ritual is to release and direct aggressive impulses in such a way as that aggressive hostility is kept under control, while aggressive love (moving toward) is enhanced within the group. In pig exchanges among the Enga in the New Guinea highlands (see chapter 3), these two forms of aggression are kept in careful balance. The pig exchange is designed to enhance friendships and loyalties through song, dance, the giving of gifts, and the repayment of debts; yet it employs the same costumes, including weapons carried, as are used in battle; and its tone, expressed in oratory, music, and body decoration, varies from the gentle and joyous to the fierce. Similar ambivalences may be observed in military and quasi-military rituals throughout the world, in sporting events, fraternal associations, and in many religious rituals as well, where love and bloodletting may be found as two aspects of the same event. As dangerous and frightening as these ambivalences may be, they should not surprise us, for a close association between fighting and lovemaking is experienced, at least part of the time, in most sexual relationships.

Ritual's work of directing aggressive impulses in ways that will be beneficial to the group is a complex matter. It is not only that the impulses are controlled by being made to follow the pattern of the ritual: It is also that sometimes they are ritually decontrolled, released from some of the restraints that social law and custom impose upon them. For example, rituals may be employed to work up hostile, aggressive energies in preparation for battle, or to stir up the determination to win a sporting contest, as cheerleading squads attempt to do. The stimulation of energies hostile to an adversary is often accompanied by a rise in feelings of friendship toward members of one's own performance group.

It is not the case, however, that the aggressive love stimulated by ritual is merely the by-product of antagonisms being directed toward an out-group. On the contrary, ritual often provides space and freedom for loving aggression within a group, while at the same time lifting up visions and symbols of universal love. It may even be part of the genius of ritual activity that it can tap deeper into wellsprings of aggressive love than can any other cultural activity. The communal character of ritual provides a grounding for the more exclusive intimacies known to individuals in their fantasies, to lovers and friends in mutual exchange with each other, and to solitary souls in prayerful relation to God. This is one of the principal reasons for the appeal of public and communal performance. Bereft of their grounding in ritual assemblages, personal relationships, and even political alliances, grow thin, lacking the nourishment of more comprehensive group life.

The coming together that rituals occasion always has something of the quality of a good-time gathering, a party. Many rituals are grandly festive; but even when they are not, in the most solemn ones—be they funerals, requiem masses, dedication ceremonies, or prayers for relief of suffering—a tendency toward festival may be seen. In Western traditions, for example, almost any liturgical order may find a fitting conclusion in the phrase, "Let the people say Amen!" The people's chorus of "Amen" is a party-shout, a coming together around a Yes; and it moves toward joy even when it is pronounced in a season of death, fear, or disaster.

Ritual controls emotion while releasing it, and guides it while letting it run. Even in a time of grief, ritual lets joy be present through the permission to cry, lets tears become laughter, if they will, by making place for the fullness of tears' intensity—all this in the presence of communal assertiveness.

A ritual is a party at which emotions are welcome. If the emotions are too strong, threatening to swamp the party, the ritual scenario can be used to guide and moderate them; and if the emotions are too weak, draining the event of its energy, the ritual can invoke them, like spirits, to be present, through the use of rhythm, display, and other summoning techniques. Any ritual performance is an invitation for energies to come together, to multiply their power by fusion, coupled with performative norms—that is, the ritual's own form—to guide the energies' expression.

Along with the idea of ritual as party goes that of ritual as play. Any theory of ritual must recognize that, however factitive, efficacious, and socially necessary the performance of certain rituals may be, their manner of work is different from that of ordinary labor and from (what shall we call it?) secular technique. As the Mbuti said of the *molimo*, "It was all dance, it was all song, it was all work, and it was all play."

We have already touched upon ritual's playfulness in our analysis of the ritual mode of performance, where we took note of the element of pretense that belongs to all performance in that mode. The "showing forth" that belongs to ritual lifts it into an orbit of play, in which imagination runs ahead of visible, tangible reality, and things that may be, and might be, and ought or ought not to be, are given permission to happen in the play-time, the pretend time, of the ritual occasion. Rituals characteristically perform very serious and important work; but it is work done playfully, with that marveling combination of serious pretense and pretended seriousness that belongs to children and is revived in adults in the ritual mode of performance.

The communal and free-playing qualities of ritual have been addressed most cogently by the late anthropologist Victor Turner in his twin concepts of communitas and liminality. These have proven so appealing to students of ritual that the words now turn up in almost all writing about rituals. They are, in fact, so bandied about as to be in danger of losing their force. They are very much to the point, however, and it will be worth our time to review their meaning in the way that I understand it.

Turner's idea of liminality takes its departure from Arnold Van Gennep's *Rite of Passage*.[175] Van Gennep had concentrated upon rituals that effect a passage from one social situation to another—from childhood to adulthood, perhaps, or from outsider to insider, from foe to ally, from the realm of the living to that of the dead, and so on. He viewed rites of passage as falling into three types, depending on their relation to the passage being made. Rites of separation (washings, cleansings, and other "purifications," for example) came first, to detach the subjects of the rite from their old status or condition. Rites of incorporation (presentation of salt or the sharing of food, for example) came last, enabling the subjects to reenter society on a new basis. In between came transitional rites, rites of the threshold (sequestrations, nakedness, and introductions to various mysteries, for example), in which the persons in passage were neither in their previous state, from which they had been separated, nor yet in that subsequent, reincorporated state to which the rites were conducting them, but rather were between two conditions, neither here nor there. Employing a term taken from the Latin word for threshold, which is limen, Van Gennep spoke of the transitional stage as comprised of liminal rites, flanked on the one side by preliminal (the separating) rites, and on the other by postliminal (the reincorporating) rites.[176] Thus Van Gennep saw the liminal rites as the core of the sequence. Rites of passage conducted persons through a nothingness, a temporary loss of identity in a time that was no time and a place that was nowhere.

In *The Ritual Process*, Turner elaborated upon liminality as he observed it in his own field researches among the Ndembu in Africa:

The attributes of liminality or of liminal *personae* ("threshold people") are necessarily ambiguous, since this condition and these persons elude or slip through the network of classifications that normally locate states and positions in cultural space. Liminal entities are neither here nor there; they are betwixt and between the positions assigned and arrayed by law, custom, convention, and ceremonial. . . . Thus, liminality is frequently likened to death, to being in the womb, to invisibility, to darkness, to bisexuality, to the wilderness, and to an eclipse of the sun or moon.[177]

During initiations Ndembu neophytes are submitted to ordeals and humiliations, "often of a grossly physiological character." Turner comments that "they have to be shown that in themselves they are clay or dust, mere matter, whose form is impressed upon them by society."[178]

Extrapolating from the data concerning liminal states that he gathered in field research, Turner proposed a list of binary oppositions expressing the difference between the properties of liminality and those of society's status system, from which the "threshold people" are temporarily separated. It will be sufficient to reproduce here only a part of his list:[179]

Liminality	*Status system*
transition	state
homogeneity	heterogeneity
equality	inequality
anonymity	systems of nomenclature
absence of status	status
nakedness or uniform clothing	distinctions of clothing
minimization of sex distinctions	maximization of sex distinctions
sacredness	secularity
foolishness	sagacity

Liminality is characterized by a destructuring in relation to what Turner calls "social structure." The latter is the sum total of rules, norms, and status-markers that society keeps in place to define and govern its institutions and to control the processes of material production. The relativity of ritual's liminal destructuring needs to be appreciated. That is, ritualized liminality is by no means the complete absence of any and all structure, for in that case it could not exist. On the contrary, as our discussion of ritual's ordering function has shown, rituals are concerned with their own ordering as well as with the ordering of the world. Ritualized liminality, then, employs structures of its own; but these are different from the structures of society, and they are often utilized to emphasize homogeneity, equality, anonymity, and foolishness *when compared with* the heterogeneous, status-marked, name-conscious intelligence of the social order.

Turner's thought, initially prompted by Van Gennep's, proceeded to a far broader conception of the liminal. In Turner's eyes, liminality, the character of being neither here nor there but "in between," belongs to rituals as such and is not confined to rites of passage, let alone to one particular type of them. Without contradicting Van Gennep's analysis, Turner proposed a new conception, which may be described as follows: When people engage in ritual activity, they separate themselves, partially if not totally, from the roles and statuses they have in the workaday world. There is a threshold in time or space or both, and certainly a demarcation of behavior, over which people pass when entering into ritual. The day-to-day world, with its social structure, is temporarily suspended. Turner has written:

Just as the subjunctive mood of a verb is used to express supposition, desire, hypothesis, or possibility, rather than stating actual facts, so do liminality and the phenomena of liminality dissolve all factual and common sense systems into their components and "play" with them in ways never found in nature or in custom, at least at the level of direct perception.[180]

Because ritual is essentially playful and imaginative, it does not constitute a realm entirely independent of social structure. The terms of its playing take their initial cues from mundane life, and the time of ritual is but a limited time. When it is over, the duties pertaining to the social structure must resume. Hence ritual activity, existing *as if* outside the structures of society, existing in a subjunctive mode of play and pretend, is neither here nor there. It is liminal.

I may observe in this connection that much ritual boredom and ritual misapprehension in post-Enlightenment societies arises from the fact that ritual liminality has been suppressed. As the powers of nation-states have grown in modern times, so has the desire on their part to eliminate as much liminality as possible from ritual performance, because liminality can lead to a weakening of state control over people's ideas, emotions, and behavior. This same desire for control spills over from the state into various religious institutions as well, those that see themselves allied with hegemonic political powers. By education and practice, then, much of the liminality of ritual comes to be suppressed. This end is brought about also by certain cultural factors, particularly the exaltation of scientific reasoning and the dominance of middle-class values. Thanks to them, the playfulness and irrationality of ritual have come in many quarters to be viewed with suspicion. Ritual comes to be seen more as dutiful form than as release from social pressure. Its liminality ceases to be strongly experienced.

However playful, foolish, subjunctive, and pretense-ridden liminality may be, there is yet a substance to it. By its temporary suspension or distancing of social structure, ritual liminality makes room for something quite different, which Turner calls communitas. Why, we may ask, did he resort to a Latin term and use it in his own peculiar way instead of speaking simply of "community?" The answer has to do with the peculiarities of liminality, of ritual as a "threshold" phenomenon having a relation to the social order that is full of dialectical complexity. In my discussion of communitas I shall perhaps read more into the concept than Turner himself intended, yet this is the only interpretation of his argument that makes good sense to me.

Turner seems to think of communitas as something like the soul or essence of ritual. It is less empirical but more substantive than what the term "community" denotes. The latter word, he tells us, refers to an "area of common living," in other words, a village, town, neighborhood, and so on.[181] Communitas belongs to a different logical category. He calls it "an essential and generic human bond, without which there could be *no* society."[182] In other words, communitas is not itself a part of social structure but is one of society's reasons for being. Turner sees this *raison d'être* becoming manifest in ritual.

If communitas were a physical entity or a measurable force, it would not require the liminality of ritual for its instantiation. It would be amenable to the empirical techniques used in society's work and would find its place entirely within the social structure. But since communitas is a bond among human beings that is "essential and generic," it transcends empirical categories and has to be comprehended in a subjunctive rather than an indicative mode. In philosophical terms, we could say that it is a potentiality, not a fully actualized thing in the ordinary world; and that is why it requires an "as if" mode of thinking and acting in order to find expression. Communitas is and is not "real." It is and yet is not part of society. It is both present and absent at any time. Hence it is liminal, existing in between logical categories, like all potentialities. It lives by ritual.

If ritual were all work and no play, if it were a technique of an ordinary sort, it would not loosen the hold of the social structure upon experience and would not provide time, place, and playfulness for communitas to become manifest. It would belong to society as a part belongs to the whole and not as something antithetical to, something basically "other" than, the very society to which it does, yes, belong. Language concerning ritual liminality is driven to paradox because of the fact that threshold phenomena have a dialectical relation to the realities that surround and define them; and it is this dialectic of the liminal, hinted at in the Turnerian term "antistructure," that opens a way through which communitas and other invisible potencies may arrive upon the human scene.

The section in *The Ritual Process* in which Turner introduces the concept communitas is worth quoting at length, even though some of the language in it is tortured. It may be taken as testimony to the logical contradictions that abound in all discussion of liminality:

> What is interesting about liminal phenomena for our present purposes is the blend they offer of lowliness and sacredness, of homogeneity and comradeship. We are presented, in such rites, with a "moment in and out of time," and in and out of secular social structure, which reveals, however fleetingly, some recognition (in symbol if not always in language) of a generalized social bond . . .[183]

In his writings up to and including this one, Turner gave more attention to symbolism and less to performance than he was to do later on. Hence he fails to notice in this important passage that a people's "generalized social bond" is primarily expressed in ritual *behaviors*, the gestures and actions through which persons relate to each other during a ritual's performance, and which are not so much of a symbolic as a participatory nature. The paragraph continues:

> . . . a generalized social bond that has ceased to be and has simultaneously yet to be fragmented into a multiplicity of structural ties. These are the ties organized in terms either of caste, class, or rank hierarchies or of segmentary oppositions in the stateless societies beloved of political anthropologists. It is as though there are here two major "models" for human interrelatedness, juxtaposed and alternating. The first is of society as a structured, differentiated, and often hierarchical system of politico-legal-economic positions with many types of evaluation, separating men [sic] in terms of "more" or "less." The second, which emerges recognizably in the liminal period, is of society as an unstructured or rudimentarily structured and relatively undifferentiated *comitatus* [sic], community, or even communion of equal individuals who submit together to the general authority of the ritual elders.
> I prefer the Latin term *communitas* to "community," to distinguish this modality of social relationship from an "area of common living."[184]

When Turner speaks (awkwardly) of the recognition in ritual of a generalized social bond "that has ceased to be [fragmented] and has simultaneously yet to be fragmented into a multiplicity of structural ties," I take it he is thinking of communitas as a spirit of unity that is ordinarily disrupted or compromised by social stratification. He does not go so far as to speak of *alienation*, but he might well have done so, for the acid of social stratification that is so inimical to communitas is the alienation that results from social distancing and the exploitation of the weaker by the stronger.

It is of crucial importance to realize that ritual holds the possibility for social alienation to be partly and temporarily overcome. While it does not always achieve this possibility, to the extent that it fails to do so it falls away from being ritual, declining into mere routine, or into what Turner calls "ceremony" (by which he means the celebration of the social structure), perhaps becoming an instrument of regimentation, the very opposite of authentic ritual. "Communitas cannot manipulate resources or exercise social control without changing its own nature and ceasing to be communitas."[185] This means that ritual is itself not immune to processes of alienation.

When social conditions are such that a split is introduced between consciousness of a ritual's form and awareness of the creative human activity through which the ritual has been made—in other words, when people lose sight of the fact that rituals are the result of human activity carried on in specific historical conditions—then ritual becomes a fetish, just as commodities become fetishized in a consumerist society. Ritual can then be manipulated by those who hold power in society, used to protect their privileged positions by surrounding them with an aura of sacredness or inevitability. Such uses of ritual pervert the phenomenon by seeking to destroy its liminality, and hence its capacity to be the bearer of communitas.

When its character has not been subverted, ritual offers an occasion for social alienations to be suspended. They are not exactly eliminated, but they are for a time transposed in such a way as to lose whatever semblance of ultimacy they otherwise have. The liminality of ritual, then, is a recourse from society's alienating structures to a generalized bond of unity (communitas) that is felt or intuited among humans and other beings.

With preindustrial tribal societies in mind, Turner speaks of a "communion of equal individuals who submit together to the general authority of the ritual elders." Although submission to "ritual elders" stands in some contradiction to the "generic human bond" that is the essence of communitas, it is true that "elders" can loom large in ritual. They may be priests authorized to preside over the ritual's performance; or perhaps bold warriors or other powerful figures with some standing also in the social structure; or they may be certain "experienced ones" known for their ritual expertise, like shamans or "wise old women" whose authority comes from adventures in the spirit world or from the practice of healing arts, or is, like that of the prophets in Israel, the result of a special calling from on high. What needs emphasis, however, is ritual's tendency to subordinate all privileged authority, whether derived from social structure or from spiritual life, to the overarching value of communitas, the bond of affection, or at least mutual recognition, that unites all members of the group with each other and sometimes with all other creatures in the universe.

Broadly speaking, as we have argued in our previous chapter, rituals generate, maintain, and celebrate order; but they do so in a peculiar way, by grounding the sense of order in something that is other than itself, something fundamentally at odds with order—namely, participation in an undifferentiated core of life.

"For me," Turner writes, "communitas emerges where social structure is not."[186] That is, it emerges liminally, in times and spaces generated ritually. He cites Martin Buber, who used the term "community" to denote what Turner himself calls communitas:

Community is the being no longer side by side (and, one might add, above and below) but *with* one another of a multitude of persons. And this multitude, though it moves towards our goal, yet experiences everywhere a turning to, a dynamic facing of, the others, a flowing from *I* to *Thou*. Community is where community happens.[187]

Contrasting communitas with social structure, Turner finds the former to be "spontaneous, immediate, [and] concrete . . . as opposed to the norm-governed, institutionalized, abstract nature of social structure."[188] In other words, communitas is not only an ideal or a principle of bonding, but is also the experience of it. It exerts a pressure upon society both from below (as ritually generated experience) and from above (as a ritually generated ideal). It becomes manifest in its difference *from* society:

. . . communitas is made evident or accessible, so to speak, only through its juxtaposition to, or hybridization with, aspects of social structure. Just as in *Gestalt* psychology, figure and ground are mutually determinative, or, as some rare elements are never found in nature in their purity but only as components of chemical compounds, so communitas can be grasped only in some relation to structure.[189]

Turner illustrates this point with Lao-tse's parable of the chariot wheel, in which the spokes of the wheel, attached to the central block (the nave) holding the axle, "would be useless . . . but for the hole, the gap, the emptiness at the centre"—in other words, the still point on which the wheel turns. Turner says that communitas, which is unstructured and represents "the 'quick' of human interrelatedness," is "indispensable to the functioning of the structure" of society.[190]

Communitas breaks in through the interstices of structure in liminality; at the edges of structure, in marginality; and from beneath structure, in inferiority. It is almost everywhere held to be sacred or "holy," possibly because it transgresses or dissolves the norms that govern structured and institutionalized relationships and is accompanied by experiences of unprecedented potency. . . . I am now inclined to think that communitas is not solely the product of biologically inherited drives released from cultural constraints. Rather is it the product of peculiarly human faculties, which include rationality, volition, and memory, and which develop with experience of life in society.[191]

Let me summarize the Turnerian view I am advancing in this chapter: Rituals are inherently communal, while at the same time being imaginative and playful, even when most serious. They become bearers of communitas, which is a spirit of unity and mutual belonging that is frequently experienced in rituals of high energy, particularly those that are closer to the shamanic than to the priestly type of ritual pathway.

In their liminality, rituals exist outside many of the rules and expectations society normally imposes upon behavior. Rituals partly substitute for society's codes of behavior special codes of their own (the understandings of what one is supposed to do and not do during a particular ritual, and the tone or style of behavior that is appropriate), and partly they foster spontaneous performance and "inspired" words and actions. Much goes on in rituals that would not be tolerated at other times: Hand-clapping, ecstatic dancing, rhapsodic speech, cross-dressing, speech-song recitations, direct address to invisible beings, the treating of a statue or an entranced person as if it, she, or he were a god, public exchange of affection, mystical union with other participants, the telling of dreams, mind-altering music or drugs, the public sharing of sacred food, and more.

The liminality of rituals means that they are informed, on the one hand, by a greater than usual sense of order and, on the other, by a heightened sense of freedom and possibility. Being imaginative, rituals can experiment with both ideal order and ideal freedom, releasing feelings of love and participation in the process. Being playful, rituals can afford to fail. Freedom from the tyranny of having to succeed enhances, paradoxically, the likelihood of their achieving their goal.

■

In middle-class life in Western societies, it is difficult to find rituals that provide much experience of communitas. Here we keep our rituals close to the social shore, so to speak. We do not often let them head for high water, and this is our great loss. No doubt we dwellers in comfort in the privileged societies that consume most of the world's natural resources, leaving two-thirds of the world's population at starvation level, are fearful of losing what we have. Perhaps we do not want any strong reminder of a "generic human bond," lest it cause us to lose our heads and identify with those dying of hunger. Dream of a common humanity, especially when ritualized and therefore brought into experience, can threaten a socially privileged way of life.

It is different among the exploited and the marginalized. That is why, in order strongly to experience communitas manifest in ritual one must belong to or associate with groups of people who have little invested in the present social order. At carnival festivities attended by large numbers of the poor, at pilgrimages to which the common people flock, in very popular religions such as *vodou* in Haiti or Hinduism in southern India, in some types of evangelical Christianity not dominated by reactionary politics, in black American churches serving the urban and rural poor, in the churches of East Germany prior to the bloodless revolution of 1989, among women turning to ritual to help them find viable alternatives to patriarchy, and in some other settings, ritual is loved because it gives space for communitas to flow. There people can say that it is all dance, it is all song, it is all work, and it is all play.

When a spirit of rebellion against unjust social structures is rising, an understanding of ritual as an alternative order fostering freedom, creativity, and deliverance will take precedence over the idea that rituals enforce rigid notions of order. Community will come to mean something like Turner's idea of communitas. Ritual will be seen as the occasion for both symbolizing and experiencing relationships in which spontaneity, affection, and unity replace unwanted law and compelled obedience. Under these conditions, communities will put ritual in the service of personal and social transformation, which is the subject of our next chapter.

9

Transformation

Liminality is the mother of invention!

—VICTOR TURNER[192]

Having considered two of the three great gifts that rituals make to social life—the establishment of order and the deepening of communal life—we are now to take up the third and most important, which is to assist the dynamic of social change through ritual processes of transformation.

From a purely theoretical point of view, if that were possible or desirable to achieve, it would be an open question whether rituals should be thought of first as instruments of order that happen to enhance communal bonds and to facilitate various kinds of transformation; or primarily as community-making events that incidentally generate order and transform it; or first of all as techniques of transformation that help to order life and to deepen communal relationships. Theory, however, is always affected by a thinker's social orientation and ideology. In my own case, although I belong to the privileged gender (male) and race (white) in the North American middle class, my theory is that ritual is best understood from a vantage point created by a "preferential option for the poor." That is to say, we cannot well appreciate the power of ritual unless we see its usefulness to those in need, especially those who, having little social power and, being the victims of injustice, have a need for the social structure to be transformed.

Here is the most difficult part of our entire discussion, for here ritual misapprehension is apt to be the greatest. Many persons in Western society are skeptical of any transformative powers that may be claimed for ritual, except perhaps the inducement of changes that can be taken as primarily subjective or psychological in nature. This skepticism, being partly a matter of ideology, is strongest in those sectors of society that would have the most to lose were any major social transformation to occur.

One way of guarding the status quo against change is to deny the rationality of any expectation that rituals can do much to alter it. The entire tradition of Enlightenment thought, with its strong antipathy to rituals, lends plausibility to such denial. This means that in order seriously to consider the idea that a ritual can serve as a technique of transformation, we must come straight out with the M-word and face the question of magic.

■

People educated in the Western style tend to assume that only cultures or subcultures less enlightened than our own have recourse to magic. Most Western intellectuals regard magic as superstition, and most theologians equate it with paganism as well. In these matters, it often seems that one person's "magic" is another person's "religion." Ronald Grimes's words are therefore refreshing: " 'Magic,' as I use it here, does not refer only to other people's rituals but to ours as well. It is not a pejorative term."[193]

In our chapter concerning order, we quoted a Haitian woman, Mme. Victor, describing how to cure the *move san* (bad blood) that she and her culture understand to afflict women who have difficult pregnancies. We were interested then in the precision of her instructions, their being rooted in a received sense of order in nature, implying a structured cosmos, and at the same time their *making* order, in the sense that her formulae are what she, the "doctor," orders. What she does as a practitioner of local herbal medicine, of course, is to *reorder*: The medicine she prescribes, together with her instructions about how to prepare and administer it, are designed, as she says, to "make the milk return to its rightful place." At the same time, her metaphor of order and right place suggests also a transformation, since the aim of the cure is to transform the flow at the nursing mother's breast from a toxic to a nourishing substance. As outsiders we may suppose that Mme. Victor's intention is also to reorient the distraught mother to her child, her family, her friends, and herself, so that she will come to occupy her *own* rightful place.

Researcher Paul Farmer rightly noticed that Mme. Victor's magic is ritualized;[194] but to say so is to speak redundantly, since *all* magic is ritualized and, as we shall see, all ritual employs magic.

Techniques of transformation that are *not* magical, such as those based on scientific analyses or empirical observation without any transcendent reference—like building a car or boiling water—have a claim to being culture-invariant. They are understood to employ forces and "laws" that are the same in any cultural milieu. The techniques of ritual, however, appeal to forces, agents, and "laws" (understandings of how things work) that are culture-dependent. Magic operates within socio-cultural frameworks of reality.

Thorough analysis would show that "science" and "magic" overlap. On the one hand, while magic does not confine itself to empirically grounded methods, neither does it exclude them. For example, medical anthropologists often discover empirical bases for herbal cures that have been practiced and transmitted ritually. On the other hand, the procedures and understandings of science are by no means independent of local culture, even though science aims to achieve a body of knowledge that is universally valid.[195]

The bugaboo of regarding magic as nothing more than bad science is hard to shake off, but Suzanne Langer made a nice try when she wrote this:

The apparently misguided efforts of savages to induce rain by dancing and drumming are not practical mistakes at all; they are rites in which the rain has a part. . . . A "magic" effect is one which *completes a rite*.[196]

In other words, the world seen by magic is the world as ritually ordered, a world in which society and nature usually are fused in a single vision. But it is not this vision alone to which I call attention. It is the vision as the enabler of transformative action.

We are on the best footing when we think of magic as what Grimes calls "ritual work." He says that if a ritual "not only has meaning but also 'works,' it is magical."[197]

This way of thinking about the subject is close to that of Van Gennep, who had used "magic" to refer to the ceremonies, rites, and services that are the principal techniques of transformation employed by religion.[198] More than Van Gennep, however, Grimes directs attention to the presence of magic in "our own" culture:

Magical acts seldom displace pragmatic or scientific ones [see Malinowski (1954), 85–87], and we have no reason to assume that magic is absent from technological societies, although it is probably adumbrated in them. I suspect magic is minimal in modern agriculture, but modern therapy and modern sexuality are as laden with magical thinking as healing and fertility rites ever were. In addition, advertising is full of it. People deny that they believe in magic, but ingest this pill and use that shampoo expecting "somehow" (the cue for magical transcendence) to become what they desire. A more responsible example of modern magic is Carl Simonton's [1975] use of imagery in therapy for cancer patients. A person treated in his clinic wills and imagines a cancer as soft or dissolvable and surrenders images of it as a rock, army, or steel armor. Considerable success is had in directly using symbols for such concrete ends.[199]

This is insightful, but it still holds magic at arm's length. More nearly on target is this:

> . . . a prayer, if one expects it to precipitate specifiable results such as healing or world peace, is magical. If the person praying is simply adjuring us to be peaceful, the prayer is hortatory and ceremonial. . . . Magic depends on the declarative to reach the imperative: "This is how things work; therefore, let this be the case."[200]

To reach from the declarative to the imperative requires a technique. The carpenter, aiming to let it be the case that the nail goes into the wood, uses a technique of hammering. For magic, the technique is ritual: What the act of hammering is to the carpenter, the performance of ritual is to the worker of magic.

Within the context of religion, as Van Gennep saw it, practice and theory are inseparable. If they do separate, religion dissolves, "the theory without the practice becoming metaphysics, and the practice on the basis of a different theory becoming science."[201]

Using the term *magico-religious*, Van Gennep expressed the conjunction of religious practice and theory. His point is excellent, for it reminds us that religion cannot be religion without performance, in all the senses of "performance" that we have earlier elaborated. The aim of religion is not simply intellectual understanding; it is also, and primarily, transformative action, for which the principal technique is "ceremonies, rites, and services." Ritual-making may not be a religion's first or last word but is surely its most essential. A religion is a *praxis*, a certain way of acting or attempting to act in the world, and this is established through a certain way of acting ritually.

Van Gennep's emphasis upon magic as the technique employed by religion should not blind us to the occurrence of magic outside religion also. Social life in general and political life in particular require ceremonies and rites, those quasi-dramatic enactments that express and define people's relationships and also make possible their trans-formation as part of the social dynamic. When the king is anointed, the President inaugurated, the scholar hooded, the couple wedded, or the dance floor rocked by the celebrators of Saturday night, we have instances of magical transformation. These events change things, and do so by the technique of ritual—that is, by magic.

While the literature on magic being published today offers no consistent point of view, there is considerable criticism of the idea, put forward most influentially in Frazer's *The Golden Bough*, that magic is primitive science, born of ignorance.[202] Here is Wittgenstein reflecting upon Frazer:

When we watch the life and behaviour of [human beings] all over the earth we see that apart from what we might call animal activities, taking food &c., &c., [people] also carry out actions that bear a peculiar character and might be called ritualistic.

But then it is nonsense if we go on to say that the characteristic feature of *these* actions is that they spring from wrong ideas about the physics of things. (This is what Frazer does when he says magic is really false physics, or as the case may be, false medicine, technology, &c.).[203]

Ridding himself of the notion that magic, the action of ritual, is bad science, Wittgenstein helps us to glimpse the affinity between ancient or primitive ritualizing and modern instances:

The religious actions or the religious life of the priest-king are not different in kind from any genuinely religious action today, say a confession of sins. This also can be "explained" (made clear) and cannot be explained.

Burning in effigy. Kissing the picture of a loved one. This is obviously not based on a belief that it will have a definite effect on the object which the picture represents. It aims at some satisfaction and it achieves it. Or rather, it does not aim at anything; we act in this way and then feel satisfied.[204]

If I understand Wittgenstein's point, it is that magic should not be understood within the logic of cause and effect but rather in terms of symbolic and linguistic associations. This may be too little to claim for magic, but at least it avoids thinking of magic as false logic, and it does allow for a certain understanding of ritual as technique of transformation. Desire is transformed into satisfaction: "we act in this way and then feel satisfied." There is change, of however subjective a kind.

Some views of magic more recent than Frazer's challenge his idea of magic's being a "primitive" phenomenon but agree with him that it is unscientific and false. Instead of being false because primitive, magic is said to be false because decadent. "We are often told," says Suzanne Langer, "that savage religion begins in magic; but the chances are, I think, that magic begins in religion."[205] She assumes this to be a downhill course, as does Daniel O'Keefe, who expands the point with subtlety throughout his lengthy interpretation of magic as Promethean: *Stolen Lightening: The Social Theory of Magic.*[206]

Gregory Bateson's thoughts on the matter, lofty as they are, reveal a common misunderstanding of religion. For him science and religion are closely allied, and magic is "a degenerate 'applied' form of either":

My view of magic is the converse of that which has been orthodox in anthropology since the days of Sir James Frazer. It is orthodox to believe that religion is
an evolutionary development of magic. Magic is regarded as more primitive and
religion as its flowering. In contrast, I view sympathetic or contagious magic as a
product of decadence from religion; I regard religion on the whole as the earlier
condition.[207]

Bateson is right, of course, that magic is an application of knowledge,
a technique, as Van Gennep called it. What is interesting, and erroneous,
is the vaguely Neoplatonic point of view entertained by Bateson (and
many others) that the application of knowledge for practical ends is a
corruption. The following passage seems based upon an idealization of
knowledge divorced from praxis:

Consider such rituals as rain dances or the totemic rituals concerned with [the
human's] relationship to animals. In these types of ritual the human being
invokes or imitates or seeks to control the weather or the ecology of wild
creatures. But I believe that in their primitive state these are true religious
ceremonials. They are ritual statements of unity, involving all the participants in
an integration with the meteorological cycle or with the ecology of totemic
animals. This is religion. But the pathway of deterioration from religion to magic
is always tempting. From a statement of integration in some often dimly
recognized whole, the practitioner turns aside to an appetitive stance. He [sic]
sees his own ritual as a piece of purposive magic to make the rain come or to
promote the fertility of the totemic animal or to achieve some other goal.[208]

In other words, rituals are all right as long as they are not supposed
to have any practical result. Then, in a second thought, Bateson allows
that they may have results directed toward the celebrants, but not
toward anything external to them:

The criterion that distinguishes magic from religion is, in fact, *purpose* and
especially some extrovert purpose. Introvert purpose, the desire to change the
self, is a very different matter, *but intermediate cases occur.* If the hunter performs
a ritual imitation of an animal to cause that animal to come into his net, that is
surely magic; but if his purpose in imitating the animal is perhaps to improve
his own empathy and understanding of the beast, his action is perhaps to be
classed as religious. (Emphasis added)[209]

Rushing to repudiate magic, Bateson fails to notice that the
"intermediate cases," in which introvert and extrovert purposes are
mixed, are the most prevalent and the most interesting. They express, I
would argue, the genius of religion, in which change in the self and
change in the outer world are bound into an intimate connection.

It would be a poor anthropology, in the theological as well as the
social-scientific sense, to categorize all desire as bad or corrupting. The

better moral and theological question is not *whether* there is appetite or whether people perform rituals and other acts out of desire to change their situations, but *what* they desire, in what situations, and with what sense of responsibility for the common good. Bateson's assumption that an appetite for change in the external world makes religion degenerate flies in the face of the fervent desire present in many religions for transformation of the external world—that crops may grow, that disaster may be avoided, that illness be cured, or that justice roll down like a mighty stream. Religion is not about the elimination of desire but its *transformation* from lower to higher forms—the transformation of the suffering world into one more compassionate, loving, and just.

While Frazer, Bateson, and many other writers try to defend religion by denigrating magic, Van Gennep's position, holding magic and religion together, is better. We may say that some forms of magic and magical belief are less intelligent than others, remembering that the magico-religious, as Van Gennep called it, has crass as well as admirable examples; but without magic, religion is powerless. Since the rites of religion are techniques of transformation, Van Gennep realized, when people divorce religion from magic they end up with metaphysics on the one hand, empirical science on the other, and religion gone. This is the fate to which much liberal religion in Western society has very nearly come. Having mostly turned away from its own magic, it has little to offer, and its numbers are declining.

While some persons would like to preserve religion, if only it could be purified of all magic, some others hold that religion, no less than magic, is a system of illusion. The best argument against religion, however, is not that it is illusory but that because it is powerful it is dangerous. Since this argument could be used against *all* forms of power in the world, it proves not that religion should cease but that it should be subject to moral and intellectual critique. What is wanted is not the elimination of all power, without which life could not continue, but its transformation into beneficent forms. Religion should be judged by its contribution to that end.

The business of religions and their rituals, then, is to effect transformations, not only of persons' individual subjectivities but also transformations of society and the natural world. In a religious perspective, the personal, societal, and physical realms are not isolated from each other but participate together in a single field of divine power. The word "magic," which serves to remind us that ritual is a means of confronting power with power, is also a reminder that not all power is physical and material.

"From the viewpoint of the actor," Edmund Leach tells us,

rites can alter the state of the world because they invoke power. If the power is treated as inherent in the rite itself, the analyst calls the action magic; if the power is believed to be external to the situation—a supernatural agency—the analyst says it is religious.

Leach is well aware of the tendency to analyze religion and magic into two different things, and the dichotomy bothers him. He continues:

Current argument on this theme is highly contentious, and I must declare my own position: I hold that the rite is prior to the explanatory belief. This will be recognized as essentially the view of Robertson Smith.[210]

It was also the view of Wittgenstein, as we have seen, and the Cambridge anthropologists before him. Instead of holding the question of power at arm's length, Leach proceeds to discuss it. Of interest here is his conclusion that

. . . every act by which one individual asserts his [sic] authority to curb or alter the behavior of another individual is an invocation of metaphysical force. The submissive response is an ideological reaction, and it is no more surprising that individuals should be influenced by magical performances or religious imprecations than that they should be influenced by the commands of authority. The power of ritual is just as actual as the power of command.[211]

This is well said, reminding us that ritual and its magic cannot be understood except in relation to the socio-political world.

Perhaps we should add to Leach's comment the following: The power of ritual is not only just as actual as the power of command but also as actual as the power to *resist* command when the latter is unacceptable. Rituals of disobedience are perhaps less frequent but no less significant than those which induce conformity.

If the power of ritual to effect change is denied, causing religion to become, as Van Gennep said, metaphysics, then in that case the understanding of the world becomes the task of pure intellect, and its transformation the work of scientific technology. That is a dangerous situation because it masks two truths that are best known through the practice of ritual: first, that the agencies affecting human destiny, whether they be human or divine or aspects of nature or some combination of these, are of a personal character and should be addressed performatively; and second, that communal life without such performance becomes a mockery of itself, drained little by little of the experience of communitas and the recognition of the human as human.

Ritual, as I have indicated, refuses to recognize clear lines of demarcation between the psychological, the socio-political and the material worlds. It tends to personalize the latter and to objectify the former two, lessening the sharp distinction that scientific method likes to make between a material world of impersonal forces and a societal world of consciousness, custom, and choice. Ritual acts as if everything is alive and personal. We have already heard Wittgenstein on this:

In magical healing one *indicates* to an illness that it should leave the patient.
    After the description of any such magical cure we'd like to add: If the illness doesn't understand *that*, then I don't know *how* one ought to say it.[212]

If one speaks *to* an illness and not just about it, if one *speaks* to an illness and does not just treat it as an impersonal condition, and if one expects that this speaking, done ritually, will affect the illness, is one's magic crass? I submit that a judgment about that should rest more upon ethical and practical considerations than upon metaphysical ones. It is necessary to judge the total situation of those performing the ritual. One needs to understand the situation personally, psychologically, socially, politically, culturally. What we can say in general, I think, is that there is something healthy about ritual's assumption that human reality is essentially dramatic, that at bottom life is not something to be *treated*, as scientifically based medicine *treats* a disease, but something to be *enacted*, as in the enactment of one's own being in the world or the enactment of a cure. Although this insight can perhaps be defended metaphysically, it is beyond my present purpose to do so. The clearer case is moral: when we understand ourselves as agents active in a world made up of other purposive beings, our sense of self and responsibility is heightened. The person who performs a rain dance or goes to church to pray for rain is at least *doing* something, and probably with more self-awareness than the person who watches the TV weather report and waits with passive impotence for the sky to change. Of course, there is nothing to prevent one's doing the ritual and also watching the TV weather, but in that case the passivity is gone.

■

Like any technique or value, magic is subject to distortion; and this happens especially when magic is viewed as a technique in direct competition with more empirical methods for transforming a situation. If we are to give up the Frazerian idea that magic is bad science, while retaining the knowledge that rituals do in fact bring about certain kinds of change, we must cease looking at magic and science as two means to the same end and realize instead that they are different means to different ends. At times the ends of magic and science may overlap, but they are not identical. Compared to science, magic is more holistic in its methods and aims.

Grimes helpfully points out that "the force of magic lies in its use of desire as a contributing factor in causing hoped-for results."[213] In other words, magic takes subjectivity seriously and includes it in its view of the overall situation that is to be transformed. The inclusion of subjectivity, of "the human factor," as inherent in all aspects of any situation is part of what is meant by calling magic holistic; and it is this which most distinguishes it from scientific techniques. Science is primarily analytic and works by putting subjectivity in brackets and carefully delimiting the field of reference pertinent to any problem. By contrast magic is primarily synthetic; it works by emphasizing subjectivity and seeking to include as much as possible within the field of reference. When magic apes science by viewing its own techniques as valid without reference to subjectivity, and when it concentrates on narrow results narrowly achieved, then it is corrupted.

These considerations underscore two observations about ritual magic we have already made—its appeal to transcendent reference and its dramatizing character. Instead of narrowing its focus, as the pursuit of scientific techniques tends to do, magic broadens its view, always aware that the problem and situation of immediate concern is transcended by relevant factors that are likely to be hidden from view and probably lie on another plane of reality. In Haiti the *mambo* Melanie said to me, "If a disease has physical origins, then it can be cured by scientific methods; but if its causes are spiritual, then the *services vodou* are required." Such a view of the relation between science and magic, which one may encounter in many parts of the world, implies that the spiritual realm includes, yet surpasses, the physical. To put the point more clearly, the spiritual is the very act of transcending, while not excluding, the mundane.

Spirit is life. To call it transcendence is to speak abstractly. The same point is made more concretely by saying that spirit is personal. To view the world spiritually is to view it as full of personal agency, and this is precisely what ritual does: It takes reality as something to be enacted, a point we may also state the other way around by saying that ritual takes enactment as reality. The persons who perform a ritual are inserting their own present actions, their own subjectivity and interactions with others, into a holistic understanding of the world. They aim at a transformation of the world, or some part of it, through the *work* that they do; not as detached manipulators of objectified things that behave according to invariant rules, but as free agents actively impinging upon other free agents in a spirited world. Ritual is the arena in which such action and interaction takes place. Hence in ritual, as in magic, the most distinctive feature is *not* the repetitive pattern but the performance of direct address to the powers being confronted or invoked.

Magical transformation, then, is not simply a transformation of subjectivity, leaving the external world unchanged except perhaps in appearance. Neither is it a transformation of the external world only, leaving subjectivity out of account and untransformed. Rather, it is transformation of a total situation by means of an enactment undertaken with strong subjective desire and producing an effect upon a number of subjects and objects together. It is, in short, a reordering of a totality. Let us take two examples: (1) a magical cure in Korea, and (2) exorcising apartheid in South Africa.

1. A Magical Cure

In Seoul, Korea, in 1983, I attended a *kut*, a ritual that employs song, dance, trance, and spirit possession. This one was led by a shamaness, known in Korea as a *mudang*, with several assistants. It took place in a medium-sized room in a large house where several similar services were going on simultaneously in other rooms. Attending were some fifteen or twenty persons, including the family who had requested the service. The father was going blind and needed a cure. He had received treatment in several hospitals and clinics, but his eyes continued to worsen, and so the *kut* had been arranged. At the request of my Korean host, David Suh, the *mudang* gave me permission to observe.

Except for a low altar at one end, laden mostly with food set out in colorful display, the room had no furniture. Three female drummers, one of them the *mudang* herself, sat on the floor along one wall near the altar. There was a male assistant who did little drumming, much more dancing and singing. The family sat along the wall opposite the drummers but not as near the altar. We observers, who included several apprentice *mudangs*, sat at the end of the room facing the altar. Not a lot of floor space was left over. Our arrangement resembled that of a quite intimate theater without chairs. Staring at me from among the food platters on the altar was a roasted pig's head.

I wondered how anything likely to go on in this room could cure blindness. Now that it's over, I am not sure that it did. At least no such cure was evident during the three hours I was present, and I did not learn what happened to the man's eyesight later. Nevertheless, the following things did happen.

The room became filled with a prodigious energy, emanating mostly from the *mudang*, her musicians, and their drums. There was, most of the time, a pounding, ebullient rhythm causing everyone's pulse to rise and leading to a keen level of anticipation. The *mudang* and her assistants danced vigorously. Some went into trance. At various times they became possessed by spirits, the two who impressed me most being the "petty official," with his felt hat, rapid-fire speech, and constant demands for money; and the "birth grandmother," with her huge fan, broad-brimmed straw hat, and flowing white robe.

The money that the "petty official" dunned out of the supplicating family and stuffed into his pockets, sleeves, collar, ears, and hat, as well as into the mouth of the pig's head, was, I learned, an amount that had been agreed upon ahead of time, a point which an uninformed observer would never have guessed, what with the "petty official" becoming ever more demanding in voice and gesture, the very picture of a small-time extortionist, and the family looking frantic and digging into pockets, purses, shopping bags, and bosoms in an apparently desperate effort to come up with ever more cash. The passing of money had been turned into a game. It is most likely that a bit more money was asked than had been agreed to, and equally likely that the family anticipated that. This serious play with money—serious because the money changed hands "for keeps," playful because of the conspiratorial and almost mocking style in which it was performed—increased the energy-pulse in the room.

Spirit possession, in my view, has also to be regarded as a kind of serious game. By that statement I definitely do not imply that there is nothing to it more than conscious role-playing. On the contrary, in many instances of spirit possession (some people would say in all) the possessed person loses consciousness throughout the trance and later has no recall of what occurred. I am as ready as any person to give this a theological, or if you please a mystical, interpretation. I take visiting spirits with much seriousness, whether they show up in a Korean *kut* or in a Christian service of worship. However, the seriousness and the truthfulness of spirit possession does not mean that it involves no role-playing, as is made obvious by the fact that costumes and props are made ready ahead of time, prepared for a panoply of spirits that is just as recognizable as the dramatis personae of any familiar script.

Is it sacrilege to use these theatrical terms? I think not, especially if we are willing to use them to speak respectfully of *our own* religion and its most hallowed traditions. Liturgical vestments are costumes; and bread, wine, baptismal water, pulpit, and Bible are props for Christian worship, in just the same sense as props are used in the theater: They are the materials that need to be made ready for the anticipated action. In themselves they are not much. In the final analysis, it is the action, not the dress, that counts.

In spirit possession, "playing for keeps" is escalated to a very high level, as I could tell by watching not only the tone of the possessed performers at the *kut* but also the faces and demeanor of the family who needed help. They got it.

Thanks to David Suh's translation, I was able to follow what went on in the numerous exchanges between the visiting spirits and the family. Each member of the family was addressed, not just the father. They were told that hard times lay ahead. They were not to give up hope. Financial burdens would increase. The father would need much care. Everyone needed to see things they had not seen before, otherwise the family would find itself on the rocks. When the father regained his sight, everyone would have to readjust. And if he did not, who could tell what lay ahead? The family's roots were emphasized and interpreted as part of the historic roots of the nation. Each of the visiting spirits had died unjustly and carried, like the Korean nation itself, long victimized by its imperial neighbors, a spirit of *han*, a term that means both pride and resentment.

Courage and wisdom, I realized, were the ointment being applied to the father's eyes, and the "cure" was being given not to him only but to all his family network, and even to the rest of us present who cared about Korea.

The situation addressed was total. The father's particular affliction had been taken up into an entire cosmos of affliction. Everyone was being reoriented, renewed. Relationships were being transformed. You could see and feel it occur then and there, no matter how long or short it would subsequently endure.

Is this magic? I call it so, and think I do not misuse the word. If the transformation that occurred was not the one that had been anticipated by the family, it was nevertheless real and included a transformation of expectation. That there be a transformation is one half the definition of magic. The other half is that the technique for achieving it is ritual. I departed that room rather amazed, remembering the tag-lines with which Euripides often ended his plays:

> The gods bring many things
> to their accomplishment.
> And what was most expected
> has not been accomplished.
> But god has found a way
> for what no one expected.[214]

"But surely," someone will object, "this way of defining magic is equivocal." How shall we answer such a sober-minded critic? Magic's power rests upon the power of equivocation, through which not only blind eyes but also meanings and signifiers are transformed in a twinkling. If we cannot equivocate in speaking of magic, we cannot speak of it at all. It collapses into "bad science" or "falsehood" and is gone. Meanwhile, however, the ritualizing of the world and its sufferings continues, and because of it the world and its history come to be what they were not.

Consider a different example.

2. Exorcising Apartheid from South Africa

In 1987 two United States citizens, Walter Wink, the author of *Violence and Nonviolence in South Africa: Jesus' Third Way*,[215] and Richard Deats of the Fellowship of Reconciliation, were invited to South Africa to do workshops on nonviolent direct action. Because he had spoken against apartheid on a previous trip in 1986, Wink's visa application was denied outright. Deats's was granted after a long delay. The sponsors decided to hold a single large workshop in Lesotho, where Wink could legally go, inviting people from all over Southern Africa. This took place in May 1988. My account of the event is based on information given me directly by Walter Wink.

The workshop participants, thirty-eight in all, of whom about a third were black, were native to South Africa, Lesotho, Botswana, Swaziland, and Mozambique. They included a number of prominent religious leaders of South Africa, among them Sheena Duncan, president of Black Sash and vice president of the South Africa Council of Churches (SACC); Joe Seremane, acting justice and reconciliation secretary of the SACC; Sid Luckett, director of the justice division for the Cape Town diocese of the Anglican church; Emma Mashinini of SACC, subsequently elected to the steering committee of the Emergency

Convocation of Churches; Richard Steele and Anita Kromberg, South African staff persons of the International Fellowship of Reconciliation, cosponsors of the event; the staff of the Transformation Resource Centre in Lesotho, cosponsors; Peter Kerchhoff, organizer of the Pieter-maritzburg Agency for Christian Social Awareness; Rob Robertson, a leading spokesperson for nonviolence; three Quakers; four radicalized Afrikaners; and a contemplative Anglican nun. All the black participants had experience of detention and torture for their opposition to apartheid.

The workshop was held in a nondescript room about forty feet square in a Catholic seminary and retreat center in Roma. Chairs were set in a circle in one half of the room, which was furnished with a coal stove. The sponsors had covered the walls of the otherwise barren room with banners and political posters opposing apartheid. For the first worship service, someone had made a large wooden cross about eight feet high and four feet wide, and during the service participants were asked to affix their names to it. With this act, we may speak of ritual and the ambiguity of performance.

The reader may guess, as indeed the participants could only guess, at the symbolism of affixing one's name, along with others', to a large wooden cross during a Christian worship service improvised for a workshop concerning resistance to apartheid. I do not mean that the symbolism was secret, only that it was richly polyvalent and was not verbalized at the time.

What the North American reader might not guess is that the act was risky. Although Lesotho is purportedly an independent country, in fact it is completely under the control of South Africa. As Wink reported to me, "We fully expected the security police at any time." The name-bearing cross would have provided the police with a ready-made roster of those apprehended in a raid. Hence the act of placing one's name upon a cross during a service of worship—in itself a performance in the *ritual mode,* combining doing and showing—took on in this context the additional implications of performance in the *confessional* and *ethical* modes.

The act signified: "I am a person who is willing to suffer in the struggle against apartheid." And this declaration entailed also a transformation, even in the case of those who had *already* endured such suffering, for it amounted to a rededication of the self, a renewal of commitment, a reenactment of devotion, and hence a *movement* (passage) of the self from an old stage to a new one. This is transformation effected in the confessional as well as the ritual mode.

The act further signified: "Not only am I willing in principle to suffer and risk for the sake of opposing apartheid, but I do put myself at risk here and now, by giving up the possibility of remaining anonymous on this occasion." Because the risk was actual (not only symbolic) and because it was undertaken for the sake of greater social justice, the act was transformational in the ethical mode of performance, too, in addition to the ritual and confessional modes. People often ask whether rituals "work." In cases like this one, we know that the ritual works from the simple fact that it has inescapable consequences. The risk that is here ritualized is real risk. In this sense, rites of passage always "work," since their enactment places their participants in a new social situation.

At the second worship service in the Lesotho workshop, the large cross was laid on the floor and the participants stood lighted candles upon it. Wink has not provided me with enough comment on this service to enable any analysis, but it is clear that the wooden cross was taking on additional layers of meaning through repeated usage. Meanwhile, the workshop sessions employed Bible study, some improvisational enactments of biblical stories, and reflections upon violence and nonviolence in South Africa today. The theme was the opposition that Christians faithful to God and Christ are required to make against the "principalities and powers" that are responsible for social injustice and oppression:

For we are not contending against flesh and blood, but against the principalities, against the powers, against the world rulers of this present darkness, against the spiritual hosts of wickedness in the heavenly places. (Ephesians 6:12)

. . . to make all [people] see what is the plan of the mystery hidden for ages in God who created all things; that through the church the manifold wisdom of God might now be made known to the principalities and powers in the heavenly places. (Ephesians 3:9–10)

He disarmed the principalities and powers and made a public example of them. . . . If with Christ you died to the elemental spirits of the universe, why do you live as if you still belonged to the world? Why do you submit to regulations . . .? (Colossians 2:15, 20)

The workshop ended with a third service of worship. Wink asked each participant to write down on a piece of construction paper the name of the particular power that had him or her most in its thrall. Naming is always performative and is among the most obvious and consequential of the workings of ritual. Wink's aim was to provide occasion for persons to become conscious of the powers that prevent, or try to prevent, their being faithful to the Kingdom of God in their own

Southern African context. As he expected, people wrote phrases like "Fear of Death," "Fear of Torture," "Separation from Family," and "Fear of Detention." Holding these insignia aloft, the people now formed a procession, at the head of which was the great cross with their names attached. The procession circled the room and sang:

> Thine be the glory,
> Risen, conquering Son!
> Endless is the victory
> Thou o'er death hast won.

The tune was from Handel's *Judas Maccabeus*, familiar wherever this hymn is sung. When the procession and the hymn ended, the cross with its names attached was placed against a wall. Participants carried the signs bearing the names of the powers they feared to the coal stove. They burned them. Someone said a prayer, and the event was over.

If we speak of such a ritual as accomplishing transformation, we are not entitled to say that its direct result has been the tumbling of the Jericho-walls of apartheid in South Africa, for they are still standing. Perhaps they are weakening. What we can say is that certain transformations, as mentioned above, took place *during* the ritual, that these now become part of the history of the struggle for black liberation in Southern Africa, and that the rituals themselves are part of the movement for freedom that is now going on. We can say one thing more: If no people in South Africa were willing to undertake rituals of transformation in which they anticipate the liberation for which they long, then that freedom would never come. Ritual is, at the least, the preparation of groups of people for the spiritual work they must do; and the struggle for liberation is a spiritual work—that is, a work of moral courage—however physical and violent or nonviolent it may be.

Rob Robertson had persuaded Wink to try to enter South Africa illegally after the workshop ended. He thought it could be done at a certain border crossing and was worth the try. In a letter to friends written on June 16, 1988, Wink described how it happened:

Sister Camilla, a contemplative nun in our group, arose at 2 A.M. to begin praying that we would get in. Others in the States were also focusing their prayers on that day. As we came in sight of the border we stopped and prayed that, as God had opened the prison doors and let Peter and Paul and Silas out, God would let us in! Then in a pouring rain, we drove up to the border post, jumped out, and ran under the shelter of the porch, where the senior soldier in charge was whistling—"Thine be the glory, risen, conquering Son . . ." The rain-darkened room was so dim that I virtually had to read my passport to the other soldier; he never even looked for a visa.

Synchronicity, to be sure—only, it is rather awkward to give praise and thanksgiving to synchronicity.

In *Unmasking the Powers*, Wink has spoken of the historic 1965 civil rights march from Selma, Alabama, to the state capital at Montgomery as an "exorcism." His words are pertinent:

Waving holy water and a crucifix over Buchenwald would scarcely have stopped the Nazi genocide of Jews, but think about it—what if the church in Germany *had* staged ritual acts of protest outside those gates? What if, in churches all over the land, pastors had read from their pulpits prayers exorcising the spirit of Satan and Wotan from the national psyche? It could not have happened, of course, because the prior understanding of collective possession and the church's task in unmasking the Powers was not in place. . . .

The march across the Selma bridge by black civil rights advocates was an act of exorcism. It exposed the demon of racism, stripping away the screen of legality and custom for the entire world to see. . . .

Exorcism drives the devils first to reveal their names and then casts them out. Most do not come out without a struggle. When Phil and Dan Berrigan poured blood on the files of the Selective Service System, they were attempting to expose the demon of American messianic imperialism in Vietnam. They paid for it with stiff prison sentences.[216]

Actions such as these fit the definition of ritual that Bobby Alexander has proposed (see Appendix B): "planned or improvised performance that effects a transition from everyday life to an alternative framework within which the everyday is transformed."[217] The everyday in Nazi Germany was the state's program of mass murder. In Alabama in 1965, the everyday was racial segregation. In South Africa in 1987, it was the apparently insuperable force of government by apartheid. The Selma march and the cross-bearing procession in Lesotho were the deliberate enactment of something different. They were magical acts. The word "magic" is not invoked here because of such things as the synchronicity that occurred for Walter Wink at the border crossing but rather because the Lesotho workshop and the Selma demonstration employed ritual as a technique in a holistic process of transformation. Without such ritualization, the Civil Rights Movement in the United States could not have occurred, nor can any other liberation movement in the world. It was the genius of Martin Luther King, Jr., inspired by Mahatma Gandhi, Jesus, and others, to recognize this. At certain stages of their struggle, ritual magic is the principal technique available to oppressed peoples for the transformation of their historical situation. As one veteran of the Civil Rights Movement has said:

. . . I came of age in the civil rights movement, in those demonstrations—in Mississippi, North Carolina, some parts of Alabama. We had white policemen coming at us and we had our spirituals, our songs. That's all we had.[218]

Rational political methods alone cannot bring about transformation of society from a less to a more just condition, because they cannot fuse the visionary with the actual (the absent with the present) as rituals do, thus profoundly affecting the moral life. Nor can ideas alone do this, for in order to bear fruit ideas require flesh-and-blood performance. Ritualization is required, as when the names are placed on the cross for the police to see if and when they come, or the marchers move across the Selma bridge, or (earlier) the freedom-loving people of Montgomery got off the segregated busses and walked in the open streets. They walked to get to their jobs, of course; but the magic is that they walked to get ever so much further than that. Dignity was their destination, and dignity is what they gave themselves by performing it, in public, in the dusty street, where the doing and the showing were one and the same.

■

The ability of rituals to assist in the transformation of society, which I have called part of their magic, is not magic in a fantastical sense. This is a point I want now to pursue by emphasizing that rituals not only can change, or help to change, a situation but that they themselves are subject to change in the course of time. In other words, rituals belong to human history. Ritual process belongs to historical process. It is not some kind of detached thing remote from the events that it influences. Agents of transformation, rituals are themselves transformed by the histories to which they belong.

This thought no doubt seems obvious to persons in the social sciences, but it can encounter resistance in some religious communities and some theologies. Even where it gains intellectual assent, there may be much resistance to change in a group's practice, especially if ritual is prized so highly for its ordering function that its ability to transform and to be transformed is feared.

Many people in fact think of a ritual as something that follows a set script and is always performed more or less the same way. However well sanctioned by usage such a meaning of ritual may be, it is very misleading, for it runs the risk of identifying ritual either with purely formal repetition or (what is similar) with a corrupted sense of magic.

I have argued that magic is corrupted by attempting to leave subjectivity out of account. By the same token, rituals are corrupted by trying to objectify them in such a way as to protect them from change. Instead of their being taken as part of the holistic situations they would transform, rituals are treated as impersonal objects. An effort is made to remove them from ongoing history, preserving as sacrosanct some form they have already assumed. The result is what theologians call *ritualism*. Its aim in some instances is to effect change in everything except the liturgical tradition, in others to ward off every kind of change whatever. In either case, such opposition to change amounts to corrupted magic, since it falls short of viewing transformation in a holistic way.

Rituals are in fact not changeless, and the attempt to make them so violates their nature. Instruments of transformation, they are themselves transformed by the processes of which they are a part: "To perform a ritual the same way twice is to kill it," said Stanley Walens, "for the ritual grows as we grow, its life recapitulates the course of ours."[219]

The changing of rituals under changed social conditions is so obvious that it would require no emphasis if it were not frequently denied. One example of such change was documented by Monica Wilson in "The Wedding Cakes: A Study of Ritual Change," which reports the influence of European wedding practices on nuptial ceremonies among the Nguni people in Pondoland and the Ciskei in Africa. Weddings, of course, are rites of passage in which the status of two persons, and the community's expectations concerning them, are transformed; but the rites themselves undergo change as they are employed in shifting circumstances. Wilson concentrated upon alterations in patterns of display in Nguni weddings that followed upon the arrival of missionaries and other Europeans prominent in the colonial system. Before long, she recounts, "the clothes worn and the parade of bride and groom [became] a copy so far as resources permitted of white patterns of display."[220] A European-style wedding cake was introduced, taking its place in the ceremony along with the type of cake that was already traditional. Changes like this did not amount simply to personal preferences:

The style taken over by the converts tended to become the norm, and the black fringed shawl and kerchief survived a century longer among Nguni women than they did among the whites with whom they originated.[221]

Wilson generalizes that

within a short space of time *new* forms are accepted as "traditional" in ritual. Some of the details of the contemporary marriage ritual . . . derive from traditional Nguni patterns, others from Europe, and others (such as *two* cakes) are brand new, but they are spoken of as *customary* among Christians, with an implication of antiquity.[222]

Wilson's is an example of ritual adaptation. In her description, it seems to include little or no critique of the social situation. There are times, however, when changes in familiar rituals are made deliberately to encourage social protest, and I choose an example from an unlikely source: the Anglican Book of Common Prayer. To find the example I have in mind, we must turn to the edition published in Philadelphia, the birthplace of American independence from Britain, by the Protestant Episcopal Church in 1789. The Preface to this edition declares:

It is a most invaluable part of that blessed "liberty wherewith Christ has made us free," that in his worship different forms and usages may without offense be allowed, provided the substance of the Faith be kept entire; and that, in every Church, what cannot be clearly determined to belong to Doctrine must be referred to Discipline; and therefore, by common consent and authority, may be altered, abridged, enlarged, amended, or otherwise disposed of, as may seem most convenient for the edification of the people, "according to the various exigency [sic] of times and occasions."

The authors of this passage were surely wrong to think that liturgy and doctrine can be so clearly separated one from the other, as if doctrine can remain immutable while forms of worship are altered; but they were right to recognize, as had their forerunners in the Church of England, that ritual does and must respond to "the various exigency of times and occasions." The preface continues with a quotation from the Prayer Book as published by the mother church:

The particular Forms of Divine Worship, and the Rites and Ceremonies appointed to be used therein, being things in their own nature indifferent, and alterable, and so acknowledged; it is but reasonable that upon weighty and important considerations, according to the various exigency of times and occasions, such changes and alterations should be made therein, as to those that are in place of Authority should, from time to time, seem either necessary or expedient.

The American liturgical changes, like some that had preceded them in the Church of England, especially at the time of the English church's separation from Rome, were made in deliberate response to a changed political scene. Far from being simply adaptive, however, the American changes represented a conscious desire for the rituals to contribute to the new nation's experiment in democracy independent of the British crown.

In addition to their adaptation and responsiveness to particular occasions of social change, rituals are also transformed by processes less conscious and rational but no less consequential in the long run. This seems to be what Stanley Walens had in mind when he said that a "ritual grows as we grow." He might have added that *we* grow as our *rituals* grow. Thomas Peterson writes that the

meaning of ritual is never fixed and is always shifting because its meaning comes from its use. There can never be exactly the same meaning for any ritual act, because, while the form might be held constant, the context which is inseparable from the form will always vary.[223]

Theodore Jennings has pointed out that one reason rituals change is that they not only transmit ancient knowledge but also assist the discovery of new knowledge. He identifies three "moments" or types of knowledge provided by ritual, one of which, the most relevant here, is often overlooked. Calling this "the aspect of 'discovery' or 'inquiry' characteristic of ritual action," he writes:

If we concentrate our attention upon ritual as an entirely fixed and unvarying sequence of actions, we are likely to overlook this aspect of ritual knowledge altogether. But such a "synchronic" approach to ritual is misleading when it is taken as the sole mode of gaining an understanding of ritual action. The problem might best be illustrated if we sought to compare the enactment of the Latin rite Mass in Western Africa, Central Mexico, a suburb of Chicago, and St. Peter's in Rome. Even if all are "performed" in Latin (the situation prior to Vatican II) the trained observer would notice significant variation which it would be at least premature to dismiss as incidental. Even if we attend to repeated performance of the same ritual in the same cultural setting over a period of time we would also notice differences in detail which eventually become very important. Even the liturgies of Eastern Orthodox churches with their strong emphasis on historical continuity and tradition have a history characterized both by development (amplification, elaboration) and by discarded alternatives. . . . A diachronic perspective on ritual, together with a cross-cultural comparison of putatively identical rituals, brings to light considerable variation which cannot be accounted for in the view of ritual as sheer repetition.[224]

Jennings argues that the changes rituals undergo are neither accidental nor incidental. As he says,

variation in ritual performance is by no means the incidental and extraneous phenomenon it has often been thought to be by those who define ritual action in terms of unvarying repetition. Instead, the variation in ritual performance may be understood as a decisive clue to the character of the ritual action as a relatively autonomous form of noetic exploration and discovery.[225]

We learn by doing. This includes the doing of ritual. What we learn by doing ritual is not only the ritual and how it has been performed before. We discover how to do it *next* time. We discover something of the world the ritual belongs to and aims to transform. "Ritual knowledge," Jennings holds, "is gained by and through the body . . . not by detached observation or contemplation but through action."[226]

One has to think here of the kinds of knowing that come to persons through physical activity rather than through the interpretation of words and icons. Jennings uses dancing as an example, and we might also think of athletics, carpentry, weaving, or lovemaking. On the radio, Davie Johnson, manager of the New York Mets, speaks of things that a pitcher can know only through "muscle memory," and Jennings speaks of learning how to use a chalice by handling it, just as the axe he himself had used elsewhere to chop firewood taught his hands, arms, and shoulders how it needed to be swung.

With such doing-knowledge in mind, Jennings goes on to observe that

> Ritual knowledge is gained through the alteration of that which is to be known. Even if we reduce the field of the object of ritual knowledge to the ritual itself—that is, claim that that which I seek to know is the ritual or the ritual action itself—even then we must say that the exploratory "doing" is a doing which alters the ritual complex or its constituent parts in some way. . . . Ritual knowledge is gained not through detachment but through engagement—an engagement which does not leave things as they are but which alters and transforms them. . . . ritual knowledge is not "descriptive" but is prescriptive and/or ascriptive in character. . . . Marx's formula that it is important not so much to understand the world as to change it is one which also neatly summarizes this aspect of ritual action.[227]

Jennings offers no specific evidence for his claim that ritual knowledge alters what it comes to know, but in my view the claim is defensible for the reason that Jennings assumes: Ritual is neither a detached contemplation of the world nor a passive symbolization of it but is the performance of an act in which people confront one kind of power with another, and rehearse their own future. At the least, as Jennings points out, this will result in the ritual itself being transformed over time; but the implication is that the world of which the ritual is a part will also be changed.

■

The transformative action of rituals is coming more and more to prominence in recent analyses, stimulated most perhaps by the thinking of Victor Turner and Richard Schechner, his sometime collaborator. The index of a recently published symposium edited by Schechner with Willa Appel lists thirty-one places in the volume where transformation is discussed. Colin Turnbull, for example, says that transition and transformation are "two basic elements of any ritual" and that "the latter is essential to our full understanding of liminality."[228] Schechner speaks of "the deconstruction/reconstruction process that performers use to effect transformations of self,"[229] and Turner, especially in his earlier writings, was interested in a dialectic between ritual and social structure which contributed to the dynamic of socio-historical change.

Although some of Turner's thoughts about this subject invite criticism of the kind that the interested reader may find in Appendix B of this book, Turner's contribution to the understanding of ritual process is immense. The concept of liminality, which he broadened and deepened beyond its origin in Van Gennep, and which I have discussed in the previous chapter, has become indispensable.

Turner showed that "ritual is not necessarily a bastion of social conservatism; its symbols do not merely condense cherished sociocultural values. Rather, through its liminal processes, it holds the generating source of culture and structure."[230] He argued cogently that "liminality is the mother of invention."[231]

The idea, however, is not simply that ritual is a cornucopia of inventiveness or a factory of fantasies. Rather, this inventiveness is related dialectically to the powers and structures of society as they exist at the time of the ritual performance. This means that ritual stands in contradiction to society, while at the same time being a part of it. We might say that ritual embodies the principle of growth or dynamic process through which a society transcends itself, praising, evaluating, rebuking, and remolding life as it is presently lived. As Turner puts it, "performance is often a critique, direct or veiled, of the social life it grows out of, an evaluation (with lively possibilities of rejection) of the way society handles history."[232] It follows that

cultural performances are not simple reflectors or expressions of culture or even of changing culture but may themselves be active agencies of change, representing the eye by which culture sees itself and the drawing board on which creative actors sketch out what they believe to be more apt or interesting "designs for living."[233]

Turner is certainly not the only scholar to entertain a view of ritual as innovative and transformative. Here, for example, is Erik Erikson:

. . . it should be noted that there can be no prescription for either ritualization or ritual, for, far from being merely repetitive or familiar in the sense of habituation, any true ritualization, while ontogenetically grounded, is yet pervaded with the spontaneity of surprise: it is an unexpected renewal of a recognizable order in potential chaos. Ritualization thus depends on that blending of surprise and recognition which is the soul of creative interplay, reborn out of instinctual chaos, confusion of identity, and social anomie.[234]

Roland Delattre has correctly insisted that ritual action, whatever else it may be, is always political action:

For in ritual action we not only seek to articulate the state of affairs as we experience it, we also exercise in ritual action our creative capacities to re-order that state of affairs. Rituals may celebrate and confirm the rhythms and shape of an established version of humanity and reality, but they may also celebrate and render articulate the shape and rhythms of a new emergent version.[235]

The "social magic" of rituals, their character as "transformative performance" (Turner) or simply "transformance" (Schechner),[236] is only partly the result of their power to envision a reordering of the world. It comes also from their power to expose society's injustices and contradictions. Turner speaks of ritual as "a *transformative* performance revealing major classifications, categories, and contradictions of cultural processes."[237] He rightly assumes that such revelations are themselves transformative, and further supposes, again rightly, that revelation through *performance* is particularly potent. The liminality of ritual is the power of transcendence, of no-saying, of expressing what society and culture deny, of unmasking pretension, of elevating persons and things of "low degree," of "putting down the mighty from their seats" (Luke 1: 52–53). It is the power Shakespeare called imaginative, to "give to aery nothing a local habitation and a name."[238]

While it is the business of literature to give names (the right descriptive words), that of ritual is to give "local habitation." Performance makes present. Because it is performance and not verbal description or exhortation, ritual brings the far-away, the long-ago, and the not-yet into the here-and-now. Because it is performance, ritual produces its effects not simply in the minds but also in the bodies of its performers. When it is imbued with the spirit of liberty, ritual becomes part of the work through which a body politic (a people) throws off its chains. But it is not always so imbued, and the transformations it brings about are not always liberating.

■

We have already noticed that ritual, employed as a means for the transformation of society is a kind of "social magic." It is important to remember that the morality of magic is determined by its practitioners. Nothing in the nature of ritual per se insures that the social transformations achieved by it will necessarily be good ones, for this depends upon the aim and will of the performers.

The insight of most religions is that the performers in sacred rite are not limited to the human ones. Rituals invoke the participation of spirits, animals, deceased ancestors, or gods, not simply as *objects* of ritual attention but as performers in their own right. For them also, the ritual is a technique of communication and transformation, and they seek to use it for purposes in line with their own natures.

As we have said earlier, the ritual world is a *personal* one, not the impersonal realm postulated by science. It is a world in which personal agents direct their interactive performances toward the reordering of social relationships. This is a moral project through and through, in the sense that it is never morally neutral but always aimed at something desired. Ritual is the work of beings who are characterized by their capacity to *perform* and hence to fabricate a social world that is not simply given to them but is compounded of desires and actions that are subject to moral evaluation.

Since the transformative potential of rituals is very high and not always directed toward ethically justifiable ends, it is fearsome. The totalitarian uses of ritual in our own time (and before) have shown that it holds the power to transform people not only into creatures of freedom but also into destructive armies and mass murderers. If the latter is not to be our own fate, we must learn to employ rituals as part of a more beneficent magic aimed at the transformation of society toward ever greater justice, peace, and freedom. We must see to the redemption of our rituals. Doing so in the context of Christian praxis will be the subject of our concluding chapter.

Conclusion

10

Christian Sacraments as the Performance of Freedom

Bless Thou the truth, Dear Lord,
Now unto me,
As Thou didst bless the bread
By Galilee;
Then shall all bondage cease,
All fetters fall;
And we shall find our peace,
Our All in All.[239]

And befo' I'd be a slave,
I'll be bound and in my grave. . . .
Oh, freedom!
Oh, freedom over me![240]

Jesus . . . is the eternal event of liberation in the divine person who
makes freedom a constituent of human existence.

—JAMES CONE[241]

That something is wrong with the sacramental life of most churches is a thought so widespread it scarcely needs arguing. In the introductory chapter of this book, I confessed to repeated churchly experiences of ritual boredom, knowing that many other persons have felt the same. In this final chapter, I wish to reflect upon performance of the sacrament known as Holy Communion or Eucharist, considering the way it is often performed and suggesting how it might be done if it were taken more seriously, yet also more playfully, as the enactment of a God-inspired freedom.

I shall begin by commenting upon a specific service of worship that I chanced to attend a few days before writing this chapter, following this with reflection upon two recent interpreters of sacraments—the anthropologist Victor Turner and the liberation theologian Juan Segundo. Noticing conflicting ideas about the sacraments in these two Roman Catholics, whose thought is as relevant to Protestant as to Catholic practice, I find Turner, to whom I am otherwise much indebted, to be off the mark. The last part of the chapter will focus upon the ritual performance of freedom, imagining how a revitalized sacrament of Holy Communion might be performed.

■

At the seminary in which I teach, it is the custom to celebrate communion during a half-hour service on Thursdays at noon. Because we are an interdenominational school, the leadership and the form of the services varies from week to week. I select the service on this particular Thursday as my example because in certain ways it was typical of Protestantism, while in others it was better than average.

The chairs in the Gothic-style chapel on this day were arranged in arcing rows facing a pulpit, which was placed beside a large, semipermanent rough-hewn cross some ten feet in height. A few feet away, on the other side of the pulpit, a table held the communion elements, covered with several small cloths. The organ prelude, full of life, was an "Antiphon" by jazz composer Calvin Hampton. After a call to worship, the congregation sang, "When I Survey the Wondrous Cross." Drawing upon his African-American Baptist heritage, the presiding minister interrupted the hymn a couple of times to stir the congregation into a full-throated, fervent singing, which was vigorously accompanied by both organ and piano. Spirits rose. Then we sat, and the minister, following the script (program) we all had in our hands, said, "Let us confess our sin unto God." Spirits sank.

"What sin?" I asked *sotto voce*, beginning to search myself and feeling a vague sense of guilt for not having brought along a sin to confess, like being empty-handed when faced with a collection plate. So, instead of making an *act* of confession, which would have required a fuller intentionality on my part, I recited a formula about "our" sin and God's forgiveness. An argument in favor of this can be made: It brings the idea of the forgiveness of sin to consciousness; it plants words about it in memory, for recollection when needed; it rehearses an act that is sure to become appropriate at another time, perhaps before the present service of worship ends. And yet the timing of this act, or pseudo-act, seems wrong, seems to arise more from a theological a priori (we are first of all sinners and must confess it before we can hear the Word of God) than from specific awareness of our situation.

Over the years, I have formed an objection to being asked to confess sin near the start of a worship service. The practice reflects a theology not mine, for it presupposes that the relation between God and person is based upon the person's sinfulness. The congregation gathers, invokes God's presence, and immediately says, "We're sorry." Although this sequence is time-honored, especially in the Reformed tradition, it is not conducive to what the Westminster Shorter Catechism in 1648 beautifully said was humanity's chief end, to glorify and enjoy God forever.[242]

After the short litany of confession came scripture lesson and homily. The latter was, to my ears, adequate as these things go but not very stimulating. Like the prayer of confession, it stated its theme in rather general terms and left it there, concluding with a segué into the communion prayer. This prayer was rather long, covering almost two full pages in the program, most of it spoken by the minister. It rehearsed the mighty acts of God that are of a liberating character: "You delivered us from captivity . . . Blessed is your Son Jesus Christ. Your Spirit anointed him to preach good news to the poor, to proclaim release to the captives, . . . to set at liberty those who are oppressed, and to announce that the time had come when you would save your people. . . . By the baptism of his suffering, death, and resurrection you . . . delivered us from slavery to sin and death. . . . When he ascended, Jesus promised to be with us always, in the power of your Word and Holy Spirit." The prayer continued by reciting the words of institution that refer to the bread and wine which Jesus gave his disciples at the Last Supper: "This is my body . . . This is my blood. . . ." Toward the end, the prayer implored that the gifts of bread and wine "be for us the body and blood of Christ, that we may be for the world the body of Christ, redeemed by Christ's blood."

It was a majestic prayer, announcing in clear tones the heart of the Christian gospel as a promised freedom from oppression, imprisonment, sin, and death. However, I thought to myself, it is all words. We are hearing about these things, but we are not seeing them, nor touching nor feeling them. The prayer is mostly a narrative recalling what the Bible says God did some time ago. It is on the mythic or storybook plane. It is not, in any specific way, addressing what is here and now, this Thursday in September in the year 1990. It goes as far as to ask for transformation—"Pour out your Holy Spirit on us gathered here, and on these gifts of bread and wine"—but it does not linger over this. It does not wait for this to happen. Rather, it takes the petition for granted, uttering it as a formula usually said in the ritual. (How much of Christian Eucharist has become formulaic? How much of people's attention to it has come to rest on the expectation that it *will* be the saying of routine things and thus not magical in the sense I have given to this term but simply mysterious?) Of course, I do not know what is being thought and felt by all the individuals in the room at this moment, but I can certainly sense what is public. I can take in the *corporate* tone, and I see that it is pro forma. The reason is not, I think, that the minister lacks conviction or leadership. It is that the ritual itself, as here conceived, rests content within its own form. It is *about* transformation and liberation, but it has no intention or method for them to take place now. Jesus might have been a wonder worker, but we are sheep.

The program instructed the congregation to receive bread and wine (or grape juice) passed to them in their seats and to wait until all were served so that all might "commune together." Servers passed the elements to us, while soft organ music played. It was at this point that I noticed, as so often I do, that Christian communion services have become funereal. The music would not have waked a baby, let alone rouse the dead from slumber. I suppose that for some this communion hush suggests mystery, but for me and many others it covers a vacuum. What must strike an observer of this scene is how utterly individualistic it has become. Although we were invited to "commune together," we became at this time nothing more than rows of isolated atoms, mostly avoiding any recognition of one another. I looked about and saw a few people, eyes closed, withdrawn into prayer or contemplation, while most looked at the ceiling or floor in a kind of embarrassed waiting. I glimpsed the profile of one of my colleagues, an ordinarily genial person of whom I am quite fond, looking as if he had been called up before a judge whom he was afraid to look in the eye.

At the minister's cue, we ate our tiny squares of bread and swallowed our little shots of wine or juice. We joined in reading a final prayer—"Grant that we may go into the world in the strength of your Spirit, to give ourselves for others ..."

Then we started to sing "How Firm a Foundation." Much to my surprise, at this point the ritual reached its climax.

The same minister had been conducting the noontime services every day since Monday, a series that ended with this communion service. Each day he had concluded the service with this same hymn, and each day the singing of it had become more free, less dutiful, more playful, and also more fervent. In some circumstances, the song might have gone dead from so much repetition, but this particular minister drew upon certain shamanic qualities that are present in his African-American church tradition. Other people might call them part of evangelical tradition. I refer to a knowledge of how to employ ritual order in the service of Spirit.

"Now, I want you to sing that verse one more time," he called out while we were still holding the last note. "Sing it as if you meant it: 'The SOUL . . .' " The word soared from his mouth like a bird from a limb. It reverberated in the chapel. "The SOUL that on Jesus hath leaned for repose, I will not, I WILL not desert to his foes." This interruption, exhorting us while we were busy singing and modeling a freedom to let out all that was within us, broke through our isolation. In that moment, we became a corporate body. We began to listen to each other as we sang the verse again. But there was more.

"Now listen," he said as we came to the end of the verse. "Turn to those near you and pass the peace." This was done eagerly. Handshakes, embraces, words of peace and affirmation moved warmly through the room. "Amen!" said the minister. "Now turn to someone near you, and let's sing again. Sing that verse one more time, and this time sing it directly to your neighbor." JoAnn was next to me. She is a gospel singer herself, while I have much less training, but no matter. Away went the programs holding the now-familiar words. We looked into each others' faces and sang and sang: "That soul, though all hell should endeavor to shake, I'll never, no never, no never forsake."

The minister raised his hands and prayed a blessing over us. We began to disperse. Tapping me on the shoulder, someone said, "Have some more." She held a tray of leftover cups of wine and juice in one hand and a platter of bread in the other. Several of us ate, laughed, and talked together. I went home refreshed.

The service ended well, but something is wrong, I mused later: We have got the bread and wine in one place and the Spirit in another. The "elements," as they are called in liturgical tradition, have become mystical, privatized, and funereal, causing us to look elsewhere for fellowship and the ritual enactment of freedom. The heart of the rite, focused upon Christ's body and blood, has become so orderly that it does not much partake of liminal antistructure. One might be tempted to say it has come entirely under the shadow of the cross, except that there is not much agony in it. It feels more like a funeral for some good person without the liberty to weep, wail, or moan any grief. In short, the communion with bread and wine has ceased to be the enactment of much of anything, becoming instead the symbol of someone else's sacrifice, the one made by Jesus long ago. This is suitable for encouraging the sheep to dwell quietly in the fold (hoping they don't get too bored there), but it does little to bring about revolutionary freedom in the world.

■

An event that deserves truly to be called a sacramental performance is not simply *about* the freedom that the Christian gospel proclaims but is also an *embodiment* of that freedom. Therefore it carries within itself the freedom to change and experiment. Far from standing quiet in the dead seriousness of a funeral, or even the high seriousness of a museum, and far from confining itself to the safety of good taste, a sacrament of the grace of Christ tends toward improvisation and irony. It thrives on laughter, not only because laughter may express joy but principally because laughter is the sign of liberty.

The real presence of Christ supports what may be called in today's jargon a "postmodern" understanding of Christian sacraments, by which I do not mean a totally new understanding but one that breaks free of the self-important seriousness that has characterized so much of neoclassicism, romanticism, and modernism. Victor Turner once wrote that

Postmodern theory would see in the very flaws, hesitations, personal factors, incomplete, elliptical, context-dependent, situational components of performance, clues to the very nature of human process itself, and would also perceive genuine novelty, creativeness, as able to emerge from the freedom of the performance situation, from what Durkheim (in his best moment) called social "effervescence."[243]

If the sociologist and anthropologist can talk of social effervescence, the theologian and liturgist might speak of "sacramental effervescence," which would be the liturgical and gospel-based example of what Turner brilliantly calls "the freedom of the performance situation."

Although Turner's praise of performative freedom was insightful, he refused, more's the pity, to apply the insight to Christian sacraments.[244] Describing himself as "Catholic by faith and anthropologist by profession," Turner published an article in *Worship* magazine in 1976 in which he identified Catholic ritual with the forms it took following the Council of Trent (1545–63).[245] He began well enough by noting that rituals are indeed open to change:

Ritual is . . . not only many-leveled but also capable of creative modification on all or any of its levels. Since it communicates the deepest values, it has a paradigmatic function; ritual can anticipate change as well as inscribe order in the minds and hearts of participants.[246]

This is true. Yet Turner proceeded in the same article to castigate the liturgical reforms of Vatican II, holding that while the traditional Mass released men and women from bondage to "the secular structures of their own age" and confronted them with eternity, "which is equidistant from all ages," the new liturgy "has been conceived . . . as a suitable 'expression' or 'reflection' of contemporary social structures and processes, even fashions and fads."[247] He concluded with a plea, couched in grand rhetoric,

that the living tradition of spiritual knowledge cognizantly preserved in the traditional Roman Rite should not be lightly abandoned to the disintegrative forces of personal religious romanticism, political opportunism and collective millenarianism. We must not dynamite the liturgical rock of Peter.[248]

The last sentence is most revealing. In Turner's imagery, the liturgy has ceased being "capable of creative modification on all or any of its levels" and become a rock in danger of demolition.

Turner strongly objected to the translation of the Mass into words the people can understand. Assuming Latin to be a kind of liminal language, he confused the liminal with the esoteric. In the article mentioned, Turner gave detailed analysis of the Tridentine Mass but offered no example of any liturgy that is post-Vatican II. Contrary to his insights elsewhere, on this occasion he construed liminality as eternity, "equidistant from all ages." Worse, he identified this timelessness with the particular form that the Mass took on in the sixteenth century. To regard a particular historical form of a rite or a text as sacrosanct is a temptation of all those who like to think that their religious practices are timeless. It is an attitude that seems particularly absurd in Christianity because it stands in such obvious contradiction to both the message and the style of Jesus. ("The sabbath was made for humanity, and not humanity for the sabbath.")[249]

The long and short of it is that Turner championed postmodernism in the arts, while fiercely opposing it in the sacraments. His was a familiar, yet in his own case exceptionally sad, misunderstanding of ritual life in relation to Christian gospel, owing more to nostalgia than to theological, or even anthropological, judgment.

From the perspective that is today often called postmodern, reality cannot be made to fit within traditional forms. Reality is a matter of breaking form. Although postmodern aesthetics is full of references to tradition, it employs tradition in ironic and contradictory ways, affirming and denying it simultaneously, in order to express a playfulness of spirit that transcends the givenness of form, perhaps especially the heroic forms of high modernism.

Since the message of the gospel is liberation, and since a sacrament celebrating that gospel is the performance of a freedom, a Christian sacrament tends to break through any particular form. It refuses to be entirely at home in any liturgical tradition, whether the most ancient and venerable, the most customary, or the most modern. Fidelity to the gospel turns out to require treating liturgical form not as sacrosanct but as an occasion for creative expression. There is a gospel-based reason as well as anthropological reasons why the sacraments have adapted themselves to varying cultural situations. Attempts to prevent this are always grounded in an imperialism that is at once cultural and ecclesiastical.

In communities where liberation theology has taken root, notably in various parts of Latin America, the liturgy has taken on a highly participative quality as people have moved, in Juan Segundo's words, from being "gospel consumers" to "gospel creators." Language, music, vestments, and the relation between laity and clergy all change in order to take part in the freedom that is discerned as the soul of the Christian gospel.

Christian sacraments are ritual enactments, in present time, of a freedom that is granted to all who worship in the spirit of Christ. To be sure, this divinely inspired freedom has been bought at a price and requires for its continuance a life of costly discipleship, which is why both Baptism and Eucharist include reminders of death and dying: To be baptized is to surrender one's life to flooding waters, and to take communion is to drink blood. But these rituals are certainly not about the finality of death. Rather, in them dying becomes a rite of passage, in which the "children of Israel" move from bondage to freedom.

Christian sacraments celebrate something that is humanly absurd, something literally unbelievable and beyond all worldly expectation. The sacraments are about deliverance from oppression, including the grip of death. The outlandishness of this in the face of our natural mortality and in the presence of pervasive human misery is what puts the sacraments in an ironic relation to their own tradition. Full of tradition, the sacraments are not fully at home inside tradition. Made fresh by their rehearsal of spiritual power, the sacraments are neither ancient nor modern nor timeless, unless, as can sadly happen, their form comes to be valued more than their spirit.

Because they are celebrations of the breaking of bondage, Christian sacraments have repeatedly to break open their own forms. They cannot always repeat themselves. They must find, in particular situations, in quite immediate contexts, the means to laugh, cry, play, and shockingly truth-tell their way into the world-altering liberty of Christ's presence.

■

In 1971, prior to what became his best-known work, *The Liberation of Theology*, Uruguayan Jesuit Juan L. Segundo brought out the original (Spanish) version of *The Sacraments Today*, which was volume four in a five-volume *Theology for Artisans of a New Humanity* that he wrote in collaboration with the staff of the Peter Faber Center in Montevideo. Based on lectures given at Harvard University, technical in its vocabulary and too concerned with the interpretation of church dogma to appeal to a vast readership, *The Sacraments Today* is no longer in print. It is nonetheless among the most trenchant discussions of liturgy published in modern times, because it combines the perspective of liberation theology with a well-reasoned concern for the liturgical life of the church. Segundo rightly saw that a reforming of the sacraments is required wherever the church acknowledges that the gospel calls it to become engaged in struggles for justice and freedom.[250]

Although Segundo's terms of reference are entirely Roman Catholic, a Protestant reader of his book is repeatedly struck by the similarity between the sacramental situation he describes in Catholic parishes and that which prevails in most of Protestantism. The reason for this is not far to seek: Most of Protestantism, like most of Catholicism, has popularized an understanding of sacraments that obscures, or even denies, their having any direct relevance to the *social* conditions of the worshipers and the transformation of these into conditions more just. The lack of an adequate social-justice dimension means that the rationalism in Protestant thinking about sacraments (or the emotionalism that often substitutes for thinking) turns out to be just as mystifying as the sacerdotalism of the Roman and other priestly traditions.

Segundo sees that the modern-day crisis in sacramentalism is really a crisis of the church's understanding of its social situation and role:

... our difficulty and our crisis with respect to the sacraments does not stem from the sacraments or their decrepit liturgical entourage. It stems from the fact that we do not see the necessary correspondence between what they signify and the reality of the Christian community in the world. ... There are times when it seems that our yearning and zeal for ritual reform and liturgical renewal is a superficial way of solving a much deeper problem. For it enables us to hide from the real problem: the problem of community.[251]

Hence, unlike some traditional and even recent sacramentalists both Protestant and Catholic, Segundo does not define the mission of the church as arising from the sacraments but instead defines the sacraments according to the mission: "The sacraments are made for the Church, not the Church for the sacraments."[252] This reversal of priorities makes a world of difference, making clear that the sacraments are not ends in themselves but instruments employed in a divine and human work.

The church's mission, as Segundo sees it, is that of "forming a community and leading it to its commitment in history. Outside of this function the sacraments are devoid of meaning."[253] This amounts to saying that a sacrament cannot be "rightly administered" unless it signifies a social as well as a spiritual liberation. A sacrament must signify not merely the *idea* of liberation but its *actuality* as a work in which both God and the people move against all forces of enslavement.[254]

Rejected, then, is the "substantialist" conception of sacraments, according to which the presumably sacred elements (bread, wine, water, anointing oil, and so on) signify and convey a spiritual substance called grace. Along with such an idea, Segundo also casts aside the notion that a sacrament imparts to a recipient something "accumulable."

Borrowing an expression from Paulo Freire, Segundo rejects the "bank deposit" approach to sacraments, according to which

as in the banking system itself, what accumulates for the recipient also accumulates for the benefit and insurance of the bank too. The sacramental grace becomes a bond that maintains a certain membership in the Church and guarantees a minimum degree of conformity with her.[255]

At present, says Segundo, the

process of sacramental administration is that of the ruling classes. Words, gestures, and values are deposited in the faithful without any effort being made to have them speak their own word. . . . More than anything else in the Church, the sacraments appear to be the *gift* which the "ordained" give to those who are not ordained. . . . In no way do they appear to be the preparation of the whole community for its interpretative, prophetic, liberative task.[256]

In short, the faithful become "gospel consumers" rather than "gospel creators."[257] Where this happens, the sacrament renders the laity essentially passive, for it is not any kind of act which they perform.

Either it is no act at all, but only a kind of show without any true consequences (no efficacy), or else it is an act of a special class of persons (the clergy) with effects that are invisible and presumedly spiritual. The latter conception Segundo ridicules as "magical."

As I have argued in a previous chapter, it is not wise to employ the word "magic" as a pejorative term. However, Segundo's underlying thought is not only valid but of crucial importance: The efficacy of the sacraments is genuine rather than illusory only where it becomes "a rhythmic, dialectical dimension of societal and historical activity."[258] The vanity (call it magic or whatever) is to look for "divine efficacy in certain procedures without any relation to historical efficacy."[259] That is, sacraments lose their power and their reason for being when they are severed from divine and human work aimed at ending oppression.

Since the Second Vatican Council, Segundo proposes, there have been three principal ways of understanding the relation between "temporal progress" in human history and the "kingdom of God"; and these bear directly upon the interpretation of sacraments and their efficacy.[260]

In the most traditional interpretation, the "kingdom of God" and "temporal progress" are entirely different, the one being religious and the other profane. They belong to two different histories (a salvation history versus a temporal one) that occur on two different planes of reality; and the modes of working that are pertinent to each of them amount to two different kinds of efficacy. The religious efficacy is sacramental and works in the sphere of the soul, while the profane one is rational and pragmatic and works within the social sphere. There are thus two histories with two efficacies.

In the second way of understanding, there is but one history and one efficacy. In this light,

the efficacy of the Church is measured by its effective contribution to the liberation of [humanity], even when it is a question of the Church's most distinctive features such as faith and the sacraments. This criterion and goal, however, is exactly the same one that all [people] of good will seek in their commitment to the tasks of history.[261]

In such an understanding, the sacraments seem more or less useless, for they have no efficacy that is at all different from that of the secular world, and so the "function and the very nature of the parish are called into crisis."[262] Lacking any kind of distinctive efficacy, the sacraments become nothing more than instruments of education or propaganda, with an all too familiar impoverishment of the spiritual life necessary for the renewal of expectation.

A third way of understanding discerns only one history in the providence of God, with the religious and the secular united in a single destiny, while at the same time it discerns a twofold efficacy, two modes of working for the same end. This interpretation "stresses the specific contribution that revelation about the growth of the kingdom can bring to that which, for nonbelievers, is only earthly progress."[263] Political consciousness-raising and Christian evangelization "are closely tied together but are not to be confused with each other."[264] Within the one human history, to which the secular and the religious both belong, the religious has a particular function, and the sacramental life of the church a distinctive role. This is Segundo's position on the matter, and I share it.

The two "efficacies" of which Segundo speaks may also be called two modes of Christian praxis, the ritual and the ethical. The discussion in Part II of this book has shown that there is also a third mode, the confessional. These three are often split, sacramentalists devoted to ritual, activists emphasizing work in the ethical mode, and evangelicals urging confession of faith. Yet the church is an adequate instrument of grace only where all three come together as distinct modes of a single Christian praxis.

The distinctive role Segundo identifies for Christian sacraments is that of being "signs" of the realm of God. He does not sympathize with those who regard sacraments as "rites," for he thinks this terminology belongs to the two-histories-two-efficacies point of view. If we call sacraments signs, however, we run the risk of reducing them to conveyors of information, thus missing the peculiar power they have for causing situations to change. It is vital to understand that sacraments do not only point to something transcendent or something not yet in being: They also actualize something in present time and place, making possible, if only for a time, a kind of life otherwise remote. They are not simply rich means of communication: They are ritual instantiations of powers and potentialities not usually visible. In theological terms, they invoke and celebrate the presence of God in the midst of the gathered community. In the sacraments, one actually partakes, here and now, of that which is going to be. One does not merely hear about it or have a visible reminder.

Christian sacraments can be regarded in two complementary ways: (1) they are rituals designed, as all Christian ritual should be, to summon and welcome the presence of God into a gathered company of worshipers; (2) at the same time, they are instruments for bringing nearer to fulfillment the freedom that God has promised to the world, which Christians see in the story of Jesus' life, message, death, and resurrection. Hence a Christian sacrament may be defined as *an action of God together with the people of God, ritually performed to celebrate freedom and to hasten the liberation of the whole world.* If this way of stating the purpose of sacraments seems rather ambitious, it should be remembered that the ambition resides in the gospel itself. "For God so loved the world . . ." It needs saying that Christian sacraments have no exclusive claim to the divine work of liberation, but instead find their place alongside sacraments in other religions in which God also is active.

In speaking of a Christian sacrament as *an action of God and the people of God*, I imply more than an action *about* God. I mean to say that a Christian sacrament is performed not only by the people present but by God collaborating with them. A ritual in which deity is not active is no sacrament.

The end toward which Christian sacramental action turns is the health and harmony of all creation. This ultimate aim wants emphasis precisely because a sacrament may often (and legitimately, I think) have a more proximate end as well. A baptism, for example, is often focused upon an individual or small group. A Eucharist may be performed to bring relief from a drought, to end a war, to give thanks for rain and peace, or to reinforce the fellowship of persons, and so on. Yet the presence of proximate ends—which, if they are just, are of as much concern to God as to the people—should advance and not obscure the ultimate aim, which is the overcoming of evil (oppression) and the transformation of the whole earth into the commonwealth of God. One of the greatest powers resident in Christian sacraments is their ability to locate immediate needs within a framework of eschatological expectation.

We may say, then, that a sacrament is a true sign if, and only if, it is more than a sign. It is a sign not simply because it means something but primarily because it actually does something. It is the part that stands for the whole, the little communion given in earnest of the great feast for one and all that is promised in the gospel and requires human dedication.

As leaven in a loaf signifies the rising of bread by bringing it about, so a true sacrament does not merely point toward the eventual consummation of God's realm but is part of the action that causes justice and peace to rise. The work of leaven in bread always seems magical, even though it can be explained scientifically; and sacraments are magical in the same sense. The baker-magician does not have to know the biology of the yeast organisms but does have to know the techniques of bread-making. Likewise, the performers of a sacrament do not need to know ritual theory nor even sacramental theology but must know the ways of justice, freedom, and love within a gathered community. Still, ritual techniques themselves are not the principal effective agents. They serve only to facilitate a collaboration between the people and God, who, to the extent that they encounter one another sacramentally, generate transforming power together.

■

The liminality of rituals has been discussed at some length in the previous chapter. Here we need stress only the importance of this concept for Christian sacraments. As liminal, antistructural occasions, sacraments provide a temporary surcease from the pressures of social structure. That is, they offer in ritualized time a freedom from what the New Testament calls "the world," their ritual form becoming a tabernacle for the enactment of an alternative mode of being. In sacraments the "kingdoms of this world" are first acknowledged and then set ritually aside. Instead of conforming to the roles expected in everyday society, which pertain to the "old Adam,"[265] worshipers may follow St. Paul's injunction to "let your bearing towards one another arise out of your life in Christ Jesus."[266] That is to say, in the Eucharist, persons may become possessed by the spirit of Christ, in whatever form that spirit chooses to be present.[267]

It is a matter much to be regretted that a wide gulf so often separates Christian liturgists and sacramental theologians, on the one hand, from the advocates of spirit possession, on the other. Equally regrettable is it that where this gulf is occasionally bridged, as in some quarters of the Episcopal and Roman Catholic churches, more emphasis is placed upon personal salvation than upon the liberation of the whole world from the evil of oppression.

Although Pentecostal churches are not known for their sacramentalism, this has more to do with word usage than with actuality, as anyone may be aware who has attended anything as powerfully God-present as a foot-washing ceremony in old-time Pentecostal congregations. To "get the spirit"—that is, to become filled with the immediate presence of deity—is the essence of a sacramental act, although this truth has been obscured, not to say suppressed, in those churches that have come to put high value on their social respectability and thus to shy away from experiences that are strongly antistructural,.

preferring the shelter of this world's customs even in ritual. In these circumstances, the experience of possession (being filled with something) during a sacrament has been more or less banished, its place taken by an emphasis upon symbolism. The water of baptism, the bread and wine of communion, have in the "respectable" churches become symbolic substitutes for the true presence of Christ in the sacramental performance. Originally, we should suppose, the water, bread, and wine belonged to rituals in which persons were ecstatically possessed by a power they identified as "the risen Christ."

Precious little seems to be known about early Christian worship. There are some indications that it may have been, at least part of the time, ecstatic; and this hypothesis, if true, would go far to explain the early Christians' conviction that Christ was risen and would return. To base this belief entirely upon reports of an empty tomb and the ransacking of scripture for proof texts seems far too rationalistic. It surely was based upon strong experiences of Christ's presence, and these, for most people, must have occurred during moments of ecstasy in ritual gatherings. They are epitomized in the story of Pentecost, recorded in Acts 2:

While the day of Pentecost was running its course they were all together in one place, when suddenly there came from the sky a noise like that of a strong driving wind, which filled the whole house where they were sitting. And there appeared to them tongues like flames of fire, dispersed among them and resting on each one. And they were filled with the Holy Spirit and began to talk in other tongues, as the Spirit gave them power of utterance.[268]

Such a scene is scarcely intelligible except against a background of ecstatic ritual, where it becomes plausible enough. The gathered group "together in one place" is said to have been sitting, but this was not likely a sitting with folded hands in quiet contemplation, much less listening quietly to a homily. We know that on some occasions hymns were sung,[269] bread and wine consumed,[270] greetings made with kisses,[271] and other ritual actions performed that were so much against the grain of social custom that they evoked charges of unseemly behavior, even orgy.[272] When the Spirit possessed the group during Pentecost, observers accused them of drinking too much.[273] Peter's sermon, which followed the Spirit's arrival, began by addressing this charge, putting the event in the context of Hebrew scriptures:

These [people] are not drunk, as you imagine, for it is only nine in the morning. No, this is what the prophet spoke of: "God says, 'This will happen in the last days: I will pour out upon everyone a portion of my spirit; and your sons and daughters shall prophesy; your young men shall see visions, and your old men shall dream dreams. Yes, I will endue even my slaves, both men and women, with a portion of my spirit, and they shall prophesy. . . .' "[274]

The Emmaus story indicates that the risen Christ was known to at least some of the early Christians "in the breaking of bread."[275] That is, during the ritualized eating and drinking the cult members did together, the living Christ became present among them. What is most likely is not that the experience of the risen Christ gave rise to a memorial meal taken in his name, but that eating and drinking together in his name engendered experiences of his spirit strong enough to suggest that no tomb could hold him. Such engenderment, evocation, and recognition of spirit in the course of ritual activity is very familiar in the world. Eucharist is (or should be) its Christian version. The Eucharist is sacramental not because its elements are consecrated but because the Spirit that the ritual invokes is Holy.[276]

The history of the Eucharist during the patristic period (second to fifth centuries) should be seen not as the rise of sacramentalism but as its decline. The repudiation of Montanism (roughly 172 to 220 C.E.) was fateful. This movement, which included Tertullian among its adherents, originated in Phrygia (now central Turkey).[277] Named for Montanus, its first leader, the movement clung tenaciously to ecstatic ritual. According to standard texts, "Montanism antagonized the Church because the sect claimed a superior sanctity arising from divine inspiration";[278] but we should remember that Montanism was part of the church, not something outside. Calling it a sect is merely to say that it was repudiated by its eventually victorious adversaries. That "enthusiastic" (spirit possessed) worship carries with it a number of dangers is certainly true, but so does the avoidance of enthusiasm. The patristic church repudiated Montanism at the same time that it rejected women in leadership roles, sought acceptance within the Roman Empire, and centralized its own ecclesiastical structures.

During the patristic period, the sacraments lost much of their liminality. Shamanic components gave way to priestly ones, while the sacraments were gradually reinterpreted as structures mediating a mysterious grace, not antistructures through which the risen (and unpredictable) Christ could become directly known in experience.

In the high Middle Ages, it was the genius of sacramental theology to emphasize the "real presence" of Christ in the Eucharist. Yet there was a fault in the doctrine as it was expounded in terms of Aristotelian philosophy: Christ's presence was identified with the sacramental substances (bread and wine) rather than with a spirit invoked by the liminality of the ritual performance. This turned Christ into a reified (spurious) object. It also gave to the priest a dubious authority as one who could, using liturgical formulae, cause bread and wine to become Christ's body and blood. Even when belief in transubstantiation was devout, the focus was upon the substances ingested by the individual believer rather than upon Christ's participation in a communal act. Here lies the root of that separatism that characterizes most celebrations of Holy Communion to the present day.

It is better doctrine to affirm that the real presence of Christ is the spirit of Christ active and experienced in the ritual performance. Christ's presence is marked by an ecstasy arising from ritual-granted experience of the liberty whereby "Christ has set us free."[279]

Genuine presence is mutual presence. As one human being experiences the presence of another in the exact same measure in which she allows her own self to be present to her neighbor, so also God becomes present to worshipers in the same measure in which they present themselves as "living sacrifices."[280] Much of the language in Paul's epistles is chosen to communicate with persons who, like him, had experience of the immediate presence of Christ. Controversy surrounded the interpretation of such experience, and Paul's letters are often polemical; but if the experience is not assumed, the letters make little sense.

Liturgically, sacrifices are gifts: They unite human donors with divine recipients in a single act.[281] Sacraments, like sacrifices, are acts that generate intense presence: Worshipers make themselves present to each other and to God, receiving in return the shock of God's presence among them. Sometimes the presence of God in worship is palpable. Every act that brings this about is, in general terms, "sacramental," even if it is not one of the specific sacraments recognized by tradition.

Jesus' saying that the second of the commandments is like the first, equating love of God with love of neighbor, suggests that in a Christian sacrament the way of God's becoming present to us, and allowing God to be present in return, is for one human being to become radically present to another. The mysterious One who is sacramentally present in worship is not one but two—both the neighbor and God. The experience of such mutual presence is the experience of blessed freedom, a spirit radically opposed to the authoritarianism of the principalities and powers that rule the world in the present age.

■

How can the concepts discussed here and in the rest of this book be brought to bear upon real-time sacramental performances? As a first step in answering that question, a set of maxims may be useful:

Fifteen Maxims for the Planning of Christian Rituals

1. To *do* something while *displaying* the doing equals *performance.*
2. In theater the display is paramount; in ritual, the doing.
3. A ritual is a "transformance"—a performance designed to change a situation.
4. Church ritual often becomes mere display, either just flashy or merely symbolic, with no hint of transforming power.
5. In ritual active participants should outnumber the passive ones.
6. Art is *play* done workfully, but ritual is *work* done playfully.
7. All rituals invoke powers. A ritual is religious when those powers receive adoration. It is Christian when the powers are God, Christ, and Holy Spirit.
8. A Christian ritual "works" only when its participants are willing to make demands upon God. ("Ask and you shall receive.")
9. To be boring is to bear false witness.
10. To be sensational is to bear no witness at all.
11. Ritual loves not paper.
12. The form of a Christian ritual may be very traditional or very innovative or both at once, since form in ritual is nothing but technique, and substance is spirit.
13. Christian ritual is liminal and authentic when the people of God receive the spirit of God into their midst. ("The kingdom of God is among you. . . . Where two or three are gathered together, there am I. . . .")
14. The liminality of ritual can be used by God to weaken the grip of oppressive powers. In fact, God has no other use for it.
15. Christian ritual is the opposite of servitude: It is the performance of a freedom.

Since these maxims are distilled from the ideas about ritual and sacrament set forth throughout these pages, it would be redundant to comment further upon most of them. But what does their implementation suggest for Eucharistic performance?

Beverly Harrison's insight, similar to an emphasis I have tried to make in this book, provides an apt word of caution: "I'm beginning to see the goal to be ritualizing more than ritual."[282] If indeed the most important thing about ritual is the ritual-making process, and if a Christian sacrament is, as I have said, the performance of a freedom, then it would be foolish to provide, especially at the conclusion of this book, one single model for an ideal Eucharistic celebration. Inasmuch as a sacrament is not merely the *sign* of the gospel but is itself a transformative act, its form is less important than its willingness to be guided by the spirit of God.

What follows, then, is not to be taken as the only possible conclusion to the arguments of this book, let alone the only acceptable direction that Eucharistic ritualizing may take. The value of these specific suggestions will lie not in their being adopted straight from the page but in whatever stimulus they may give to the free play of imagination and faith together when a Eucharist (or other worship) is being planned.

I will first discuss four performance qualities—space, time, word, and rhythm—of the kind of ritual I have in mind. Then I will make a few suggestions concerning the series of actions that a performance of Holy Communion might include. In this I make no attempt to follow the order of service that exists in any one tradition but instead offer a variation upon some traditional usages, reminding the reader that the ability to innovate while at the same time echoing ancient custom is what keeps any tradition alive.

■

1. Space. Although I would not like to encourage spending huge amounts of money on new church architecture, the space in many churches is very poorly designed for the Eucharistic performance of freedom. One of the main problems is the presence of church pews, which I have long regarded as an invention of the Devil to keep the people of God apart. It is exceedingly difficult to envision, let alone perform, the freedom of the gospel while confined to pews. In such a fix, the most one can do is to hear about freedom, not touch it or feel it. Although flexibility of space is a very important principle for Christian worship, since spontaneous movement is the analog of liminality and freedom, this principle has been violated by most church architecture, which has reflected a hierarchical structure and an ethic of obedience in the church. The design of church space usually separates laity from clergy, fixes attention upon a pulpit or alter (usually presided over by a male, not a female), and regiments the seating of the people in a manner far more alienating than what they experience in most other gatherings, whether in the sports arena or the theater. In the stadium the audience's encounter with itself is palpable. In the theater this is accomplished by laughter, tears, applause, and intermissions. In the church, more's the pity, we have to stretch for it. Usually the stretch is not even made, the space not designed for it, the freedom of the gospel remaining abstract.

The sameness of church space from one week to the next also deserves comment. Perhaps the rigidity of the architectural design is a major reason for this, but thought should be given to ways to get around that. When one enters a place of worship where a service is soon to occur, the arrangement and decoration of the space ought to arouse expectation by suggesting either a pronounced emptiness waiting to be filled, or the presence of careful planning for this particular occasion, or perhaps both at once. The closest analogy is the preparation of a space where a party or a festival is to happen, though I do not mean that the tone must always be festive. It is just that the setting ought to communicate that people who care have made things ready. Flexibility of space tends to make this need more apparent, which is one of its advantages.

2. *Time.* If worship space in churches is often inflexible, so is time. The prevalence of the idea that the worship of God can regularly be confined within a little box of time, often less than one hour long, shows the degree to which church ritual is afflicted by consumerist attitudes. It is difficult to engage oneself in a creative process while watching a clock. The clipped pace of many Communion services suggests not the preparation and sharing of a holy meal in a liminal "time outside of time," but a kind of franchised ecclesiastical fast food operation. This image is not far-fetched in a day when churches have been known to advertise that they offer "self-service communion." Liminal time, as in a good jam session, or when one "could have danced all night," is neither long nor short but simply lasts until it is finished.

3. *Word.* Contrary to popular opinion, and the assumption of many persons who sit down to "write" a worship service, a ritual is not made up primarily of words, nor even of gestures, but of actions. In the sacrament of Holy Communion, the basic action is identical with one of the principal cultural actions that is practiced all over the world—the eating of food together. Particular words and gestures interpret this action inside Christian sacramental contexts, but these words and gestures must be considered ancillary to the action itself. When words are "suited to the action," as Hamlet advised the players, they become performative. In ritual, words shift from being mainly descriptive or

informative to become, in one degree or another, carriers of transforming power. However much they may refer to things past or future, performative words mainly work, along with music and other artistic techniques, to constitute the immediacy of ritual's present moment. They have more affinity with heart, throat, mouth, lips, ears, and expressive bodies than they do with eyes looking at cold print. This is why maxim number 11, above, states that ritual loves not paper. Few aspects of latter day worship are more alienating than the so-called church bulletin with its printed order of service, yet this prop is so customary that the suggestion to dispense with it seems almost unthinkable. People's attachment to a "program" is a measure of how far their sacrament has drifted from being the performance of freedom.

A printed order of service has two unwanted effects: it directs people's attention 1) away from each other and 2) away from what is happening in present time. Instead of taking cues from real live people, individuals tend to take instructions from the sheet of paper. Instead of living in the moment, the worshiper reads a scenario that tells him or her how the plot will go and how many steps there are to the end. When the service gets boring, one reads the announcements, or the names of the church staff, or the excerpt from a book that may be on the cover. (Nowadays the cover is more likely to display an example of bad art or a sentimental photograph.) All this is safe, very safe, but has little to do with freedom. When paper is given up, worship leaders and participants are thrown on their own. They must learn from each other what is happening. The shape of things to come must be heard with the ears and seen with the mind's eye. The ritual becomes less like a scripted drama and more like a well-hosted party. Imagine the dullness of a party that had a scenario for everyone to read as it went along! Since ritual is work done playfully, it does not love words on paper. In male-stream religion, this may be the most frightening part of the counsel I have to give.

4. *Rhythm.* Paper gone, rhythm can become what it is meant to be— the soul, the heart-beat of worship. I mean something very serious here, but not solemn. Since the playfulness and freedom of ritual have largely disappeared from churches, the soul of worship often disappears, leaving behind only skeletal bones in the form of an "order." The service is then envisaged not as something musical, danceable, and expressive but rather as the recitation of certain prescribed words. To recover from this barrenness it is necessary to think a lot about rhythm and to be bold in its performance.

The sacramental performance should start by establishing a strong rhythm. This can be done with piano, drums, organ, hand-clapping, singing, or whatever. In what follows I shall think of rhythm set and maintained by drums, for these are dear to my heart. Recently I was present at a ceremony honoring a Christian liberationist from South Africa. When he was introduced, a company of African drummers and dancers made entrance and raised the roof, pulling the congregation into a storm of hand-clapping, screaming, and cheering. This was fine, but when it ended the rhythm was lost, the ceremony reverting to an ordinary Protestant solemnity. I envisage a Eucharist that does not lose its rhythm.

Softly now, softly. Let the drummer drum. Drum. Darrrumm. Darum. Drum. Drum-drum. Softly.

> It will resound
> Clearly
> The sky
> When we come
> Making a sound.[283]

Keeping these four performance qualities in mind — space, time, word, and rhythm — let us think about a number of the actions that might belong to a sacrament of Holy Communion, including the principal one of taking food together.

■

1. *Invoking the presence of God.* Too often the invocation is a pious formality. Let it be performed as a summons. God is needed. God is called. God is asked (told?) to come forth here and now. The presence of God may take surprising forms. For example, in a macho culture, God might arrive as a woman. In a white racist culture, God may arrive black. It is not inconceivable that God may arrive as a white or black male racist, for with God one must take one's chances. Otherwise, the Holy One is reduced to ideology (wish-fulfillment). We may wish to avoid this relativity but cannot honestly do so; for God is not God all alone but only in relation to human desire, sometimes affirming it and sometimes rebuking.

2. *Giving praise of God.* Let this be a hymn or other rhythmic affirmation of divine grace. Drum. Darrrumm. Darum. Drum. Drum-drum. Not so softly now. Since the ritual began with the establishment of a rhythm, here the congregation takes it up, directing it toward praise of the God who, in the previous action, has been invoked.

3. Seeing the world's oppression. This act may take the place of the more traditional "confession of sin," which I have criticized above. The worship of God requires seeing the world for what it is—a system of oppression tempting us all, hour by hour, to become oppressors ourselves. Near the beginning of worship, this world of injustice and tribulation must be recognized and distanced. "Lord, I believe. Help my unbelief."[284] Let the members of the congregation turn to each other in small groups (four to six persons) and speak of the of the world's chains, its tribulations, as they currently know them. This may be followed by a litany (with responses simple enough to be made without reading from a piece of paper), in which the "principalities and powers" of this world are named.[285] Drum. Darrrumm. Darum. Drum. Drum-drum.

4. Passing the peace. The priesthood of all believers means that members of the congregation are empowered to give to each other the peace of God, the promise of liberation contained in the gospel, and the love that belongs to the fellowship of Christ. In this moment, let the people visit each other, beginning with the small groups clustered in the previous act, making God's grace available. The formulae, "Peace be with you," "The peace of Christ be with you," "Shalom," and so on, are too cryptic and have become cliché. New phrases might be suggested, or the people encouraged to find their own words. Body contact is essential, and individuals should be encouraged to use whatever form of it suits them, from the touching of hands to the exchange of embraces and kisses. While this goes on, drums make soft but not solemn sound.

5. Calling upon those who came before. We have not given birth to ourselves. To be in the presence of Christ is to stand in a tradition line, however much we can, should, and do critique the tradition. Highlighting the present liminal and sacramental moment requires visioning it to take place in the context of a "cloud of witnesses" who have preceded us.[286] I must caution, however, that this act of remembering should not be turned into hero worship. Neither is it simply an act of bringing the past to mind. Instead, it is another act of invocation, in which those who matter to us in the history of faith and freedom are called to be present now. Here is a good place for women to be remembered, particularly their role as first witnesses to the Resurrection of Christ, their often unrecognized ministries, and their ages-long struggle to be free of male domination.[287] Recalling past witnesses prepares for the ensuing action, the reading of scripture. Drum. Darrrumm. Darum. Drum. Drum-drum.

6. Reading scripture. High church traditions have it right when they regard the reading of scripture as an important liturgical moment, not an interruption of the ritual but one of its high points. They have it wrong when they exclude women and other laypersons from this reading, and when they treat the Bible as if it were a holy object descended from the sky. The Bible belongs to the people. It is they who must read and interpret it. Drum roll or fanfare might introduce their doing so. The reading should then be ritualized in such a way as that the text (in most, but perhaps not all cases, the Bible) gets passed from hand to hand, moving through the congregation, read aloud perhaps one verse at a time, the way it is sometimes done in Bible study groups. It would not be out of place for the readers to comment briefly upon the passage they have read aloud. When this is finished, let the drum rhythm resume and accelerate slightly, then stop.

7. *Preaching.* Like the reading of scripture, the preaching should be approached not as a liturgical interrupt or digression but as a performative ritual action. A good act of preaching serves many functions at once, but the chief of them is, like that of the entire ritual, to accomplish a transformation. In America the sense of this is best preserved in parts of the black church tradition, but I think it possible to revive it in other settings. Here again one should remember that ritual loves not paper: The reading of sermons from a written text is deplorable. A sermon is the ritualization (that is, the creative enactment) of one person speaking to others a word of God as the speaker has heard it. A sermon differs from a lecture by its immediacy, personal conviction, and oratorical force. The sermonizer does not rely upon, although he or she may allude to, any authorities in "this world." Preaching comes from the heart. It is testimony less to what one thinks than to what one knows by faith. Thinking is certainly required, yet thought alone is not enough to make a good sermon, which is thought wedded to conviction and expressed in both the ritual and the confessional modes of performance. In a sermon, the word of God should be experienced as a power. (See Appendix A for the text of an excellent, brief communion sermon I recently heard.)

8. *Responding to the preacher.* Customarily, a sermon receives an implicit response, or none. It would enhance ritual to make the response explicit. In some settings, notably in African-American churches, the congregation may "bear up" the preacher with sighs, groans, shouts of "Preach!" "Amen!" and so on. It is rare to offer the congregation a time to talk back to the preacher, yet this is the custom in the church I attend, where it has become so valuable that I advocate its adoption elsewhere. No preacher has a monopoly on the Word of God. Like the scriptures, preaching belongs to the people, even if a clergy person is expected most often to perform it. The preacher is not authorized to be the sole

mediator of God's truth. In fact, the sacramental performance of freedom works against mediation. The Word of God, like the Spirit of God, "blows where it will."[288] Once the congregation has listened to the preacher, the preacher should listen to the congregation. Let public conversation ensue. When it is done, the drums may resume, leading to—

9. *Singing and dancing.* The service wants now to become more festive. The rhythms already heard punctuating or accompanying the previous actions should provide a basis for this. How much dancing can be used here, and who will and will not join in, will vary greatly from one setting to another, but certainly an effort should be made to have as many persons dance as possible. At the very least, there can be singing and hand-clapping. Children (of any age) can use tambourines, bells, and what-not to "make a joyful noise."

10. *The offering.* Since taking up a collection has become rather thoroughly routinized in church worship, ways should be found to restore its power. Much of the trouble lies in a cultural attitude that money is "dirty," the opposite of "clean" spirituality: When the offering is collected in church, an anthem is often sung. The music can sometimes be very good, but the effect is to divert attention from money changing hands. We need a ritual-based, whole-hearted conviction that the giving of money is a celebratory act. To achieve this, we might take a clue from Gestalt psychology: Take the thing you want to avoid and "build it." Specifically, counter all embarrassment over the collection by lending the act some dash. Aim attention directly at the transfer of money. This is, after all, a real economic transaction, a place in the ritual where specific, measurable change takes place. As such, it deserves the name "sacrifice." It would be best for the congregation to be on its feet, to come forward, each person making an offering accompanied by prayer.

11. *Prayers.* The concerns of the worship leader(s) and the congregation should now be offered to God in the form of prayers. These should end with thanksgiving and praise, in anticipation of God's presence at the Holy Meal that is to follow. How the prayers begin is less important. They should include petition and intercession, fearlessly asking for what is needed (see maxim 8, above). They should ask for the liberation of the victims of social injustice and the end of all unjust social structures, as well as the healing of the sick, identifying as specifically as possible the individuals and groups who need deliverance. Let members of the congregation be encouraged to add their own extempore prayers to any that are offered by the worship leadership. Like singing, dancing, and communing, the offering of prayer is a time of "coming together." Since in Jesus' mind the love of God and the love of neighbor are

inseparable, the people's attentiveness to one another's prayers is an index of the attention paid to God.

12. *Setting the table.* The offering should conclude with the bringing of food to be shared in the sacrificial meal: bread, wine or juice (or both), perhaps some fruit as well. Table linen (if any) and vessels should not be very different from what could suitably be used in an ordinary household. These foods and materials are gifts for God, but since they are *from* God as well, they should be desirable by the people who are present and whom God loves as much as self. The actual setting of the freestanding communion table (or tables) should be done now in full view, by women and men, and by clergy and laity, working together. During this, let the congregation remain on its feet and begin a chant, softly accompanied by percussion. Here is a simple chant, easily learned, rhythmically adaptable, meant to be repeated ad infinitum:

Ho   ly,   ho   ly,   ho   ly

13. *Breaking bread together.* Singing, the congregation comes to stand in a circle around the table. If numbers are large, let several circles be formed, each around its own table. The symbolism of multiple tables is greatly to be desired, particularly if the number of congregants is greater than about thirty. It keeps the meal within a personal scale; it gets away from the idea that there is only one Christ in all experience; it better reflects the reality of Christ's presence among the people, wherever and whoever they may be, instead of Christ's being imagined always at the center of one unitary church; it involves more people in leadership.

With the people gathered around one or more tables, let bread, wine, and other food be shared and consumed. I suggest doing this *without* the pronouncement of any liturgical formulae or special prayers. In a sense, and this a profound one, the setting of the table and the sharing of food speak for themselves. Perhaps someone could say, "Come, let us be together," or "Come, let us eat together." Other words can come later. The value of the drumming introduced at the start of the service is here greatest, not because the drums are loudest now, for they should be gentle, but because they can maintain through the otherwise silent eating a rhythm of expectancy. We are not now at the end of the sacramental meal but only at its beginning. Our debt to the past is obvious, but we are eating now in present time, living into a liberated future. Perhaps someone sings—"Come, thou long expected Jesus, born to set thy people free ..."

14. Telling stories together. Traditionally, the story of The Last Supper is told before the bread and wine are served, during the prayer of consecration and just before the elements are distributed. I suggest here three innovations:

1. Place the story *after* the food is consumed. This gives it a more convincing location, because it follows our usual sequence of interpreting actions after they occur. It also follows the more likely sequence of early Christian worship, which was to let the common meal evoke stories about Jesus, not holding the meal in obedience to a specific story. Now that the meal has been taken and the people are still gathered at the table, it is story time.

2. Let the story be told by the people, using their own words, one person starting it off, telling just a part, then letting someone else pick it up, then another, and so on until the story's end. This time-honored way of telling a familiar story expresses community and builds collective memory.

3. Let other stories be told, too. It is unrealistic, and perhaps a denial of the action of God's spirit, to imagine that at the common table only one story is being remembered. The emergence of others should be encouraged.

15. Sharing Christ together. As the bread is the broken (shared) body of Christ, so the sharing of Christ can be done sacramentally by the people's sharing their experiences of Christ with each other. Before the people leave the table, let each turn to a neighbor and each ask the other, "Who is Jesus Christ for you today?" Let each in turn answer this question, speaking to the neighbor who has asked it.

16. Rejoicing together. Holy, holy, holy. Drum. Darrrumm. Darum. Drum. Drum-drum. Drum-a-drum-drum. Let the chant resume. Let other songs be sung. Let the heavens rejoice. Let there be dancing. Let food be consumed, as long as anyone wishes to eat. In this festivity, the small circles, if any, dissolve into the larger whole. The sacramental meal having become a party, some persons should act as hosts, moving among the people to see if any lonely, shy, or lame ones would like company or encouragement.

17. Going out. A benediction may be said at any time now. Its purpose is not sharply to conclude the sacrament but only to make a mark, giving the permission to leave that some will feel they need. The benediction might take the form of a prayer asking God to use the church to hasten the day when all the world will find justice and be free. The people may now disperse or linger as they will. Before the last have departed, the remaining food should be taken into the street and given away. If there are no hungry people in the vicinity of the church, the church should be moved.

∎

At sacraments' end, the rulers of the present age return. Then the members of the "beloved community" pass once more into the realm of what Segundo calls "historical efficacy," where there is little magic and where the need for liberation is vast and urgent. If the sacrament has indeed been an occasion for the experienced presence of that compassionate and freedom-loving God to whom Christ bears witness, then the communicants' return to the social condition of the present age is painful. We may speak of a painful passage from sacramental service (where we are the served as well as the servants) to a more mundane kind of service aimed at liberating a world held captive to structures of social inequality.

A false gospel will pretend that if the sacraments are faithfully performed and the message of salvation loudly preached, all is well. A false gospel will be triumphalist, whether in personal, political, or ecclesiastical terms. It will be success-oriented.

A truer gospel helps the children of light to see that their sacramental experience of communion with the living God will increase the pain they feel in passing from the ecstasy of sacrament to the misery of the world's poor. Out of this sympathetic pain is born the Christian contribution to the redemption of the world.

The performance of freedom in the sacraments serves to delegitimate, in Christians' eyes, all powers in the world that enforce inequality and destroy peace. It propels Christians to move back and forth between performance in the ritual mode, the acme of which is sacramental, and performance in the ethical mode, the political aim of which is the construction of a just, creative, and peaceable society.

The Christian life is characterized by the frequent crossing of a threshold between the practicalities of working for freedom in the historical world and the magic of the performance of freedom in the sacramental community. Neither mode of performance is sufficient alone. Together they make up a twofold praxis in which God and the people of God seek to transform society's captivity to greed into a communion of liberty.

Appendixes

Appendix A

A COMMUNION SERMON

This communion sermon was preached by Jae Soon Park, a Minjung theologian from Korea, in the chapel of Union Theological Seminary in New York City on October 25, 1990. It is reproduced here with the kind permission of Mr. Park.

Today I would like to talk about the story of feeding five thousand people with five loaves and two fishes. I believe this is one of the vivid examples of Jesus working for social justice for the poor and oppressed people.

A Korean poet, Kim Chi Ha, once said: "Bread is heaven. As heaven cannot be monopolized, bread cannot be taken alone. We should take bread all together."

Jesus taught that the kingdom of heaven is like a feast of eating together. And he always ate and drank with the poor and forsaken people. The life of Jesus was like a feast with the oppressed poor people. Through his ministry he built up table-community in the midst of suffering. He held a feast with the hungry people in the desert. He fed more than five thousand people with five loaves and two fishes. All the people ate and were filled; and they gathered up what was left over of the broken pieces, twelve baskets full.

This was not a supernatural miracle but a miracle of sharing in life. Our communal life begins in the sharing of small things and becomes richer through our sharing. And sharing life leads to the eternal life of God. Jesus incarnated the principle of sharing through bread and words.

In the end he shared his life itself with the people. He gave us his body and blood for communal life.

This means, Jesus died for the oppressed people trying to create table-community. And he was murdered by the oppressors who refused to share their bread. His crying out on the cross, "My God, my God, why have you forsaken me?" is the crying out and appeal of the exploited people to God for true communal life. The suffering and death of Christ on the cross is the suffering and death of the people exploited and forsaken by the privileged few.

The Eucharist then is not only a religious symbol of Christian ritual. It is the event of breaking the chains of monopoly and isolation and opening new worlds of justice and peace. And it is unification of Jesus and me in my body. Jesus is resurrected in my body through communion. So I can feel the blood and body of Jesus Christ in me.

Remember, today Jesus Christ is still present among the suffering, dying people deprived of table-community. Now he is suffering and dying with the oppressed people. He is now shedding his blood with the people who are shedding their blood for justice and peace in this world. Therefore when we take the body and blood of Christ in communion, we should think of the body and blood of the righteous who are now shedding their blood. So when we celebrate communion, we can hear their outcry in our body.

The body of Jesus holds the power of sharing life. It has the power of breaking down the walls of political oppression, economic exploitation, sexism, and racism. It has the power of creating a new world that exceeds capitalism and totalitarianism. So that when we receive the body of Jesus, we receive power for living together. And when we share the body in communion, we are one with the suffering people in Jesus Christ. Amen.

Appendix B

SOME POINTS IN CRITICISM OF
VICTOR TURNER

Victor Turner has been the chief theorist of recent times to emphasize the transformative role that rituals play in society. Probably no anthropologist has better perceived the creative, freedom-making side of ritual. This, plus his concept of "social drama," has put the entire field of ritual studies in his debt.

Turner's writings, however, pose an interpretive problem, because his statements concerning "the ritual process" are not entirely consistent. One's understanding of ritual can be aided by raising three principal questions about Turner's theory: (1) What kind of relation does he see between social structure and ritual antistructure? (2) How useful is his distinction between the "liminal" and the "liminoid"? (3) Has he defined ritual correctly for the purposes of his own theory and in agreement with empirical evidence?

1. The Dialectical Relation Between Structure and Antistructure

Our chapter on "Community" introduced the key Turnerian concepts—liminality, antistructure, and communitas—all of which express a view of ritual as in some way antithetical to the rules, hierarchies, and duties that normally govern societal life. What seems clear is Turner's picture of a stratified and duty-ridden "social structure" on the one side; and, on the other, the periodic occurrence of rituals, which are communitas-bearing antistructures, liminal to the social structure and differing from it "deeply, even abysmally."[289] When we ask, however, about the exact *relation* Turner sees between these two parts of his picture, the answer is less than clear.

From early on, Turner employed the term "dialectic" to speak of the connection between structure and antistructure. "Social life," he wrote in *The Ritual Process,*

is a type of dialectical process that involves successive experience of high and low, communitas and structure, homogeneity and differentiation, equality and inequality. . . . In other words, each individual's life experience contains alternating exposure to structure and communitas, and to states and transitions.[290]

In this passage, the "low" phase of the process is associated with structure, differentiation, inequality, and *status.* The "high" phase has to do with communitas, homogeneity, equality, and *transitions.* The contrast between states and transitions suggests that communitas is responsible for change in social life, which would otherwise be static. But it is not clear whether Turner means transitions *within* a given social structure or transitions *of* that structure from one state to another. The former is suggested by a passage in the same book, in which the term "dialectic" again appears:

There is a dialectic here, for the immediacy of communitas gives way to the mediacy of structure, while, in *rites de passage,* [people] are released from structure into communitas only to return to structure revitalized by their experience of communitas. What is certain is that no society can function adequately without this dialectic.[291]

A close reading of *The Ritual Process* leads one to ask whether the word "dialectic" accurately names what Turner had in mind. More is at stake here than a semantic quibble. In speaking of a dialectic, Turner seems to have run ahead of himself, anticipating a view of liminality vis-à-vis social structure that he did not have when he wrote *The Ritual Process* but would adopt later on. What he actually describes in *The Ritual Process* is not a dialectic but simply a contrast, or as he says, an "oscillation":

Communitas cannot stand alone if the material and organizational needs of human beings are to be adequately met. Maximization of communitas provokes maximization of structure, which in turn produces revolutionary strivings for renewed communitas. The history of any great society provides evidence at the political level for this oscillation.[292]

These words describe neither a dialectic nor a process but simply a cyclical pattern. However, the word "dialectic" and the phrase "revolutionary strivings," not to mention the word "process" in the title of the book, indicate that Turner's thought was pulling in two directions: A cyclical view of history was competing with an idea of history as a dialectical process of change. This tension in Turner's mind seems writ into the ambiguous title of the book. Does "the ritual process" refer to a process belonging to *ritual* and not to social structure, or does it refer to a process going on in *society* in which ritual plays a key role? One cannot say for sure.

Only in a weak sense of the word may "dialectic" be thought of as mere oscillation or alternation between this and that. This weak sense appears in *The American Heritage Dictionary*, for example, as definition number 5: "The contradiction between two conflicting forces viewed as the determining factor in their continuing interaction." In *The Ritual Process*, it is clear that Turner thinks of social structure and ritual antistructure as conflicting forces, and that the contradiction between them is the key to their interaction. Yet he seems to deny that the interaction leads anywhere. He envisions significant change neither in the social structure nor in the liminal rituals.

Used in a strong rather than a weak sense, "dialectic" refers to a progression, in logic or in history, in which forward movement is induced by a contradiction within an existing state of affairs. The root of the word refers to dialogue: One point answers another with such relevance that it evokes a pointed reply. Instead of going in circles, each party endlessly repeating herself or himself, a genuine dialogue moves forward along a path of discovery. Hegel and Marx employed "dialectic" to describe the movement of history. In their views, a state of affairs during one historical period evokes an antithetical move toward an opposed state of affairs. This contradiction results in the emergence of a new synthesis. Once actualized, the new historical situation engenders a new antithesis, which eventuates in a new synthesis, and the process moves forward. In formal description, the pattern is repetitive—thesis, antithesis, synthesis, and 'round again—but substantively there is change: The new is not the same as the old, even if it incorporates some of the same features. Change is progressive, and change is the name of the game.

Upon first reading *The Ritual Process* years ago, I assumed that it used "dialectic" in the strong sense. I did not think that Turner's theory of history was the same as that of either Hegel or Marx, yet I imagined he had an analogous theory, in which the contradiction between social structure and ritual antistructure was viewed as substantive, not merely formal, and led to a genuine historical progression.

Subsequent readings suggest that the book reveals a divided mind. Turner had one eye focused upon "traditional" societies like the African Ndembu among whom he had done his field work, and the other upon "modern" societies like the United States in the time the book was written (1969). He did not quite know whether to link ritual with the former's relative stability or with the latter's striving for social change.

Turner's later writings show a strengthened sense of dialectic. In *Dramas, Fields, and Metaphors,* he held that history does not have a cyclical pattern, and societies are not static structures:

> The social world is a world in becoming, not a world in being (except insofar as "being" is a description of the static, atemporal models [people] have in their heads), and for this reason studies of social structure *as such* are irrelevant.[293]

The implication seems to be that social structure is properly understood only in relation to communitas, toward which it acts as a kind of limit and from which it receives a pressure to change.[294]

In the Preface to this book, Turner reminded his readers of Van Gennep's discovery that "in all ritualized movement there was at least a moment when those being moved in accordance with a cultural script were liberated from normative demands. . . ." Then he added:

> In this interim of "liminality," the possibility exists of standing aside not only from one's own social position but from all social positions and of formulating a potentially unlimited series of alternative social arrangements. That this danger is recognized in all tolerably orderly societies is made evident by the proliferation of taboos that hedge in and constrain those on whom the normative structure loses its grip during such potent transitions as extended initiation rites in "tribal" societies and by legislation against those who in industrial societies utilize such "liminoid" genres as literature, the film, and the higher journalism to subvert the axioms and standards of the *ancien régime.* . . .[295]

By 1983, in a paper subtitled "Dionysian Drama in an Industrializing Society" (reprinted 1986), Turner would fault theorist Roger Caillois for failing to "take into account the dialectical nature [of society], which moves from structure to anti-structure and back again to *transformed* structure. . . ."[296]

Here Turner, clearly taking "dialectic" in its strong sense, gives to antistructure a definite, even necessary role in a dialectic of *social* transformation. It is an extremely important contribution to the study of ritual.

2. The Distinction Between "Liminal" and "Liminoid."

Nonetheless, Turner had not stopped pulling his punches. What he gained from a strengthened sense of socio-historical dialectic he almost gave away by setting up a dichotomy between the liminal and the "liminoid." One should ask whether this categorization serves any useful purpose.

Turner coined the word "liminoid" when he turned his attention to modern industrial societies. Phenomena that are liminoid, he explained, resemble "without being identical with" those that are "liminal."[297] It does not seem that he intended "liminoid" as a diminished form of the liminal but as a variation upon it engendered by modern social conditions. He was thinking especially of the arts, particularly the performing arts, and more particularly the avant-garde, in complex industrial societies. This enabled him to reserve the word "liminal" for the rituals of preindustrial societies like those he had studied in Africa. He also used "liminal" to refer to traditional religious rites, such as the Mass, that have been carried over into industrial societies from earlier times.

The essay "Liminal to Liminoid in Play, Flow, Ritual" was published in 1982 in *From Ritual to Theatre: The Human Seriousness of Play*. In the book's first sentence, Turner says: "The essays in this book chart my personal voyage of discovery from traditional anthropological studies of ritual performance to a lively interest in modern theatre, particularly experimental theatre."

In Turner's eyes, the arts had inherited the mantle of liminality once worn by the religious rituals that were so vital a part of life in preindustrial societies. In other words, the liminoid is a product of the secularization that is thought to accompany the industrial revolution.

By 1982, although Turner appears not to have noticed, the theme of secularization in modern societies had already run its course in the domain of theology and religious studies. What had once been called "the secular city" turned out to be not all that secular once you looked beyond a certain educated elite. In recent years, the prevalence of religion and rituals in modern societies worldwide has seemed not to be waning but growing. To this Turner paid little attention, caught up as he was in thinking about creativity in the arts. I will suggest that creativity is creativity, and we should look for it where we find it, in religion and the arts alike.

In Turner's mind the liminoid differs from the liminal because of "the clear division between *work* and *leisure* which modern industry has produced" and which "has affected all symbolic genres, from ritual to games and literature."[298] Following the late French scholar Joffre Dumazedier,[299] Turner opposes the view that what we know as leisure has belonged to all societies past and present: To think so misses the point that in archaic and tribal societies "work and play alike formed part of the ritual by which [people] sought communion with the ancestral spirits." In those societies "religious festivals embodied both work and play."[300]

Turner supposed that when societies are industrialized and leisure and play become quite separate from work, the "capacity for variation and experiment becomes more clearly dominant."[301] The term "liminality," he said "properly belongs" to social systems that are "relatively stable, cyclical, and repetitive."[302] In those, he reasoned, the important distinction is not, as in industrial societies, between work and leisure but between some work that is profane and other work (liturgy, literally the "work of the people") that is sacred.

These considerations led Turner to regard liminality in a different light from the liminoid. There was something obligatory about the liminal, even though it was the bearer of that communitas which stands in utter contrast to the obligations of social structure. "Optation pervades the liminoid phenomenon, obligation the liminal. One is all play and choice, an entertainment, the other is a matter of deep seriousness, even dread. . . ."[303]

In industrial societies the authority of community-wide rituals declines, their place being taken, more or less, by the arts and other creative leisure-time activities:

I would suggest that what have been regarded as the "serious" genres of symbolic action—ritual, myth, tragedy, and comedy (at their "birth")—are deeply implicated in the cyclical repetitive views of social process, while those genres which have flourished since the Industrial Revolution (the modern arts and sciences), though less serious in the eyes of the commonality (pure research, entertainment, interests of the elite), have had greater potential for changing the ways [people] relate to one another and the content of their relationships.[304]

Turner warned that

failure to distinguish between symbolic systems and genres belonging to cultures which have developed before and after the Industrial Revolution can lead to much confusion both in theoretical treatment and in operational methodology . . .[305]

but he did not give examples of any such dire results. Even if we grant that liminality does undergo change as a result of industrialization (how could it not?) Turner did not make clear how far we ought to press this consideration, nor exactly what follows from it. Having made the distinction between liminal and liminoid seem very important, he did not himself employ it consistently, because it is impossible to do so.

Differences between liminal and liminoid are by no means categorical, and the same may even be true of the differences Turner mentions between industrial and preindustrial societies. Differences there are, it goes without saying, and they are quite important in some respects; but they are certainly not absolute, and they are the less clear when we keep in mind the many social classes, cultures, and ethnic traditions that coexist in large industrial cities.

A group in East Harlem practicing *santería* with a deep sense of its necessity and efficacy is no less a part of industrial society than is a corporate board of directors, a university faculty, or an experimental theater workshop. In Haitian culture (where I have done some research), the distinction between liminal and liminoid seems to me entirely beside the point. A Haitian *service*, undertaken for the urgent purpose of serving the *loa* and bringing about some needed change in social relationships, has the feel and tone of a Saturday night dance in my own country, except that the dancing is better. To ask whether the event belongs to work or to leisure is not the right question. Of course, Haiti is not New York; but what are we to say of the Haitians who *are* in New York? And of those who work in factories in Port-au-Prince while also serving the *loa*? Much the same ambiguity attends high-spirited worship in some religious congregations in the United States, especially under conditions in which a bourgeois ethos with its deadening sense of duty and good taste has not taken over.

One might point also to modern Japan, which someone has aptly called "the electronic tribe." Japanese society remains preindustrial in many important ways, even though it has undergone one of the world's most successful processes of industrialization. The Japanese engage in ritual activities that are clearly liminal, as well as in all the cosmopolitan pursuits that Turner calls liminoid. Anyone who doubts that serious work is accomplished by Japanese rituals should consider the national struggle over the deification of war heroes at the Yasukuni Shrine in Tokyo. The attempt to enshrine Japanese soldiers who died in World War II is a politically reactionary move to which many Japanese are opposed. Progressives and reactionaries alike perceive the effectiveness of the ritual in the context of Japanese life, and they fight about it because both sides are concerned with social transformation.

Turner was well aware that the liminoid arts and entertainments of our society have their "ergonic" (workful) aspects, and he took their transformative power quite seriously. He was equally cognizant of the "ludic" (playful) component in the rituals of archaic societies. Unfortunately, he chose not to dwell upon this quite striking crossover of qualities, through which the most playful in our culture is serious and the most serious in preindustrial society is playful; he decided instead to emphasize the difference.

The regrettable result is that Turner unwittingly helps to rationalize the alienation that afflicts so much of modern-day leisure-time activity, and is the complement of the alienation of labor that industrialism engenders. The alienation of leisured pursuits, including leisured religion as well as artistic creativity, is brought about by falsely regarding them as *not* belonging to the domain of productive human work—that is, isolating them from "real" work and pretending that they have no fateful consequences. When Turner or any others say that in preindustrial society leisure does not exist, we may reply that by the same token it does not exist here either, although there is a consensus of false consciousness that it does.

The Marxian tradition is on better ground than Turner when it recognizes that culture is a *productive* enterprise for which human beings are fully responsible and which has, therefore, in and through all its playfulness, some essential similarities to work done in fields, factories, and offices. The Marxian aim (which has certainly not been achieved in communist countries) is the humanization of work, to be accomplished by creating social conditions in which work may be chosen not out of necessity but in freedom; and this means that any categorical split between work and pleasurable creativity is false and needs to be overcome. Turner appears to think that such a split is a necessary consequence of industrialization; but it is better to see it as a result of the profit-motive, which has pervaded the industrial revolution and turned it in a direction exploitive of the cheapest possible labor. This use of industrialization has had a negative impact upon communist and socialist experiments as well, for it has forced them into monetary competition with capitalist industry and led to the alienation of labor in socialist lands as well as the capitalist domains.

The more that workers are dehumanized by being treated as working machines (or working animals) rather than as creative, imaginative human beings, and the more the working population internalizes a view of itself as split between work and play, the greater is people's alienation from control over their own lives. By providing experiences in which work and play present themselves as two sides of the *same* effort, ritual can begin to combat alienation and motivate the social change necessary to overcome it. This cannot happen as long as it is taken as axiomatic that industrialism *per se* destroys liminality and offers in its place only the liminoid, a creativity or playfulness divorced from work.

Actually, Turner did not regard liminoid phenomena as impotent. On the contrary, one could say that his theory is designed to show the importance liminoid activities have assumed in modern processes of social transformation. But the more we stress this latter, as I think we should, the less difference we perceive between the liminoid and the liminal. In any case, what is interesting is not how these may differ but how they are alike.

The difficulty of using liminoid and liminal for purposes of classification becomes apparent also when we think of the rites of new religions. Consider Christianity when *it* was new: Suppose one were to ask whether the rites of first-century Christianity were liminal or liminoid. They were certainly not community-wide. Participation in them was entirely voluntary. They had not the approval but the opposition of "tribal elders," Jewish and Roman alike. These considerations would suggest their being liminoid, yet this is impossible by Turner's criteria, if for no other reason than that they were preindustrial. Meanwhile, their revolutionary dimension was so great that they were soon to become the object of an imperial campaign to eradicate them, which did not work, and which was followed in the fourth century by the more successful imperial strategem of changing the political character of the rites by adopting them as the official state religion. It makes no sense to try to decide whether such a phenomenon is liminal or liminoid.

Similarly, the dichotomy does not cast light upon the rites of Roman Catholicism in places like revolutionary Nicaragua. There the church rites were (still are?) employed in two different ways. Among the clergy and laity sympathetic with Archbishop Obando y Bravo, the rites are performed in the "traditional"—perhaps we should say "old-fashioned"—manner. This turns out to mean that they are counter-revolutionary, since their traditionalism stands opposed to the Sandinistas' revolutionary process. The same rites were also performed by the "People's Church," that element of Roman Catholicism in Nicaragua which has been, as they say, pro-process. Among these clergy and laity the rites were performed in a "new-fashioned" way, the most famous example being the "Missa Campesina" that was performed regularly at the Iglesia de Santa Maria de los Angeles in Managua, with its music in the popular idiom, its messages of revolutionary hope, its liberationist biblical interpretation, and its active congregational participation. Whether one calls these two ways of performing the Mass liminal or liminoid matters little in comparison with the great significance they both have within the religious and political life of Nicaragua.

A categorization of liminoid versus liminal would be of no more help in comprehending the rites of early Christianity, present-day Haitian religion, Japanese rituals, or any others. It is possible that Turner meant "liminoid" to apply only to nonreligious, secular performances; but that is not what he said, and the concept remains vague.

If we avoid viewing all "preindustrial" societies in a romantic glow, if we draw back from idolizing the creativity of arts and letters in societies like our own, and if we recognize that religious rituals have always had a revolutionary potential at least as great as that of the arts at any one time, we see a clearer picture than Turner presented. There are powers that oppress, and there are forces that resist oppression. Performance in the ritual mode (liminality) does not *necessarily* resist oppression but it has a strong potential for doing so. That is because there is no performance without transcendence. If you can perform, you are aware that you *could* perform differently, and this is the beginning of freedom.

My treatment of performance in the ritual mode (chapter 5) moved in the opposite direction from Turner's separation of the liminal from the liminoid. I spoke of rituals as "work done playfully," and of artistic performance as "play done workfully." I chose to view *all* cultural performances as belonging to the ritual mode. One reason for that decision is that the lines we may imagine between sacred and secular, between the holy and the aesthetic, or between the traditional and the innovative have only "occasional" validity. That is to say, such lines must always be drawn relative to specific occasions and contexts, for the sake of intended performances and the liminality they may achieve. Freedom is always freedom *from* whatever blocks the way.

3. Turner's Definition of Ritual

In several places, Victor Turner has defined ritual as "prescribed formal behavior for occasions not given over to technological routine, having reference to beliefs in invisible beings or powers regarded as the first and final causes of all effects."[306]

Ronald Grimes has faulted this definition on several counts, including its inconsistency with Turner's own theories.[307] Grimes also points out that rituals employ deformalized as well as formalized behavior, that ritual and technology should not be definitionally separated, that some ritual traditions (for instance, Zen Buddhism) do not refer to mystical beings, and that technological routine itself has a ritual quality.

I have argued, in line with observations by Wittgenstein and others that ritual ought not be defined by any particular beliefs with which it may be associated, for ritual is prior to belief (see chapters 5 and 6). It is better, then, simply to observe that the liminality of rituals implies transcendence of social structure and of physical necessity. Performance always sets the world at one remove. Hence it often (but not always) gives rise to images of invisible beings or powers exercising control over the world, and may lead to belief in them; yet such belief is not inevitable. Much less is it necessary to ritual that any particular beings or powers be regarded as "first and final causes of all effects."

Bobby Alexander points out that many of Turner's own thoughts about ritual are at odds with the way he defined it.[308] By the time Turner wrote *From Ritual to Theatre*, he was stressing ritual's inventiveness, even in preindustrial societies. In the very same paragraph in which he reiterates the definition of ritual quoted above, Turner says that he likes "to think of ritual essentially as *performance, enactment,* not primarily as rules or rubrics," although the definition he has proffered gives no clue to this. He proceeds to describe ritual in very dynamic terms, giving the following excellent picture of rituals as agents of their own transformation:

The rules "frame" the ritual process but the ritual process transcends its frame. A river needs banks or it will be a dangerous flood, but banks without a river epitomize aridity. The term "performance" is, of course, derived from Old English *parfournir*, literally "to furnish completely or thoroughly." To perform is thus to bring something about, to consummate something, or to *"carry out"* a play, order, or project. But in the "carrying out," I hold, something new may be generated. The performance transforms itself. True, as I said, the rules may "frame" the performance, but the "flow" of action and interaction within that frame may conduce to hitherto unprecedented insights and even generate new symbols and meanings, which may be incorporated into subsequent performances. Traditional framings have to be reframed—new bottles made for new wine.[309]

Elsewhere Turner objects to "the prejudice that ritual is always 'rigid,' 'stereotyped,' 'obsessive,' " calling this prejudice

a peculiarly Western European one, the product of specific conflicts between rituals and antiritualists, iconophiles and iconoclasts, in the process of Christian infighting. Anyone who has known African ritual knows better—or Balinese or Singhalese or Amerindian.[310]

Or, we might add, anyone who has known worship in the "free" traditions of American revivalism or in the African-American church. Turner points out that "even in tribal ritual, in which interest in custom is keen, behavior ranges from 'prescribed formal,' stereotyped action to a free 'play' of inventiveness."[311]

Holding that Turner's overall theory and his particular observations are more accurate than his formal definition of ritual, Alexander proposes to amend the latter so that it will better fit the rituals Turner actually describes and the ones Alexander has investigated. He proposes, as we have already noted in chapter 9, that ritual be defined as "planned or improvised performance that effects a transition from everyday life to an alternative framework within which the everyday is transformed."[312]

This is helpful. It takes the emphasis off prescribed or stereotyped behavior, which has mesmerized so many commentators (including Turner, against his own better judgment), to focus attention where it belongs, upon transition and transformation.

In point of fact, the patterns of behavior we meet in rituals are no more formal and prescribed than those of hard-at-work traffic cops, barbers, cooks, or tailors. If certain behaviors are repeated frequently and in familiar ways in rituals, that is because the rituals are techniques. As such, they are subject to formalization in the same way as a barber's handling of scissors, and by the same token they are equally subject to variation.

Notes

CHAPTER 1

1. The phrase "ritualized abuse" is attributed to Lawrence Pazder. See Clifton, "The three faces of Satan" (1989); Pazder and Smith, *Michelle remembers* (1981).
2. Kertzer, *Ritual, politics, and power* (1988).
3. Pottebaum, *The rites of people* (1975).
4. Pazder and Smith, *Michelle remembers* (1981).
5. Mud Flower Collective, *God's fierce whimsy* (1985), 176.

CHAPTER 2

6. Klaaren, "The genesis song" (1986), 15.
7. Grimes, *Beginnings in ritual studies* (1982), 36.
8. "Two Songs of a Fool," Part I, in *Collected poems*, by W. B. Yeats (New York: The Macmillan Company, 1919). Here quoted from Driver and Pack, *Poems of doubt and belief* (1964), 16.
9. Discussing animal ritualizations, Julian Huxley goes so far as to speak of "behaviour-organs," thinking of patterned behaviors as analogous to anatomical organs and subject to similar evolutionary principles—"exaggerating one component, reducing another to a functionless vestige, or altering a third to subserve a new functional role." Huxley, "Introduction" (1966), 250.
10. Huxley, "Introduction" (1966), 255.
11. Webster, "Bird of myth" (1981). See also Brody, "Designing birds" (1991).
12. Lawick-Goodall, *In the shadow* (1971), 113.
13. Lawick-Goodall, *In the shadow* (1971), 113.
14. Whether this similarity is due to genetic transmissions or simply to formal resemblance is immaterial here, because all I am stressing is what we and the other animals have in common. Julian Huxley, as we have noticed, while emphasizing that human and animal ritualizations are "not genetically homologous," observes that they are "functionally analogous." Huxley, "Introduction" (1966), 258. It reminds me of Ludwig Wittgenstein pondering the idea of evolution: " . . . one might illustrate the internal relation of a circle to an ellipse by gradually transforming an ellipse into a circle: *but not in order to assert that a given ellipse in fact, historically, came from a circle* (hypothesis of evolution) but only to sharpen our eye for a formal connection." He added: "But

equally I might see the hypothesis of evolution as nothing but a way of expressing a formal connection." Wittgenstein, *Remarks* (1979), 9e; emphasis in original.

15. Huxley, "Introduction" (1966), 257.
16. Jane Lancaster says that "babies born blind still begin to smile at the same time and in the same way as do normal infants." Lancaster, *Primate behavior* (1975), 66. However, Ray L. Birdwhistell noticed that "smiles do not override context." *Kinesics and context* (1970), 32. I take his point to be that although the behavior pattern may be innate, its meaning and use depend on interaction with others. This provides a clear example of the bio-cultural character of human being.
17. Lancaster, *Primate behavior* (1975), 45.
18. Leach, "Ritualization in man" (1966), 403.
19. Bateson and Bateson, *Angels fear* (1987), 110 ff.
20. Compare Victor Turner on the mixture of genetic and cultural factors in ritual:
    . . . if ritualization, as discussed by Huxley, Lorenz, and other ethologists, has a biogenetic foundation, while meaning has a neocortical learned base, does this mean that creative processes, those which generate new cultural knowledge, might result from a coadaptation, perhaps in the ritual process itself, of genetic and cultural information? (Turner, "Body, brain, and culture" [1983], 228)

    The weight of scholarly opinion today seems to support Konrad Lorenz in his opinion that "the astonishing analogies between" genetically produced ritualizations and culturally produced rites "find their explanation in the similarity of their functions." Lorenz, *On aggression* (1967), 55. By contrast, Leach's position implies a radical disjunction between nature and culture that is not sustainable and has unfortunate social implications.
21. Grimes, *Beginnings in ritual studies* (1982), 36.
22. This point has recently been emphasized by Eugene G. d'Aquili and his collaborators in a line of research into rituals using a method called "biogenetic structuralism." D'Aquili et al., *The spectrum of ritual* (1979); d'Aquili, "The myth-ritual complex" (1983). I am not in agreement with many of the structuralist assumptions of this method, including the primacy it gives to myth in the generation of human rituals. I also suspect that the method is over-specific in its determination of particular structures and operations of the brain. However, I am in sympathy with the aim of placing "ritual in phylogenetic and evolutionary perspective." D'Aquili et al., *The spectrum of ritual* (1979), 26. I, too, would wish to reject "any definition of ritual, or of any other behavioral phenomenon, that renders the concept incapable, in principle, of application and test among other species"; and I agree that restricting attention to human beings "is the bane of behavioral science, posing as it does a major barrier to an evolutionary account of Homo sapiens" (27).
    R. W. Burhoe, partly influenced by biogenetic structuralism, writes that a
    view that some of us recently have been developing pictures a human culture as a supergenetic and superindividual, phenotype-shaping agency. It is made possible by the coadaptation or integration of two semi-independent information sources: first, the basic information in a human population's gene pool (which is only about one or two percent different from the information in a chimpanzee gene pool) and the organic expression of those genes in the absence of culture (an expression which lies largely in the lower levels of our brains and produced ape-men); and, second, "a new creation" of relatively stable, nucleated systems of environmental information remembered in and transmitted by a living sociocultural system. (Moore et al., "Human adaptation" [1983], 214)
23. Geertz, *The interpretation of cultures* (1973), 33–54.
24. Firth, *Symbols: Public and private* (1973), 324–25.
25. Leach, "Ritualization in man" (1966), 405.
26. Leach, "Ritualization in man" (1966), 407.
27. Wittgenstein, *On certainty* (1969), 62e.
28. Wittgenstein, *On certainty* (1969), 28e.
29. Baker and Hacker, *Scepticism, rules and language* (1984), 53.

30. Moore et al., " Human adaptation" (1983), 212.
31. Huxley, "Introduction" (1966), 258, citing Haldane (1955) and Schenkel (1964).
32. Leach, "Ritualization in man" (1966), 404.
33. Gerald Vizenor, "The Sky Will Resound," *Summer in the spring: Lyric poems of the Ojibway,* 59. Quoted in Grim, *The shaman* (1983), 208.
34. Grimes, *Beginnings in ritual studies* (1982), 36. Grimes uses "ritualization" in a somewhat different sense from mine. He says that we "cannot escape ritualization without escaping our own bodies and psyches, the rhythms and structures of which arise on their own. . . . Among the modes of ritual action, ritualization leaves us the least choice. Whether we are involved in ritualization is not ours to decide. . . . [Ritualization harks back] to what is given, preconscious, or determined about the patternings so characteristic of us as animals" (36–37). With these words, he draws attention to the preconscious, hence predetermined, side of ritualization. There is also the other, the inventive and improvisational, side, of which Grimes is as well aware as am I.
35. Huizinga, *Homo ludens* (1964).
36. Turner, "Body, brain, and culture" (1983).

CHAPTER 3

37. *Encyclopedia Britannica* (1964) 23:329.
38. Heider, *Films for anthropological teaching* (1977), 51.
39. See Benford and Kurtz, "Performing the nuclear ceremony" (1989). I find unpersuasive the first part of their article, in which they seem to view ritual pejoratively, mounting an objection to the arms race on the grounds that it has become a ritual. Furthermore, their definition of ritual is too vague and does not recognize that the word usually refers to a specific ceremony performed on specific occasions. However, in the latter part of the article, the authors say they are not against ritual as a *form* but only against its *content* in the case of the nuclear arms race. They wisely urge the creation of new rituals more appropriate to the maintenance of peace in the atomic age.
40. Smith, *Imagining religion* (1982), 54–55.
41. Van Gennep, *The rites of passage* (1908, 1960), 12–13.

CHAPTER 4

42. Deren, *Divine horsemen* (1953, 1983), 146.
43. Deren, *Divine horsemen* (1953, 1983), 147–48.
44. Deren, *Divine horsemen* (1953, 1983), 148.
45. Brown, *The vévé of Haitian vodou* (1976).
46. Brown, "Systematic remembering" (1989).
47. Deren, *Divine horsemen* (1953, 1983), 82–84, 116–19.
48. On the importance of the shamanic roots of priesthood, see Holmes, *The priest in community* (1978):

    It is customary in anthropology to distinguish between the shaman and the priest. The shaman is typical of tribal cultures, he gets his power directly from the spirits, he is independent and part-time, he focuses on the individual, and he uses spirit possession, trance, and frenzy. The priest is typical of structural role definition. He receives his credentials as a result of special training, he is the member of an organization and works full-time, he leads groups, and he participates in routine acts of adoration, prayer, and offering. (80)
    It is my contention that the reality that was the shaman's is still part of our reality, although to our great loss it has been suppressed. . . . The challenge of the priest is, then, to learn from the shaman, but not to imitate him [sic]. (95)

49. Grim, *The shaman* (1983), 187.
50. Weber, *The sociology of religion* (1922, 1963).
51. Kirby, "The shamanistic origins" (1976).

CHAPTER 5

52. Delattre, "Ritual resourcefulness" (1978), 282.
53. Macmurray, *The self as agent* (1957).
54. Singer, *Great tradition* (1972).
55. Singer, *Great tradition* (1972), 71; quoted in Turner, *The anthropology of performance* (1986), 23.
56. Grimes, *Research in ritual studies* (1985), 17, 18.
57. Marrett, *The threshold of religion* (1909), xxxi; quoted in Comstock, "A behavioral approach" (1981), 631.
58. Comstock, "A behavioral approach" (1981), 636–37. He is following Gilbert Ryle's argument in *The concept of mind* that "emotions . . . are not causes of behavior; they are rather symptoms of action or the propensity to act in a certain way" (Comstock, 629).
59. Schechner, *Essays on performance theory* (1977), 65.
60. Gombrich, "Ritualized gesture" (1966), 398.
61. Temerlin, *Lucy* (1972), 122.
62. Lawick-Goodall, *In the shadow* (1971), 96–97. See also Rappaport, *Ecology, meaning, and religion* (1979), 225.
63. Gombrich, "Ritualized gesture" (1966), 398.
64. "In Church," by Thomas Hardy, quoted from Driver and Pack, *Poems of doubt and belief* (1964), 201.
65. The times, however, are changing. In his discussion of the writings of René Girard, Walter Burkert, and Jonathan Smith, Burton Mack says:

    Merely to have shifted the focus of investigation from myth to ritual, being to behavior, belief to enactment, may be the most challenging aspect of the new directions these studies represent. *No longer does an epiphanic object or being focus the picture for the religious imagination, providing a center around which a Sacred Order is organized by means of a system of symbols. Instead, an act (action, activity) has been noticed as a transaction of consequence, reflected on as a patterned sequence, and all cultivated in ritual as of prime importance.*

    Burkert, more than the others, has emphasized the significance of this shift for his work. (Mack, "Introduction: Religion and ritual" [1987], 58–59; emphasis in original)

    Other scholars who now interpret ritual primarily as action rather than as symbol or as reenactment of myth include Richard Schechner, Ronald Grimes, and Roland Delattre. Suzanne Langer, Victor Turner, and René Girard all give a mixed picture, sometimes holding the action of ritual to be primary and sometimes its symbolic content and character.
66. As used here, "transformation" has a different sense from the one it carries in structuralist discussions. Eugene G. d'Aquili et al. in *The spectrum of ritual* (1979) say that

    structuralism conceives of phenomena at the level of observables or "surface structure" (i.e., behavior, institution, role, expression) as being manifestations of "deep structures," that is, structures that are barely, if ever, observable and that operate unconsciously to transform patterns at the surface. Patterns at the surface may thus be viewed as content mediated by underlying structure, the arrangement of these surface patterns being termed *transforms* or *transformations*. (4)

    For structuralism, transformation is a kind of translation. In my less technical usage, "transformation" refers to changes brought about in historical time, in society and in individuals.

67. An example is J. S. La Fontaine's 1972 collection of essays, *The interpretation of ritual,* which is predicated on the assumption that " 'ritual' refers to all symbolic behaviour" and in which "ritual actions are seen as exemplifying in another medium the cultural values that find verbal expression in statements about the world, society, man [sic]—statements which we call beliefs and which are elaborated in narratives or myths" (xvii). These assumptions lead to heavily structuralist analyses in which almost all the emphasis lies upon ritual's more or less formal structures of meaning.
68. Leach, "The structure of symbolism" (1972), 240.
69. Moore and Myerhoff, *Secular ritual* (1977), 200–201.
70. Wittgenstein, *Remarks* (1979), 7.
71. Harman, *Hindu goddess* (1989), 68. Compare Ronald Grimes's observation in the essay introducing his bibliographical volume, *Research in ritual studies,* that "an important theoretical challenge to the primacy of symbolism in the study of ritual is developing." Grimes (1985), 5. He makes particular reference to Sperber (1975), Staal (1979), and Jarvie (1976).
72. Hubert and Mauss , *Sacrifice* (1899, 1964), 9–10.
73. Schechner, *Essays on performance theory* (1977), 63–98.
74. Fortes, "Religious premises" (1966), 410.
75. Fortes's observation was made while commenting upon a definition of ritual quoted from *Notes and Queries in Anthropology* (1951): "Ritual, like etiquette, is a formal mode of behaviour recognized as correct, but unlike the latter it implies belief in the operation of supernatural agencies or forces." Fortes: "To put it in Durkheimian language, ritual is a form of etiquette in the context of the sacred, etiquette is profane ritual" (175). I do not think the Durkheimian dichotomy is very helpful.
76. Durkheim, *The elementary forms* (1915, 1965), 53.
77. Hubert and Mauss, *Sacrifice* (1899, 1964), 80.
78. Smith, *Religion of the semites* (1889, 1927).
79. Durkheim, *The elementary forms* (1915, 1965), 53.
80. Psalm 23: 6.
81. Jackson, *The lottery* (1948, 1982).
82. In their monograph on sacrifice, Hubert and Mauss write:

> If the religious forces are the very principle of the forces of life, they are in themselves of such a nature that contact with them is a fearful thing for the ordinary man [sic]. . . . However much need he has of them, the sacrifier [the one making the sacrifice] cannot approach them save with the utmost prudence. That is why between these powers and himself he interposes intermediaries, of whom the principal is the [sacrificial] victim. If he involved himself in the rite to the very end, he would find death, not life. The victim takes his place. (Hubert and Mauss, *Sacrifice* 1899, 1964, 98)

The intriguing sentence here is the penultimate one, in which we are told that a worshiper would come to death if he [or she] became involved in a rite "to the very end." Instead of following up on this thought, however, the authors bury it in a Durkheimian point of view, in which an axiomatic dichotomy between sacred and profane is taken to be the source of religious and ritual life. Here is Durkheim:

> The real characteristic of religious phenomena is that they always suppose a bipartite division of the whole universe, known and knowable, into two classes which embrace all that exists, but which radically exclude each other. Sacred things are those which the interdictions protect and isolate; profane things, those to which these interdictions are applied and which remain at a distance from the first. Religious beliefs are the representations which express the nature of sacred things and the relations which they sustain, either with each other or with profane things. Finally, *rites are the rules of conduct* which prescribe how a man [sic] should comport himself in the presence of those sacred objects. (Durkheim, *The elementary forms* [1915, 1965], 53; emphasis added)

Comstock attempts to interpret this very passage from Durkheim by noting "the emphasis that it places on the sacred as rule for behavior." But that is not quite what Durkheim says. Identifying the *rites* (not the sacred) with the rules of conduct, he understands them as necessary *because of* "sacred objects." Comstock, "A behavioral approach" (1981), 638.

Following Durkheim, students of religion have made rather too much of the sacred/profane dichotomy, as if it were a given that does not itself require any explanation. Comstock pertinently recalls E. Evans-Pritchard's remark that the researcher does not observe such a dichotomy in the field. Evans-Pritchard, *Theories of primitive religion* (1965). What *is* observed is performance of ritual, and one needs to consider how its own dynamic structure gives rise to the distinction between sacred and profane.

83. Exodus 3:5.
84. Van Gennep, *The rites of passage* (1908, 1960), 12.
85. Smith, *Imagining religion* (1982), 55.
86. Nietzsche, *The birth of tragedy* (1872, 1956).
87. Artaud, *The theater and its double* (1958).
88. Cf. Schechner, *Essays on performance theory* (1977), 21–23.
89. Girard, *Violence and the sacred* (1977).
90. Mack, "Introduction: Religion and ritual" (1987), 8.
91. Girard, *Violence and the sacred* (1977), 37. Cf. ". . . sacrifice is primarily an act of violence without fear of vengeance" (13). "The sacrificial process prevents the spread of violence by keeping vengeance in check" (18). "Religion shelters us from violence just as violence seeks shelter in religion" (24). "The function of ritual is to 'purify' violence; that is, to 'trick' violence into spending itself on victims whose death will provoke no reprisals" (36).
92. Burkert, *Structure and history* (1979) and *Homo necans* (1972, 1983).
93. Mack, "Introduction: Religion and ritual" (1987), 29–30.

CHAPTER 6

94. West, "A Christian intellectual" (1987).
95. Turner, *The anthropology of performance* (1986), 48.
96. Deuteronomy 30:19 RSV.
97. Mark 9:24.
98. Smith, *Faith and belief* (1979), 12.
99. Smith, *Faith and belief* (1979), 117.
100. Smith, *Faith and belief* (1979), 106–7.
101. Tylor, *Primitive culture* (1871, 1958).
102. Leach, "Ritual" (1968), 525.
103. Goody, "Religion and ritual" (1961).
104. Durkheim, *The elementary forms* (1915, 1965), 51.
105. Durkheim, *The elementary forms* (1915, 1965), 467. For Durkheim, of course, beliefs are not freestanding; they are symbolic representations of social reality. If I understand him correctly, he thought that society generates symbolic representations of itself in the form of beliefs, which in turn generate the performance of ritual actions. See also Crocker, "Ritual and the development of social structure" (1973), 47–50.
106. Smith, W. R., *Religion of the semites* (1889, 1927), 18:

> Mythology ought not to take the prominent place that is too often assigned to it in the scientific study of ancient faiths. So far as myths consist of explanations of ritual, their value is altogether secondary, and it may be affirmed with confidence that in almost every case the myth was derived from the ritual, and not the ritual from the myth; for the ritual was fixed and the myth was variable, the ritual was obligatory and faith in the myth was at the discretion of the worshiper. Now by far the largest

part of the myths of antique religions are connected with the ritual of particular shrines, or with the religious observances of particular tribes and districts. In all such cases it is probable, in most cases it is certain, that the myth is merely the explanation of a religious usage. . . . The conclusion is, that in the study of ancient religions we must begin, not with myth, but with ritual and traditional usage.

107. More perceptive about rituals than Durkheim, Langer was not entirely consistent in her view of rituals' relation to prior symbolism. Her chapter on ritual in *Philosophy in a new key* (1942, 1948) must be read in conjunction with an earlier chapter in which she argued against the logical positivists' assumption that "all articulate symbolism is discursive" (82), rightly insisting that "language is by no means our only articulate product" (83). She saw that discursive rationality, with "language proper" as its medium of expression, should not be taken as prototype for all kinds of symbolizing, for that leads one to "misconceive all other types [of symbolism], and overlook their most interesting features" (87). She held that "presentational forms," which include ritual, have a "genuine semantic beyond the limits of discursive language" (81). This enabled her to achieve brilliant insights: "The first idea of a god is not that of an anthropomorphic being that dwells in an object, e.g. in a certain tree; it is simply a notion of the object itself *as a personality*, as an agent participating in the ritual" (142).

Even so, Langer was inclined to suppose that the *sacra* generate the rituals, rather than ritual giving birth to *sacra*. "With the formalization of overt behavior in the presence of the sacred objects," she writes, "we come into the field of *ritual*." Here she places the objects first, the ritualization subsequent. The *sacra* are "life-symbols," which "present the basic facts of human existence, the forces of generation and achievement and death." Rites are "enacted at their [the *sacra*'s] contemplation." Rituals "formulate and record man's [sic] response to those supreme realities." The attitude generated by ritual "is the worshipers' response to the insight given by the sacred symbols" (134). Here she writes as if objects, albeit very special ones, give rise to ritual. My suggestion is that such objects are not constituted as sacred *prior* to ritualization but *during* that process, as part of its dynamic. In Langer's words, the object is regarded as "an agent participating in the ritual."

108. Exodus 32:24 AV.
109. See, for example, Smith, *Imagining religion* (1982), 53–65.
110. Matthew 6:6.
111. Morton, *The journey is home* (1986), 128–29: "We empower one another by hearing the other to speech." God is "a great ear at the heart of the universe . . . hearing human beings to speech. . . ." God is "the hearing one—hearing us to our own responsible word."
112. James, *Varieties of religious experience* (1902, 1936), 30.
113. James, *Varieties of religious experience* (1902, 1936), 31–32.
114. Matthew 6:1–7 RSV, adapted for inclusive language.
115. Arendt, *The human condition* (1958, 1959), 64.
116. Arendt, *The human condition* (1958, 1959), 66.
117. Matthew 5:16 RSV, adapted.
118. Arendt, *The human condition* (1958, 1959), 66.
119. Hebrews 12:1.
120. Schechner, in his Preface to Turner, *The anthropology of performance* (1986), 19.
121. Romans 12:1.
122. Matthew 25:40.

CHAPTER 7

123. Hsün Tzu, *Basic writings* (1963), 94.
124. Lively, *Judgment day* (1981), 81.

125. Rappaport, *Pigs for the ancestors* (1968, 1984).
126. Rappaport, *Ecology, meaning, and religion* (1979), 192.
127. Rappaport, *Ecology, meaning, and religion* (1979), 197.
128. Kierkegaard, *Repetition* (1843, 1964), 52.
129. "The Animals," by Edwin Muir, taken from Driver and Pack, *Poems of doubt and belief* (1964), 79.
130. Delattre, "Ritual resourcefulness" (1978), 282.
131. Goffman, *The presentation of self* (1959).
132. Girard, *Violence and the sacred* (1972, 1977), 306.
133. Huizinga, *Homo ludens* (1964). Girard differs from Huizinga in having a somewhat over-determined idea of the basis of ritual. He claims that "the working basis of human thought, the process of 'symbolization,' is rooted in the surrogate victim" (306). Girard's way of thinking about social order has quite conservative, perhaps even reactionary, implications. He appears to think that all social order is beneficent, overlooking its frequently oppressive manifestations. But he is right to think that some social order is necessary and that it springs from ritual.
134. Huxley, "Introduction" (1966), 260.
135. Huxley, "Introduction" (1966), 260.
136. Huxley, "Introduction" (1966), 263.
137. Huxley, "Introduction" (1966), 263.
138. Langer, *Philosophy in a new key* (1942, 1948), 140.
139. Peterson, "Wittgenstein's theory" (1987), 6. Cf. Moore and Myerhoff, *Secular ritual* (1977), 3: "Collective ritual can be seen as an especially dramatic attempt to bring some particular part of life firmly and definitely into orderly control. It belongs to the structuring side of the cultural historical process." Whether the rituals and ceremonies be civil, legal, or religious, they function partly as "a declaration against indeterminacy" (16). Quoted in Turner, *The anthropology of performance* (1986), 94.
140. Quoted in Turner, *The anthropology of performance* (1986), 78.
141. See Turner, *The ritual process* (1969, 1974); *The anthropology of performance* (1986); and other works.
142. Rappaport, *Ecology, meaning, and religion* (1979).
143. Neusner, *The enchantments of Judaism* (1987), 119.
144. Neusner, *The enchantments of Judaism* (1987), 169–70.
145. Neusner, *The enchantments of Judaism* (1987), 170.
146. Green, "Romancing the tome" (1987), 151, 152, 154.
147. Green, "Romancing the tome" (1987), 155.
148. Green, "Romancing the tome" (1987), 156.
149. William Scott Green (personal communication, 27 October 1987).
150. Farmer, "Bad blood, spoiled milk" (1988), 89–90.
151. Wittgenstein, *Remarks* (1979), 6–7.
152. Rappaport, *Ecology, meaning, and religion* (1979), 186.
153. Rappaport, *Ecology, meaning, and religion* (1979), 73.
154. Rappaport, *Ecology, meaning, and religion* (1979), 41.
155. Rappaport, *Ecology, meaning, and religion* (1979), 41.
156. Rappaport, *Ecology, meaning, and religion* (1979), 73.
157. Rappaport, *Ecology, meaning, and religion* (1979), 62.
158. Rappaport, *Ecology, meaning, and religion* (1979), 174.
159. Rappaport, *Ecology, meaning, and religion* (1979), 194.
160. Rappaport, *Ecology, meaning, and religion* (1979), 194.
161. Rappaport, *Ecology, meaning, and religion* (1979), 194.
162. Rappaport, *Ecology, meaning, and religion* (1979), 195.
163. Rappaport, *Ecology, meaning, and religion* (1979), 206.
164. Rappaport, *Ecology, meaning, and religion* (1979), 206.
165. Rappaport, *Ecology, meaning, and religion* (1979), 214.
166. Rappaport, *Ecology, meaning, and religion* (1979), 232.

CHAPTER 8

167. Rappaport, *Ecology, meaning, and religion* (1979), 138.
168. Turnbull, "Liminality" (1990), 55.
169. Turnbull, "Liminality" (1990), 81.
170. Turnbull, "Liminality" (1990), 56.
171. Turnbull, "Liminality" (1990), 56.
172. Rappaport, *Ecology, meaning, and religion* (1979), 49.
173. Huxley, "Introduction" (1966), 264.
174. Rappaport, *Ecology, meaning, and religion* (1979), 174.
175. Van Gennep, *The rites of passage* (1908, 1960).
176. Van Gennep, *The rites of passage* (1908, 1960), 20–21.
177. Turner, *The ritual process* (1969, 1974), 81.
178. Turner, *The ritual process* (1969, 1974), 90.
179. See Turner, *The ritual process* (1969, 1974), 92–93.
180. Turner, *The anthropology of performance* (1986), 25.
181. Turner, *The ritual process* (1969, 1974), 82.
182. Turner, *The ritual process* (1969, 1974), 83; Turner's emphasis.
183. Turner, *The ritual process* (1969, 1974), 82.
184. Turner, *The ritual process* (1969, 1974), 82.
185. Turner, *The ritual process* (1969, 1974), 174.
186. Turner, *The ritual process* (1969, 1974), 113.
187. Buber, *Between man and man* (1961), 51; quoted in Turner, *The ritual process* (1969, 1974), 114.
188. Turner, *The ritual process* (1969, 1974), 114.
189. Turner, *The ritual process* (1969, 1974), 114.
190. Turner, *The ritual process* (1969, 1974), 114.
191. Turner, *The ritual process* (1969, 1974), 115.

CHAPTER 9

192. Turner, "Symbols and social experience" (1974), 10.
193. Grimes, *Beginnings* (1982), 45.
194. Farmer, "Bad blood, spoiled milk" (1988), 89–90.
195. These points have been much discussed in recent times. See especially the articles collected in Wilson, *Rationality* (1970); Ulin, *Understanding cultures* (1984), xi–xiii, 10–11, 171–72; Taylor, *Beyond explanation* (1986), 79 ff.
196. Langer, *Philosophy in a new key* (1942, 1948), 139.
197. Grimes, *Beginnings* (1982), 45.
198. Van Gennep, *The rites of passage* (1908, 1960), 13.
199. Grimes, *Beginnings* (1982), 47.
200. Grimes, *Beginnings* (1982), 45.
201. Van Gennep, *The rites of passage* (1908, 1960), 13.
202. See Frazer, *The new Golden Bough* (1890, 1959).
203. Wittgenstein, *Remarks* (1979), 7e.
204. Wittgenstein, *Remarks* (1979), 4e.
205. Langer, *Philosophy in a new key* (1942, 1948), 135–36.
206. O'Keefe, *Stolen lightning* (1982).
207. Bateson and Bateson, *Angels fear* (1987), 56.
208. Bateson and Bateson, *Angels fear* (1987), 56.
209. Bateson and Bateson, *Angels fear* (1987), 56.
210. Leach, "Ritualization in man" (1966), 524.
211. Leach, "Ritualization in man" (1966), 525.

212. Wittgenstein, *Remarks* (1979), 6e–7e.
213. Grimes, *Beginnings* (1982), 46.
214. Adapted from William Arrowsmith's translation of *The Bacchae,* in *Euripides V* (Chicago: The University of Chicago Press, 1959), 220.
215. Wink, *Violence and nonviolence* (1987).
216. Wink, *Unmasking the powers* (1986), 64.
217. Alexander, *Pentecostal possession* (1985), 21. For further discussion of Alexander's definition, which amends one offered by Victor Turner, see Appendix B.
218. Mud Flower Collective, *God's fierce whimsy* (1985), 121.
219. Walens, *Feasting with cannibals* (1981); quoted in Turner, *The anthropology of performance* (1986), 148.
220. Wilson, M., "The wedding cakes" (1972), 195.
221. Wilson, M., "The wedding cakes" (1972), 196.
222. Wilson, M., "The wedding cakes" (1972), 197.
223. Peterson, "Wittgenstein's theory" (1987), 7.
224. Jennings, "On ritual knowledge" (1982), 113.
225. Jennings, "On ritual knowledge" (1982), 114.
226. Jennings, "On ritual knowledge" (1982), 114–15.
227. Jennings, "On ritual knowledge" (1982), 116–17.
228. Turnbull, "Liminality" (1990), 55.
229. Schechner and Appel, *By means of performance* (1990), 41. This topic is discussed in detail in Schechner, *Between theater and anthropology* (1985). Schechner identifies performers' process of self-transformation with what Turner calls "ritual process," but I think they are not the same. See also Appendix B.
230. Turner, *The anthropology of performance* (1986), 158. The following comment by Bobby Alexander is apt: "The primary value of Turner's theory properly understood is the recognition that ritual is not an 'ephiphnomenon' but has 'ontological status'. . . . In other words, ritual does not merely mirror nor rest on the surface of more fundamental social processes that underlie or precede it; it is not simply symptomatic of more primary social activity. Rather, ritual is part of the process of social change, given its capacity to generate new, communitarian social arrangements. . . ." Alexander, *Victor Turner revisited* (1991), 19.
231. Turner, "Symbols and social experience" 10.
232. Turner, *The anthropology of performance* (1986), 22.
233. Turner, *The anthropology of performance* (1986), 24.
234. Erikson, *Toys and reasons* (1977), 113.
235. Delattre, "Ritual resourcefulness" (1978), 288.
236. Schechner, *Essays on performance theory* (1977).
237. Turner, *The anthropology of performance* (1986), 157; Turner's emphasis.
238. *A Midsummer Night's Dream* (V.1.16–17).

CHAPTER 10

239. The hymn "Break Thou the Bread of Life" was written in 1877 by Mary A. Lathbury. The verse printed here is slightly altered from one found in *The Hymn Book* (Philadelphia: The Presbyterian Church, USA, 1955). I have changed the pronouns from singular to plural in the last two lines.
240. Quoted from Cleveland and Nix, *Songs of Zion* (1981).
241. Cone, *God of the oppressed* (1975), 34 f.
242. Torrance, Thomas F., trans. and ed., *The school of faith* (1959), 263.
243. Turner, *The anthropology of performance* (1986), 77.
244. Turner's refusal to find parallels between creativity in the arts and in Christianity's sacred rites offers one among several reasons to take issue with his theoretical distinction between the liminal and the "liminoid." The distinction supported his

contention that the "human process," as he calls it here, should be manifest in the secular arts but not in the rites of the church. For a critique of Turner's distinction between liminal and "liminoid," see Appendix B.

245. Turner, "Ritual, tribal and Catholic"(1976), 586.
246. Turner, "Ritual, tribal and Catholic"(1976), 505–6.
247. Turner, "Ritual, tribal and Catholic"(1976), 524.
248. Turner, "Ritual, tribal and Catholic"(1976), 526.
249. Mark 2:27.
250. As liberation-minded as Segundo's book is, it nevertheless contains a number of egregious sexist assumptions, glaring evidence of a blind spot in the author's eye at the time of the book's publication in 1971. A feminist reader, noticing such opacity, will realize again how essential is the ordination of women and their active presence in liturgical leadership in order to free the church and its theologians from oppressive sexist habit.
251. Segundo, *Sacraments today* (1971, 1974), 38.
252. Segundo, *Sacraments today* (1971, 1974), 61 f.
253. Segundo, *Sacraments today* (1971, 1974), 61.
254. Segundo, *Sacraments today* (1971, 1974), 55.
255. Segundo, *Sacraments today* (1971, 1974), 93.
256. Segundo, *Sacraments today* (1971, 1974), 93.
257. Segundo, *Sacraments today* (1971, 1974), 33.
258. Segundo, *Sacraments today* (1971, 1974), 59.
259. Segundo, *Sacraments today* (1971, 1974), 63.
260. Segundo, *Sacraments today* (1971, 1974), 124 ff.
261. Segundo, *Sacraments today* (1971, 1974), 131.
262. Segundo, *Sacraments today* (1971, 1974), 132.
263. Segundo, *Sacraments today* (1971, 1974), 133.
264. Segundo, *Sacraments today* (1971, 1974), 134.
265. 1 Corinthians 15:45. "If there is such a thing as an animal body, there is also a spiritual body. It is in this sense that Scripture says, 'The first man, Adam, became an animate being,' whereas the last Adam has become a life-giving spirit" (NEB).
266. Philippians 2:5 (NEB).
267. On the diversity of the forms of Christ and their importance for the celebration of the risen Christ, see Driver, *Christ in a changing world* (1981).
268. Acts 2:1–4 (NEB).
269. See Ephesians 5:15–20; Colossians 3:16.
270. 1 Corinthians 11:20–22, in which Paul inveighs against abuses in the church at Corinth, implies that the Lord's Supper was a common meal furnished with much to eat and drink, for he has heard, to his regret, that because of dissension in the ranks some have gone away hungry while others were drunk. He is especially concerned about behavior that is inhospitable to the church's poorer members.
271. Holy kisses are mentioned in Romans 16:16; 1 Corinthians 16:20; 2 Corinthians 13:12; 1 Thessalonians 5:26; and 1 Peter 5:17. Not all these instances seem to refer to ritual settings, but it is most likely that the custom of greeting other Christians with a kiss, and the naming of the kiss as holy, have ritual origins.
272. See Cohn, *Europe's inner demons* (1975, 1977), chapter 1. He interprets the charges made against the early Christian services as calumnies, but shows that the slanders were caricatures of actual love-feasts:

> ". . . we are dealing with a real Christian custom, misinterpreted under the influence of a traditional stereotype. The custom was the *Agape*, or love-feast. In the first two centuries of Christianity it was customary for a private person to invite baptized Christians to his [sic] house for a communal meal. The meal was an affirmation of Christian fellowship: the poor were invited, charity was dispensed." (10)

273. Acts 2:13 (NEB).
274. Acts 2:15–18 (NEB). In this passage, Peter quotes Joel 2:28–32, which reads as if it, too,

was inspired by ecstatic ritual, a point probably not lost on Peter or the author of the Book of Acts.

275. Luke 24:13–53, esp. v. 35: ". . . and told how he had been recognized by them at the breaking of the bread." I take this to be an aetiological story, told to "explain" the origin of the Christian ritual of breaking bread together. Its factual basis is the recognition of the spirit of Christ in the ritual.
276. From this point of view, the Spirit of Christ, the Spirit of God, and the Holy Spirit are one and the same.
277. This was one of the regions of the Roman Empire missionized by Paul (see Acts 16:6; 18:23). His attitude toward ecstatic worship seems to have been highly ambivalent. I think it unlikely that new Christian communities could have been started in his day if they did not worship ecstatically. At the very least they must have heard ecstatic preaching, which is probably the way that Paul himself preached.
278. *The Columbia Encyclopedia*, 2d ed. (1950, 1312).
279. Galatians 5.1.
280. Romans 12:1.
281. Hubert and Mauss, *Sacrifice* (1899, 1964).
282. Mud Flower Collective, *God's fierce whimsy* (1985), 113.
283. Gerald Vizenor, "The Sky Will Resound," *Summer in the spring: Lyric poems of the Ojibway*, 59. Quoted in Grim, *The shaman* (1983), 208. I have changed the first-person pronoun from singular to plural.
284. Mark 9:24
285. Romans 8:38; Ephesians 6:12; Colossians 1:16; Colossians 2:15.
286. Hebrews 12:1.
287. On the role of women in the New Testament and in the early churches, see Fiorenza, *In memory of her* (1983).
288. John 3:8.

APPENDIX B

289. Turner, *The ritual process* (1969, 1974), 127.
290. Turner, *The ritual process* (1969, 1974), 83.
291. Turner, *The ritual process* (1969, 1974), 116.
292. Turner, *The ritual process* (1969, 1974), 116.
293. Turner, *Dramas, fields, and metaphors* (1974), 24.
294. Turner, *Dramas, fields, and metaphors* (1974), 50.
295. Turner, *Dramas, fields, and metaphors* (1974), 13 f.
296. Reprinted in Turner, *The anthropology of performance* (1986), 127–28; emphasis added.
297. Turner, *From ritual to theatre* (1982), 32. For a detailed discussion of Turner's distinction between liminal and liminoid phenomena, including a critique in many ways parallel to my own, see Alexander, *Victor Turner Revisited* (1991), 20–26.
298. Turner, *From ritual to theatre* (1982), 35.
299. Dumazedier, "Leisure" (1968).
300. Dumazedier, "Leisure" (1968), 248; quoted in Turner, *From ritual to theatre* (1982), 35.
301. Turner, *From ritual to theatre* (1982), 28–29.
302. Turner, *From ritual to theatre* (1982), 29.
303. Turner, *From ritual to theatre* (1982), 43.
304. Turner, *Dramas, fields, and metaphors* (1974), 16.
305. Turner, *From ritual to theatre* (1982), 30.
306. Turner, *From ritual to theatre* (1982), 79; Turner, *The forest of symbols* (1967), 19; cf. Turner and Turner, *Image and pilgrimage* (1978), 243.
307. Grimes, *Beginnings* (1982), 54.
308. Alexander, *Pentecostal possession* (1985).

309. Turner, *From ritual to theatre* (1982), 79.
310. Turner, *The anthropology of performance* (1986), 26.
311. Turner, "Variations" (1977), 40.
312. Alexander, *Pentecostal possession* (1985), 21.

References

Alexander, Bobby C. 1985. *Pentecostal possession and Grotowski's ritual projects as social protest: A critical assessment of Victor Turner's theory of "ritual anti-structure" as an interpretive tool.* Unpublished dissertation. Columbia University, NY.

———. 1991. *Victor Turner revisited: Ritual as social change.* Atlanta, GA: Scholars Press. Academy Series, American Academy of Religion, no. 74.

Arendt, Hannah. 1958, 1959. *The human condition.* Garden City, NY: Doubleday Anchor Books.

Artaud, Antonin. 1958. *The theater and its double.* Trans. M. C. Richards. New York: Grove Press.

Baker, G. P., and P. M. S. Hacker. 1984. *Scepticism, rules and language.* Oxford: Basil Blackwell.

Bateson, Gregory, and Mary Catherine Bateson. 1987. *Angels fear: Towards an epistemology of the sacred.* NY: Macmillan Publishing Co.

Benford, Robert D., and Lester R. Kurtz. 1989. Performing the nuclear ceremony: The arms race as a ritual. Chapter 5. In *A shuddering dawn: Religious studies and the nuclear age.* Eds. Ira Chernus and Tabor Edward Linenthal, 69–88. Albany, NY: State University of New York Press.

Birdwhistell, Ray L. 1970. *Kinesics and context: Essays on body motion communication.* Philadelphia: University of Pennsylvania Press.

Brody, Jane E. 1991. Designing birds impress their mates with fancy décor. *The New York Times* (Mar. 5).

Branch, Taylor. 1988. *Parting the waters: America in the King years 1954–63.* New York: Simon & Schuster/Touchstone.

Brown, Karen McCarthy. 1976. *The vévé of Haitian vodou: A structural analysis of religious imagery.* Ph. D. dissertation. Temple University, Philadelphia.

———. 1989. Systematic remembering, systematic forgetting: Ogou in Haiti. In *Africa's Ogun: Old world and new.* Ed. Sandra T. Barnes, 65–89. Bloomington, IN: Indiana University Press.

Buber, Martin. 1961. *Between man and man.* Trans. R. G. Smith. Fontana Library.

Burkert, Walter. 1979. *Structure and history in Greek mythology and ritual.* Berkeley: University of California Press.

———. 1972, 1983. *Homo necans: The anthropology of ancient Greek sacrificial ritual and myth.* Originally published in Berlin as *Homo Necans Interpretationen altgreichischer Opferriten und Mythen.* Trans. Peter Bing. Berkeley: University of California Press.

Cleveland, J. Jefferson, and Verolga Nix, eds. 1981. *Songs of Zion.* Nashville: Abingdon Press.

Clifton, Chas S. 1989. The three faces of Satan: A close look at the "satanism scare." *Gnosis* (Summer): 9–18.

Cohn, Norman. 1975, 1977. *Europe's inner demons: An enquiry inspired by the great witch-hunt.* New York: New American Library.

Comstock, W. Richard. 1981. A behavioral approach to the sacred: Category formation in religious studies. *Journal of the American Academy of Religion* 49(4): 625–43.

Cone, James. 1975. *God of the oppressed.* New York: Seabury Press.

Cornford, Francis. 1914. *The origin of Attic comedy.* London: Edward Arnold.

Crocker, Christopher. 1973. Ritual and the development of social structure: Liminality and inversion. In *The roots of ritual.* Ed. James D. Shaughnessy, 47–86. Grand Rapids, MI: William B. Eerdman's.

d'Aquili, Eugene G. 1983. The myth-ritual complex: A biogenetic structural analysis. *Zygon* 18 (September): 247–69.

d'Aquili, Eugene G., Jr., Charles D. Laughlin, John McManus, *et al.* 1979. *The spectrum of ritual: A biogenetic structural analysis.* New York: Columbia University Press.

Delattre, Roland. 1978. Ritual resourcefulness and cultural pluralism. *Soundings* 61(3): 281–301.

Deren, Maya. 1953, 1983. *Divine horsemen: The living gods of Haiti.* New Paltz, NY: McPherson & Company.

Driver, Tom F. 1981. *Christ in a changing world: Toward an ethical christology.* New York: Crossroads.

Driver, Tom F., and Robert Pack, eds. 1964. *Poems of doubt and belief.* New York: Macmillan.

Dumazedier, Joffre. 1968. Leisure. In *International Encyclopedia of the Social Sciences:* 248–53.

Durkheim, Emile. 1915, 1965. *The elementary forms of the religious life.* Trans. Joseph W. Swain. New York: The Free Press.

Evans-Pritchard, E. E. 1965. *Theories of primitive religion.* Oxford: The Clarendon Press.

Erikson, Erik. 1977. *Toys and reasons: Stages in the ritualization of experience.* New York: W. W. Norton.

Farmer, Paul. 1988. Bad blood, spoiled milk: Bodily fluids as moral barometers in rural Haiti. *American Ethnologist* 15 (February): 80–101.

Fiorenza, Elizabeth Schussler. 1983. *In memory of her: A feminist theological reconstruction of Christian origins.* New York: Crossroad.

Firth, Raymond. 1973. *Symbols: Public and private.* Ithaca, NY: Cornell University Press.

Fortes, M. 1966. Religious premises and logical technique in divinatory ritual. *The Philosophical Transactions of the Royal Society of London,* 29th series, 251: 409–22.

Frazer, James G. 1890, 1959. *The new Golden Bough: A new abridgment of the classic work.* Ed. Theodore H. Gaster. New York: Criterion Books.

Geertz, Clifford. 1973. *The interpretation of cultures.* New York: Basic Books.

Girard, René. 1972, 1977. *Violence and the sacred.* Trans. Patrick Gregory. Baltimore: Johns Hopkins University Press.

Goffman, Erving. 1959. *The presentation of self in everyday life.* Garden City, NY: Doubleday Anchor.

Gombrich, E. H. 1966. Ritualized gesture and expression in art. *The Philosophical Transactions of the Royal Society of London,* Series B (29 December): 393–401.

Goody, Jack. 1961. Religion and ritual: The definitional problem. *British Journal of Sociology* 12(2): 142–64.

Green, William Scott. 1987. Romancing the tome: Rabbinic hermeneutics and the theory of literature. *Semeia:* 147–68.

Grim, John A. 1983. *The shaman: Patterns of Siberian and Ojibway healing.* University of Oklahoma Press.

Grimes, Ronald L. 1982. *Beginnings in ritual studies.* Lanham, MD: University Press of America.

———. 1985. *Research in ritual studies: A programmatic essay and bibliography.* Metuchen, NJ: ATLA Bibliography Series. The Scarecrow Press.

Haldane, J. W. 1955. Animal communication and the origin of human language. *Scientific Progress* 71: 385.

Harman, William. 1989. *The sacred marriage of a Hindu goddess.* Bloomington, IN: Indiana University Press.

Harrison, Jane E. 1908, 1961. *Prolegomena to the study of Greek religion.* London: Merlin Press.

———. 1912, 1962. *Themis: A study of the social origins of Greek religion.* Cleveland: World Publishing Co.

———. 1913, 1951. *Ancient art and ritual.* Rev. ed. New York: Oxford University Press.

Heider, Karl G., ed. 1977. *Films for anthropological teaching.* 6th ed. Washington, DC: American Anthropological Association.

Holmes, Urban T. 1978. *The priest in community: Exploring the roots of ministry.* New York: The Seabury Press.

Hsün Tzu. 1963. *Basic writings.* Trans. Burton Watson. New York: Columbia University Press.

Hubert, Henri, and Marc Mauss. 1899, 1964. *Sacrifice: Its nature and function.* Trans. W. D. Halls. London: Cohen & West.

Huizinga, Johan. 1964. *Homo ludens: A study of the play-element in culture.* Boston: Beacon Press.

Huxley, Julian. 1966. Introduction: A discussion on ritualization of behaviour in animals and man. *The Philosophical Transactions of the Royal Society of London,* Series B, 251 (29 December): 249–71.

Jackson, Shirley. 1948, 1982. *The lottery and other stories.* New York: Farrar, Straus and Giroux (The Noonday Press).

James, William. 1902, 1936. *The varieties of religious experience.* New York: The Modern Library.

Jarvie, I. C. 1976. On the limits of symbolic interpretation in anthropology.

Jarvie, I. C. 1976. On the limits of symbolic interpretation in anthropology. *Current Anthropology* 17: 687–701.

Jennings, Theodore W. 1982. On ritual knowledge. *The Journal of Religion* 62(2): 111–27.

Kertzer, David I. 1988. *Ritual, politics, and power.* New Haven: Yale University Press.

Kierkegaard, Soren. 1843, 1964. *Repetition: An essay in experimental psychology.* Trans. Walter Lowrie. New York: Harper Torchbooks.

Kirby, E. T. 1976. The shamanistic origins of popular entertainments. In *Ritual, play, and performance: Readings in the social sciences/theatre.* Eds. Schechner and Schuman, 139–49. New York: The Seabury Press.

Klaaren, Gene. 1986. The genesis song. Paper delivered to the October meeting of the New Haven Theological Discussion Group.

La Fontaine, J. S., ed. 1972. *The interpretation of ritual: Essays in honour of I. A. Richards.* London: Tavistock.

Lancaster, Jane B. 1975. *Primate behavior and the emergence of human culture.* New York: Holt, Rinehart and Winston.

Langer, Suzanne. 1942, 1948. *Philosophy in a new key: A study in the symbolism of reason, rite, and art.* New York: New American Library.

Lawick-Goodall, Jane van. 1971. *In the shadow of man.* Boston: Houghton Mifflin Co.

Leach, Edmund R. 1966. Ritualization in man in relation to conceptual and social development. *The Philosophical Transactions of the Royal Society of London,* 29th series, 251: 403–8.

———. 1968. Ritual. In *International Encyclopedia of the Social Sciences,* vol. 13. Ed. David Sills. Glen Cove, NY: Free Press.

———. 1972. "The structure of symbolism." In *The interpretation of ritual: Essays in honour of I. A. Richards.* Ed. J. S. La Fontaine, 239–75. London, Tavistock.

Lively, Penelope. 1981. *Judgment day: A novel.* New York: Harper & Row.

Lorenz, Konrad. 1967. *On aggression.* Trans. Marjorie Kerr Wilson. New York: Bantam.

Mack, Burton. 1987. Introduction: Religion and ritual. In *Violent origins: Walter Burkert, René Girard, and Jonathan Z. Smith on ritual killing and cultural formation.* Ed. Robert B. Hamerton-Kelly. Introduction Burton Mack. Commentary Renato Rosaldo. Stanford, CA: Stanford University Press.

Macmurray, John. 1957. *The self as agent.* London: Faber and Faber Limited.

Malinowski, Bronislaw. 1954. *Magic, science and religion and other essays.* Garden City, NY: Doubleday.

Marrett, R. R. 1909. *The threshold of religion.* London: Methuen.

Matthiessen, Peter. 1962. *Under the mountain wall.* New York: Ballantine Books.

Moore, Robert L., Ralph Wendell Burhoe, and Philip J. Hefner. 1983. Symposium on ritual in human adaptation. *Zygon* 18 (September): 209–19.

Moore, Sally Falk, and Barbara Myerhoff, eds. 1977. *Secular ritual.* Amsterdam: Van Gorcum.

Morton, Nelle. 1986. *The journey is home.* Boston: Beacon Press.

Mud Flower Collective. 1985. *God's fierce whimsy: Christian feminism and theological education.* New York: The Pilgrim Press.

Murray, Gilbert. 1912, 1962. Tragedy, comedy, and ritual form. In *Themis*, by Jane E. Harrison. Cleveland: World Publishing Co.

Neusner, Jacob. 1987. *The enchantments of Judaism: Rites of transformation from birth through death*. New York: Basic Books.

Nietzsche, Friedrich. 1872, 1956. *The birth of tragedy*. Garden City, NY: Doubleday Anchor Books.

O'Keefe, Daniel L. 1982. *Stolen lightning: The social theory of magic*. New York: Continuum Books.

Otto, Rudolf. 1917, 1950. *The idea of the holy*. Oxford University Press.

Pazder, Lawrence, and Michelle Smith. 1980, 1981. *Michelle remembers*. New York: Pocket Books.

Peterson, Thomas V. 1987. Wittgenstein's theory of language and ritual change. Paper written for the Ritual Studies Group, American Academy of Religion Annual Meeting, Dec. 5–8, in Boston.

Pottebaum, Gerard A. 1975. *The rites of people*. Washington: The Liturgical Conference.

Rappaport, Roy A. 1979. *Ecology, meaning, and religion*. Berkeley, CA: North Atlantic Books.

———. 1968, 1984. *Pigs for the ancestors: Ritual in the ecology of a New Guinea people*. New Haven: Yale University Press.

Schechner, Richard. 1977. *Essays on performance theory, 1970–1976*. New York: Drama Book Specialists.

———. 1985. *Between theater and anthropology*. Illustrated. Foreword Victor Turner. Philadelphia: The University of Pennsylvania Press.

Schechner, Richard, and Willa Appel, eds. 1990. *By means of performance: Intercultural studies of theatre and ritual*. New York: Cambridge University Press.

Schenkel, R. 1964. Zur Deutung der Balzleistungen einiger Phasianiden und Tetraoniden. *Ornith. Beob.* 53: 182 and 55: 65.

Segundo, Juan L., S.J. 1971, 1974. *The sacraments today*. Trans. John Drury. Maryknoll, NY: Orbis Books.

———. 1975, 1976. *The Liberation of Theology*. Maryknoll, NY: Orbis Books.

Simonton, Carl. 1975. Belief systems and management of the emotional aspects of malignancy. *The Journal of Transpersonal Psychology* 7(1): 29–47.

Singer, Milton. 1972. *When a great tradition modernizes*. New York: Praeger.

Smith, Jonathan Z. 1982. *Imagining religion: From Babylon to Jonestown*. Chicago: University of Chicago Press.

Smith, Wilfred Cantwell. 1979. *Faith and belief*. Princeton: Princeton University Press.

Smith, William Robertson. 1889, 1927. *Lectures on the religion of the semites: The fundamental institutions*. London: A. & C. Black.

Sperber, Dan. 1975. *Rethinking symbolism*. Trans. Alice L. Morton. Cambridge, England: Cambridge University Press.

Staal, Frits. 1979. The meaninglessness of ritual. *Numen* 26: 2–22.

Taylor, Mark Kline. 1986. *Beyond explanation: Religious dimensions in cultural anthropology*. Macon, GA: Mercer University Press.

Temerlin, Maurice K. 1972. *Lucy: Growing up human*. Palo Alto, CA: Science and Behavior Books, Inc.

reformed church. New York: Harper & Brothers.

Turnbull, Colin. 1990. Liminality: A synthesis of subjective and objective experience. Chapter 3 in *By means of performance*. Ed. Richard Schechner and Willa Appel. New York: Cambridg e University Press.

Turner, Victor. 1967. *The forest of symbols*. Ithaca, NY: Cornell University Press.

———. 1969, 1974b. *The ritual process: Structure and anti-structure*. Baltimore: Penguin Books.

———. 1974a. *Dramas, fields, and metaphors: Symbolic action in human society*. Ithaca, NY: Cornell University Press.

———. 1974c. Symbols and social experience in religious ritual. *Studia Missionalia* 23: 1–21.

———. 1976. Ritual, tribal and Catholic. *Worship* 50(6): 504–26.

———. 1977. Variations on a theme of liminality. In *Secular Ritual*. Ed. Sally F. Moore and Barbara Myerhoff. Amsterdam: Van Gorcum.

———. 1982. *From ritual to theatre: The human seriousness of play*. New York: Performing Arts Journal Publications.

———. 1983. Body, brain, and culture. *Zygon* 18 (September): 221–45.

———. 1986. *The anthropology of performance*. New York: Performing Arts Journal Publications.

Turner, Victor, and Edith Turner. 1978. *Image and pilgrimage in Christian culture: Anthropological perspectives*. New York: Columbia University Press.

Tylor, Edward B. 1871, 1958. *Primitive culture: Researches into the development of mythology, philosophy, religion, art and custom*. 2 vols. Gloucester, MA: Smith.

Ulin, Robert C. 1984. *Understanding cultures: Perspectives in anthropology and social theory*. Austin: University of Texas Press.

Van Gennep, Arnold. 1908, 1960. *The rites of passage*. Trans. Monika B. Vizedom and Gabrielle L. Caffee. Chicago: University of Chicago Press.

Walens, Stanley. 1981. *Feasting with cannibals: An essay on Kwakiuti cosmology*. Princeton: Princeton University Press.

Weber, Max. 1922, 1963. *The sociology of religion*. Trans. Ephraim Fischoff. Boston: Beacon Press.

Webster, Bayard. 1981. Bird of myth reported seen. *The New York Times* (Nov. 11).

West, Cornel. 1987. The vocation of a Christian intellectual. Inaugural Lecture. Mimeographed. New York: Union Theological Seminary.

Wilson, Bryan R., ed. 1970. *Rationality*. New York: Harper & Row.

Wilson, Monica. 1972. The wedding cakes: A study of ritual change. In *The interpretation of ritual: Essays in honour of I. A. Richards*. Ed. J. S. La Fontaine, 187–201. London: Tavistock.

Wink, Walter. 1986. *Unmasking the powers: The invisible forces that determine human existence*. Philadelphia: Fortress Press.

———. 1987. *Violence and nonviolence in South Africa: Jesus' third way*. Philadelphia: New Society Publishers.

Wittgenstein, Ludwig. 1969. *On certainty*. Ed. G. E. M. Anscombe and G. H. von Wright. New York: Harper & Row.

———. 1979. *Remarks on Frazer's Golden Bough*. Atlantic Highlands, NJ: Humanities Press.

Index

Aaron, 113, 138–39
Aborigines, 26
Abuse, ritual, 8; in church, 8; of women, 3; term origin, 239n.1
Acquired characteristics (inheritance of not supported), 18
Acting, 31, 79, 82, 90, 91–92, 98, 126, 127, 131, 137, 160, 169; defined, 80, 81
Action(s), 14, 17, 19, 20, 26, 27, 28, 42, 47, 49, 60, 61, 74, 79–80, 83, 85, 91, 94, 96–97, 100, 102, 108, 111–12, 118, 123–27, 138, 143, 147, 161, 164, 168–71, 173, 175–76, 178–79, 187–91, 196–97, 207, 209, 213–14, 216–18, 221, 232, 237–38, 241n.34, 242n.58, 242n.65, 242n.66, 244n.105. *See also* Performance
Actor, 79, 80, 82, 83, 98, 125, 173, 189
Act(s), 5, 8, 10, 13, 14, 16, 19, 27, 32, 35, 46, 80, 81, 87, 92–93, 95, 97, 100–103, 108, 109, 110, 111, 112, 114, 116, 118–27, 136–38, 141, 147–48, 154, 168–70, 172–73, 175, 180–81, 183, 187, 188, 204–5, 208, 211, 213, 216–19, 241n.48, 244n.91
Adam, 208, 249n.265
Adoration, 212, 241n.48
Aesthetics, 4, 9, 99
Africa, 9, 69, 109, 157–58, 185, 231, 237
African-American churches, 9, 84, 165, 199, 218, 237
African-Americans, 116–17. *See also* Black liberation; civil rights movement
Agape, 249n.272
Aggression, 103, 154, 155
Alcoholics Anonymous (AA), 115
Alexander, Bobby, 183, 237, 238, 248, 250
Alienation, 6, 85, 162, 213–14, 215, 234
Altars, 74, 176, 213
Ambiguity, 67, 69, 75, 80, 105, 118, 135, 233
Amerindians, 237
Ancestors, 84, 97, 125, 144, 191
Androgyny, 60
Anglican Book of Common Prayer, 186
Anglican Church, 84
Anglicanism, 7, 95

Animal(s): in human ritual, 171, 191; ritual behavior of, 13–15, 17–23, 25, 26, 81; ritual display in, 85–87, sacrifice of, 103, 104, 105, 140, 141
Anointing, 112, 204
Anomie, 49, 150, 190
Anthropology, 10–11, 12, 134, 148, 152, 154; medical, 168
Antistructure, 161, 227–30
Apartheid, 183; workshop exorcising, 179–82
Apes, 240n.22. *See also individual names*
Appel, Willa, 189, 248
Appetite. *See* Desire
Arendt, Hannah, 121, 122, 243
Aristotelian philosophy, 210
Aristotle, 79, 82
Arrowsmith, William, 248
Art, 30, 31, 48, 91, 92, 99, 114, 212, 231, 234, 236
Artaud, Antonin, 101, 244
Asia, 9
Asson, 62, 64, 67, 68, 72
Atom bomb, 40–44, 47, 49, 50
Atomic weapons, 37, 104
Audience (observer), 80, 81, 85, 90, 124, 154, 214
Auschwitz (death camp), 42
Australia, 33, 35
Authority, 162, 163, 173
Avant-garde, 231
Ayizan, 60, 61, 64, 65

Bacchae, The (Euripides), 248n.214
Baker, G. P., 240
Bank deposit view. *See* Sacrament
Baptism, 92, 93, 202, 207, 209
"The Bare Facts of Ritual" (Smith), 48
Bar Kochba, 142
Bateson, Gregory, 23, 145, 170–71, 172, 240, 247
Beginnings in Ritual Studies (Grimes), 23
Behavior: absolutes, 144; animal, 14–15; patterned and repetitive, 26, 27; ritual